"Intelligent and Effective Direction"

Alan R. Sadovnik and Susan F. Semel
General Editors

Vol. 14

PETER LANG
New York • Washington, D.C./Baltimore • Bern
Frankfurt am Main • Berlin • Brussels • Vienna • Oxford

Katrina M. Sanders

"Intelligent and Effective Direction"

*The Fisk University
Race Relations Institute
and the Struggle for Civil Rights,
1944–1969*

PETER LANG
New York • Washington, D.C./Baltimore • Bern
Frankfurt am Main • Berlin • Brussels • Vienna • Oxford

Library of Congress Cataloging-in-Publication Data

Sanders, Katrina M. (Marie).
"Intelligent and effective direction": the Fisk University Race
Relations Institute and the struggle for civil rights, 1944–1969 /
Katrina M. Sanders.
p. cm. — (History of schools and schooling; v. 14)
Includes bibliographical references and index.
1. African Americans—Civil rights—History—20th century.
2. Fisk University. Race Relations Institute—History.
3. Johnson, Charles Spurgeon, 1893–1956. 4. Civil rights movements—
United States—History—20th century. 5. United States—Race relations.
6. Civil rights movements—Southern States—History—20th century.
7. Southern States—Race relations. I. Title. II. Series.
E185.61.S3   323.1'196073'0071173—dc21   2003006802
ISBN 0-8204-5035-9
ISSN 1089-0678

Bibliographic information published by **Die Deutsche Bibliothek**.
Die Deutsche Bibliothek lists this publication in the "Deutsche
Nationalbibliografie"; detailed bibliographic data is available
on the Internet at http://dnb.ddb.de/.

Cover design by Joni Holst
Cover photo of 1952 Race Relations Institute participants.
Charles S. Johnson, front row, eighth from right, holding hat.
United Church Board for Homeland Ministries Archives, Race Relations
Department, 1952, Amistad Research Center at Tulane University.

© 2005 Peter Lang Publishing, Inc., New York
275 Seventh Avenue, 28th Floor, New York, NY 10001
www.peterlangusa.com

All rights reserved.
Reprint or reproduction, even partially, in all forms such as microfilm,
xerography, microfiche, microcard, and offset strictly prohibited.

To my family

and
in memory of

Dr. Audrey Lorraine Qualls
(March 14, 1955 – December 28, 2002)
Colleague, Mentor, and Friend

I am certain, however, that man is made both good and bad by his institutions; that these institutions are responsible for the shaping of personalities, our morals, and the patterns of our social relations; and that the re-shaping of our institutions are our responsibility. This is not only a function of formal education, but of all our social concerns.
 — *Charles S. Johnson**

---

* Charles S. Johnson, "A Spiritual Autobiography", p. 11 n.d., manuscript, Charles S. Johnson Papers, Fisk University, Franklin Library, Special Collections Library.

CONTENTS

List of Illustrations xi
Acknowledgments xiii

Introduction 1
Chapter One 5
    Reconciling Philosophy and Practice:
    American Race Relations, the 1940s
Chapter Two 23
    "Intelligent and Effective Direction":
    The Fisk University Race Relations Institute
Chapter Three 47
    Closing Social Distance, Building Racial Tolerance
Chapter Four 63
    Leaning on Legislation
Chapter Five 89
    Community Reactions, Participant Evaluations
Chapter Six 105
    Winds of Change
Epilogue 113

Illustrations 115
Appendices 123
Notes 143
Index 163

ILLUSTRATIONS

Fig. 1: Charles S. Johnson, RRI founder
Fig. 2: Charles H. Houston; Willard Townsend, and Frayser T. Lane at the 1944 RRI
Fig. 3: 1952 RRI participants. Charles S. Johnson, eighth from left, holding hat.
Fig. 4: 1952 RRI participants attending a lecture
Fig. 5: 1955 Galen Weaver (far right) with Native American participants, 1955 RRI
Fig. 6: Martin Luther King Jr. at the 1956 RRI
Fig. 7: Thurgood Marshall presenting at the 1956 RRI
Fig. 8: 1956 RRI Participants at a social (women dancing together)
Fig. 9: Thurgood Marshall on a coffee break with 1957 RRI participants
Fig. 10: 1960 Young RRI participants "cutting a rug" at the RRI
Fig. 11: RRI Participants at lunch, 1956

The Illustrations section begins on page 115.

ACKNOWLEDGMENTS

In pursuing this project, I have procured many intellectual and personal debts. I'd first like to express my gratitude to my graduate advisor and mentor at the University of Illinois, Urbana-Champaign, James D. Anderson. Words can never express my gratitude for the way he nourished, encouraged, and supported my interest in the history of American education. I am indebted to the archivists, librarians, and staff members who were most generous in directing me to valuable resources and were unfailing in their support as I worked through the papers. Special thanks goes to Brenda Square and Shannon Burrell at the Amistad Research Center at Tulane University, New Orleans; Rebecca Hankins, formerly at the Amistad; Beth Howse at Special Collections in the Fisk University Franklin Library; and Thomas Rosenbaum at the Rockefeller Archives. I also owe special thanks to the family of Charles S. Johnson—Mr. Jeh Johnson and Mrs. Patricia Clifford—for sharing their time, memories, and materials of their father. Gratitude also goes to Dr. Clifton Johnson, the 1966–1969 director of the Fisk University Race Relations Institute, and Dr. John Hope Franklin for sharing their time with me.

I'd like to thank my colleagues and doctoral students at he University of Iowa. Bruce Fehn and John McLure read various chapters; Leslie Schwalm and Fred Woodard offered insight and context during informal conversations; Ernest Pascarella encouraged me weekly to keep pushing and writing; and my students who often asked "How's the book going?" I would also like to thank three excellent research assistants who worked with me on various stages of this project. Teresa Garcia, Richard Breaux, and most recently Tracie Melvin helped collect needed data and offered valuable insight as I worked my way through many ideas.

I am also grateful to the University of Iowa College of Education Postdoctoral Fellowship Program, the Spencer Foundation's Small Grants Program, the Obermann Research Center at the University of Iowa, and the Linda and Doug Paul Untenured Faculty Award. These agencies and awards provided me with the resources, time, and financial support to visit archives, conduct interviews, analyze data, and simply think about this project.

I'd like to thank my family and friends. My parents Earl and Audrey, my sister Kristie, and dear friend Erica have continuously supported my efforts on this project since day one. Michael, your encouraging words have meant a lot. Of course, there are other relatives and friends—too many to name here—who have supported me at various stages of this project. Please know that I truly appreciate your support and that it sustained me through the writing process.

Finally, grateful acknowledgment is hereby made to copyright holders for permission to use the following copyrighted material:

American Missionary Association Papers. Used by permission of the Amistad Research Center at Tulane University.
Charles S. Johnson Papers, Microfilm Copy. Used by permission of the Amistad Research Center at Tulane University.
Charles S. Johnson Papers. Used by permission of the Fisk University, John Hope and Aurelia Elizabeth Franklin Library Special Collection.
General Education Board Papers. Used by permission of the Rockefeller Archive Center.
Julius Rosenwald Papers, Microfilm Copy. Used by permission of the Amistad Research Center at Tulane University.
Julius Rosenwald Papers. Used by permission of the Fisk University, John Hope and Aurelia Elizabeth Franklin Library Special Collection.
Race Relations Department, United Church for Homeland Ministries Archives. Used by permission of the Amistad Research Center at Tulane University.

INTRODUCTION

Racial unrest was widespread in the United States during the 1940s. In 1943 alone, major race riots and revolts broke out in Mobile, Beaumont, Los Angeles, Detroit, and Harlem. Job opportunities associated with World War II triggered a large migration of blacks seeking war-related employment out of the South. This mass migration to northern and western industrial cities intensified the already stressed relationships between blacks and whites as the two groups increasingly competed for jobs, housing, and education. While America hailed to the world the virtues of democracy, it simultaneously practiced numerous unfair social, economic, and political tactics towards minorities at home. These practices hit blacks particularly hard as negative stereotypes and misconceptions flourished and hindered their employment, education, and housing opportunities. Aware of their subordinate position, and noting the obvious contradictions in America's democratic ideology and actual practice, blacks increased their quest to be treated as first-class citizens. As blacks did, the dominant white culture continued to use discriminatory practices and increased violent attacks, especially in the South, against the subordinated group in the hopes of maintaining the traditions of social and racial dominance. Thus, the tensions increased and erupted with the decade's race riots.

America also experienced an increase in social awareness amidst the smoldering tensions of the decade. Blacks, whites, researchers, laborers, activists, and social, civic, and religious organizations all worked to identify the sources of and solutions to racial tensions. This stressful climate led Charles Spurgeon Johnson, a prominent black sociologist and race relations expert, who had investigated the causes of the violent Chicago Race Riot of 1919, to fear that the current riots were the beginning of many more to come. As blacks took action to secure economic, social, and political resources, the turmoil between them and whites increased.

This book tells the story of a unique experiment initially designed to address those tensions. It examines the structure, ideology, and content of the Fisk University Race Relations Institute (RRI). Johnson proposed the RRI as a way to assemble social scientists, educators, and community leaders who would work together to build racial tolerance and promote equal opportunity for blacks. The first workshop, held during the summer of 1944, ran for three weeks beginning July 3, 1944, at Fisk University, Nashville, Tennessee. The RRI would end up running each summer for 26 years. The program, which ended in 1969, was a nonprofit organization incorporated within the framework of Fisk where the RRI's initial financial supporter, the American Missionary Association, had established the Race Relations Department (Department) in 1942 to address racial issues and tensions. The Department collected data on cities and other areas threatened with racial disturbances. The Department's major concern was identifying problem areas, developing programs and techniques that would promote constructive action, and relieving areas of racial tension.[1]

Based on his prior experiences and work in race relations, Johnson believed education was the key to dealing with racial strife. Specifically, Johnson believed scholars and researchers could offer information about blacks and other minorities that would offset the negative stereotypes and beliefs held about the groups. Once the dominant white culture understood these facts and the atrocities practiced against blacks in particular, Johnson felt that moral whites would seek and implement changes in social practices through legislation that would, in turn, promote democratic treatment for subordinated groups. With policies in place that reflected America's democratic ideals, Johnson believed that racial groups would deal with one another in a tolerant manner.

It may initially seem idealistic within our contemporary context that Johnson relied so heavily on this top-down method to foster positive race relations and civil rights in America, but his ideas are easier to understand when one situates him within the complex context of his generation. Consider first that Johnson was part of a generation of people who saw top-down policies change race relations. In 1896 the Supreme Court ruling in *Plessy v. Ferguson* legalized racial segregation in the South. By 1914 segregation was practiced throughout the region. Johnson, believed to be seven years old when his hometown of Bristol, Virginia, began enforcing the Jim Crow laws, remembered an early childhood and a pre-codified society where whites and blacks treated one another with cordial tolerance. He could also remembered seeing that tolerance dissipate almost overnight with the passage and implementation of the racially divisive measure. In *Having Our Say: The Delany Sisters' First 100 Years* (1993), Sarah L. Delany and A. Elizabeth Delany also share memories of cordial tolerance between blacks and whites in the South prior to legalized segregation.

Next, consider as Daryl Michael Scott points out in the introduction to *Contempt and Pity: Social Policy and the Image of the Damaged Black Psyche, 1880–1996* that from the late 1880s and 1920 "the experts who dominated the image of black people depicted African Americans as incapable and undeserving of participation in a modern society."[2] Johnson, trained by eminent sociologist Robert E. Park at the University of Chicago which was "committed to the social inclusion of blacks,"[3] was among a group of black scholars who relied heavily on the social sciences and education to facilitate changes in social policy and vindicate the race. Johnson, who Scott notes "divided his time between activism and scholarship," used "scholarly findings to promote racial understanding, maintaining ties with groups concerned primarily with social welfare rather than social theory."[4] He designed the RRI to utilize researchers who could provide needed information to leaders affiliated with schools, churches, industry, politics, and communities—people whose voices Johnson felt would best be heard in the struggle to change crippling social policies.

Consider too that Johnson, who also started the literary *Opportunity* magazine and was part of the Harlem Renaissance of the 1920s, was a part of a generation of black elites who held to uplift ideologies. As Kevin K. Gaines notes in *Uplifting the Race: Black Leadership, Politics, and Culture in the Twentieth Century* "uplift, among its other connotations, also represented the struggle for a positive black identity in a deeply racist society, turning the pejorative designation of race into a source of dignity and self-affirmation through an ideology of class differentiation, self-help, and interdependence."[5] Gaines goes on to explain that

> Racial uplift ideals were offered as a form of cultural politics, in the hope that unsympathetic whites would relent and recognize the humanity of middle-class African Americans, and their potential for the citizenship rights black men had possessed during Reconstruction. Elite blacks believed they were replacing the racist notion of fixed biological racial differences with an evolutionary view of cultural assimilation, measured primarily by the status of the family and civilization. Cultural differences, then rather than biological notions of racial inferiority, were said to be more salient in explaining the lower social status of African Americans. And a middle-class consciousness stressing racial solidarity and self-help, uniting blacks across class lines, promised a more legitimate basis for social differentiation than color.[6]

Again, the fight to develop a positive identity was important because there was a large body of work being produced by Southern conservative social scientists that supported notions that blacks were inferior and could not be assimilated into American culture.[7]

Finally, consider that Johnson was also a contemporary of civil rights advocates like Charles Hamilton Houston who also believed the fight against Jim Crow would be won in the courts. Known as "the man who killed Jim Crow," Houston also valued the work of scholars to refute the belief that blacks were backwards and deserved fewer resources than whites. Houston organized a cadre of black attorneys primarily from Howard University to canvas the South in efforts to chronicle the black experience and to gather data that would later be used in court cases attacking segregation.[8] Johnson had also employed similar tactics when he utilized social scientists to gather information on black farmers. The findings were published in two of his best known books, *Shadow of the Plantation* (1934) and *Growing Up in the Black Belt* (1941).

"Intelligent and Effective Direction": The Fisk University Race Relations Institute, 1944–1969 and the Struggle for Civil Rights concentrates on the RRI, Johnson's research-based social action project, and its activities and proposals for calming racial tensions and promoting civil rights. Chapter 1, "Reconciling Philosophy and Practice: American Race Relations, the 1940s," offers a glimpse into the racial mood of America during the 1940s, various attempts to address those tensions, and the developing work in race relations by liberal scholars. Chapter 2, "'Intelligent and Effective Direction': The Fisk University Race Relations Institute," offers a glimpse into the development of Johnson's philosophies and ideologies on race relations. It also examines other race projects directed by Johnson, and the formation, structure, and philosophy of the RRI. Chapter 3, "Closing Social Distance, Building Racial Tolerance," focuses on the desire to utilize the RRI to dispel the negative stereotypes whites held about blacks. There was a widely held belief during the period that if whites saw that blacks were not an inferior group, whites would be willing to accept blacks as American citizens worthy of all privileges. Chapter 4, "Leaning on Legislation," examines the RRI's belief that legislation could promote positive race relations and civil rights. The chapter also examines the RRI's desire to provide blacks with current information on legislation and other measures needed to secure opportunities. Chapter 5, "Community Reactions, Participant Evaluations," examines reactions to the project. Chapter 6, "Winds of Change," examines the final days of the RRI and how student activism and growing calls for Black Power impacted the project.

"Intelligent and Effective Direction" offers insight into the years leading up to the famed civil rights movement and shows that blacks did not have a singular view on how to achieve racial and social equality. Whereas scholars have traditionally focused their attention on the grassroots efforts for civil rights, this project highlights the attempt to utilize the social sciences, education, and legislative methods to secure social equality for blacks. This project also gives a glimpse into a unique generation of Americans who could conceptualize that government could monitor and correct itself and promote civility and democracy to the American public. This project helps to bridge the gap in our knowledge of what efforts were made to secure civil rights and equal opportunities for all U. S. citizens between the establishment of Jim Crow laws and the famed civil rights movement.

May 2004

CHAPTER ONE

Reconciling Philosophy and Practice: American Race Relations, the 1940s

America experienced intense growing pains during the 1940s as significant changes in black-white relations ignited racial friction nationwide. The promise of World War II and war-related employment signaled the end of the Depression era and prompted a massive number of blacks desperate for jobs to leave the South and head to northern and industrial areas. Blacks had been hit doubly hard by the Depression. Already excluded from the more profitable jobs because of long-standing discriminatory practices, blacks also lost access to the menial jobs once reserved for them as whites, displaced by the Depression, demanded those positions. These poor whites had also left the South in search of war-related jobs, and upon arriving in the cities, found themselves—many for the first time—competing with blacks for resources. Although blacks had also migrated to the North by the thousands during the World War I era, they did not pose a serious threat to whites who had done the same. A large European immigrant population, discriminatory employment and training practices, and restrictive housing covenants reserved prosperity for whites. This second time around, however, was different as blacks fervently pushed to obtain a piece of World War II's economic pie. Blacks were fully aware of the opportunities associated with this war and did not plan to miss out again.

The World War I era had taught blacks a valuable lesson about securing social, political, and economic opportunities. Blacks had placed their hopes for advancement in the hands of do-good white "Redeemers" who controlled southern politics and promised to include blacks in America's economic wealth.[1] That promise turned to naught and black hope changed to disillusionment when, as S.P. Fullinwider notes in *The Mind and Mood of Black America: 20th Century Thought*, the "revolution of rednecks" took over and started promoting racial prejudice instead of prosperity throughout the South and even into the North.² Blacks realized American terrorism instead of the American dream as riots broke out and the lynching of blacks became "sport."³ This time around, black leaders increasingly questioned and abandoned the once widespread and highly held portrayal of the helpless Christlike image bestowed upon blacks. This image of "humility, patience, and the ability to forgive" was supposed to ensure black survival.⁴ It did not. During the WWII-era however, Black leaders began to realize that black survival and advancement relied upon the group being proactive in securing economic resources. Fullinwider notes, "Negroes began to question, and then to reject, the white man and all his works. Negroes began to question, and then reject, the white man's standards."⁵ Now black leaders realized that black survival and advancement relied upon the group being proactive in securing economic resources. After all, whites were being proactive in maintaining resources. As Aldon Morris points out in *The Origins of the Civil Rights Movement: Black Communities Organizing for Change*:

> In the short run all members of the white group had a stake in racial domination, because they derived privileges from it. Poor and middle-class whites benefited because the segregated labor force prevented blacks from competing with them for better-paying jobs. The Southern white ruling class benefited because blacks supplied them with cheap labor and a weapon against the labor movement, the threat to use unemployed blacks as strikebreakers in labor disputes. Finally most Southern whites benefited psychologically from the system's implicit assurance that no matter how poor or uneducated, they were always better than the niggers. ⁶

The willingness of blacks to seek and secure war-related resources had a profound impact on future black-white relations. While whites as a group found black efforts threatening, the government realized that the growing momentum behind black efforts to secure parity signaled blacks were boldly challenging America to acknowledge and reconcile the blatant hypocrisy of the democratic ideals it professed to the world and the system of oppression it practiced at home. This challenge forced the government to begin addressing black concerns through federal initiatives. In doing so, numerous riots between primarily whites and blacks erupted across the country as whites retaliated against those measures.⁷

RACIAL ERUPTIONS

Perhaps the work of A. Philip Randolph and his supporters is the best example of the growing willingness among blacks to confront discriminatory practices and seek the full benefits associated with being American citizens. After talks with President Roosevelt in January of 1941 failed to secure war-related jobs for blacks, Randolph, president of the Brotherhood of Sleeping Car Porters, threatened to have 100,000 blacks march down Pennsylvania Avenue in Washington, DC, the following June to protest for jobs and an integrated military.⁸ As the deadline approached, Roosevelt feared Randolph could make good his threats and thus attract significant media attention. Fearing the negative impact the publicity would have on international politics and the quickly approaching war, Roosevelt consented to banning racial discrimination in war-related industries.

In June 1941 Roosevelt signed an executive order forbidding racial discrimination in industries securing war contracts. The order, Executive Order 8802, also provided for the organization of the Fair Employment Practices Committee (FEPC), which would handle discriminatory complaints and grievances. Roosevelt also established the President's Committee on Civil Rights to investigate civil rights issues.⁹ Some black leaders criticized Randolph for agreeing to call off the march because neither of these committees had the authority to legally sanction violators. The formation of these committees, however, signaled several things. First, they were a public acknowledgment that racial discrimination was not confined to the rural South. Second, they signaled that the government knew the world was watching the way the country practiced democracy. Third, the committees signaled that blacks' efforts for advancement were gaining strength.

Roosevelt's actions showed that legislation could be utilized to provide opportunities for blacks, but attempts made by blacks to exercise those mandates were often met with white anger. For example, prior to the development of the FEPC and the President's Committee on Civil Rights, blacks in several urban areas took advantage of a federal housing program. The U.S. Housing Authority, the first exclusive public housing agency, had approved the development of approximately 134,000 low-rent dwelling units in over 360 projects in 162 different communities during the 1930s. Although blacks occupied approximately one-third of those units by 1940, their presence sparked violence in some areas.¹⁰ A 1942 riot erupted in Detroit, Michigan as black tenants attempted to move into their homes at the Sojourner Truth Housing Project. Tensions between whites and blacks dated back to 1932 when the Detroit City Planning Commission suggested that a public housing project be located near two white neighborhoods. Even though whites had vehemently opposed the project and had circulated petitions claiming that "disorder, violence, rape and mayhem" would occur when the black families arrived, counter-pressure from blacks held the commission to the project.¹¹ When the black families arrived on February 28 to move in, they found 200 white protestors armed with clubs surrounding the project. The whites had gathered that morning and were refusing to let the black tenants unload their possessions. A few minutes after the tenants arrived, another truckload of about 15 black supporters armed with clubs appeared. The two races clashed. Observers of the riot said that city officials and police didn't try to disperse the white crowd, nor did they try to protect the black tenants from the attacks. The tenants did not move in that day.¹²

The Sojourner Truth Housing Project riot not only foreshadowed the larger Detroit Riot of June 1943, it also, illustrated the fear E. Franklin Frazier theorized that whites held about the possibility of integration. In the revised edition of *The Negro in the United States*, Frazier maintained the fear whites had about losing status was related to the status blacks held in the larger community. Noting that "[o]ne of the obstacles to racially mixed housing projects [was] the fear on the part of whites that they will lose status" he went on to write:

> The integration of Negroes into public housing projects is significant not only from the standpoint of changes in the nature of the contacts between the Negro community and the white community. The growing importance of public housing is itself indicative of those changes in the organization of American life which are favoring the integration of Negroes into American society.[13]

Tensions between whites and blacks also increased as black soldiers began to challenge the existing racial practices in the U.S.[14] As black soldiers stationed abroad realized social freedoms that were not allowed in the U.S., it became a contradiction to fight to obtain freedoms for others that they, themselves, did not enjoy.[15] Although more than one million blacks participated in World War II, they continuously faced the social order of the day while serving on and off their posts.[16] The Army segregated black soldiers by restricting them to all black units commanded by white officers. The Marines remained mostly white, and the Navy relegated its black sailors to kitchen duty. When most officer candidate schools desegregated in 1942, the flight training programs remained segregated. Black pilots trained at Tuskegee Institute in Alabama. In the South, the black enlisted rode segregated buses off base and were often denied service at white restaurants while their white Nazi prisoners were served.[17]

The Harlem Riot of 1943 illustrates the developing tensions surrounding the black soldier's newfound awareness. The riot, which ran August 1 and 2, erupted after a white police officer attempted to arrest a black woman for disorderly conduct.[18] When a black military police officer tried to interfere with the arrest, the two officers began fighting. When the black officer overpowered the white officer and took his nightstick, the white officer shot and slightly injured the black officer. The black officer went to a hospital, where, as word got out, a crowd of approximately 3,000 developed.[19] Reportedly, the mob became agitated when someone threw a bottle from the roof of the hospital. As the crowd dispersed and smaller groups formed, they began moving through the main arteries of Harlem smashing shop windows. Some time later in what was described as "an afterthought" the groups began looting shops. Although it first seemed that the violence was not racially motivated, the shops that blacks vandalized were white owned. The shops that were known to be black owned were skipped. Although some civilians were attacked, the mob mostly attacked police officers who were trying to stop the activity and who blacks associated with the shooting. Just about all the white injured were cops.[20]

The ability of blacks to unite as a collective force concerned both non-liberal and liberal whites. Realizing that blacks had strength in organized numbers, many whites looked to old political strategies such as poll taxes and all-white primaries to suppress the black vote and thus restrict the group's progress. When Roosevelt and his liberal supporters sought to strike down poll taxes and all-white primaries during the presidential election of 1944, smoldering racial hostilities once again erupted as agitated whites took to their old social methods of fear, hatred, and violence to control blacks. Many southern politicians went on alert and publicly supported white supremacy. They threatened to establish new parties as they fought over civil rights. There were even calls for purchasing land in the colonial areas of Africa and sending all blacks there.[21] While southern lawmakers made political threats, southern renegades utilized physical threats, attacks, and lynching.

As Americans continued to promote democracy over fascism and racism, it became increasingly hard to ignore the ills at home. Although Americans wanted to believe that race was an issue only in the South, Randolph's March on Washington Movement, racial eruptions, and a segregated military mirrored the country's true face. Even the end of World War II contributed to racial unrest as many whites in the South feared the black soldiers' newfound and growing awareness of racial discrimination, while whites in the North feared the returning black soldiers' ability to compete for jobs.

Racial Conflict Theories

The bellowing display of racially based violence seen during the 1940s sent Americans scrambling to find the causes of the eruptions. Although some simplified explanations charged the poor whites and blacks who migrated to the North brought along their old southern racial baggage, other explanations took on a more scientific tone. The most popular explanations could be categorized into three groups: the natural instincts theories; the symbolic theories; and the status competition theories.[22] The natural instincts theories held blacks were inferior to whites. According to these theories, black inferiority limited the group to a backwards culture that made it impossible for them to take on European culture. Even if blacks could somehow assimilate, it would only be to the demise of the European culture. Natural instincts theories also held that race consciousness and a deep-seated hatred were a matter of instinct.[23]

Symbolic theories held that prejudices occur when people or groups see in certain racial and ethnic groups a symbol of something to be despised, feared, or envied. With symbolic theories one thing can represent another. The connection, however, between what is thought to be true and what is true doesn't have to actually exist because the unconscious mind makes the connection.

Another aspect of symbolic theories is that racial prejudice satisfies some psychic need of the individual or compensates for some defect in the personality.[24] Although only certain types of people develop prejudices that influence their lives, these people seem to be insecure and anxious and deal with life in an authoritarian way. Because of this they tend to deal with and only trust people within their own racial group.[25]

Two of the most popular symbolic theories during the 1940s were scapegoating and frustration-aggression. The scapegoat theory held that people are reluctant to blame themselves for their problems and will try to lay the blame on someone or something else.[26] Blacks made excellent scapegoats because for the most part, they represented many of the qualities needed to be successful scapegoats. Generally blacks as a group had distinguishing, salient features; were not strong enough to retaliate; were readily accessible and generally concentrated in one locality; and were previous victims of blame and hostility.[27] The frustration-aggression theory held that racially based group hostility is a "socially approved channel for the expression of the aggressive tendencies which people acquire as a consequence of their being frustrated."[28] All people are subject to considerable inhibition and restraint because of societal pressures, and will, therefore, need an outlet. Venting irrational and latent frustrations on blacks then becomes the socially permissible outlet in America.

The status competition theories were, perhaps, the most popular for explaining racial conflicts. Various forms of these theories attributed racial prejudice and conflict to change. Whites felt threatened by blacks' unrelenting push for self-development and improvement and feared losing security, status, and prestige. Whites also feared the technological changes that were impacting the country and needed to control something in their world. Whites felt they needed to control blacks or else blacks would infringe upon the privileges whites enjoyed.[29]

Many of the status competition theories were born out of the work of Robert E. Park, a University of Chicago sociologist who theorized on the effects of change on group or individual status. Park's take on race relations had provided a reorientation for the empirical studies of race relations. Previous work on race in the nineteenth century focused primarily on defining race, classifying racial groups, and constructing theories of racial superiority and inferiority. Scientist pondered if race was a biological term that dealt with inherited physical features based on blood or genetic relationships, or if it was a subdivision of a species which inherits its characteristics. They pondered if there were three "races" of humankind or up to 150 different races. They pondered and even had an entire discipline—craniology—devoted to measuring skull sizes. The thought was brain size reflected intelligence. The larger the skull, the larger the brain. The larger the brain, the more intelligent.

As Park placed the study of race relations within a cycle of contact, conflict, assimilation, and accommodation, he gave scientists a framework to conduct empirical studies of race relations. He shifted thoughts to the role change played in cultural conflicts and race prejudices and believed cultural conflicts played a major role in race prejudices because groups claiming superiority were unwilling to compete on an equal basis with those they believed to be inferior.[30] Because the groups would, however, eventually compete for status as changes occurred, it was only natural for them to respond to conflict situations through race consciousness. He wrote:

> The point is that every change in states, whether of an individual or of a group, involves a change in social organization. Prejudice—that is caste, class and race prejudices—in its more naive and innocent manifestations, is merely the resistance of the social order to change.[31]

That black efforts to improve status was met with opposition, prejudice, and racial animosities only meant that "[r]ace prejudice, so conceived [was] merely an elementary expression of conservatism."[32]

Park also held that changes in racial structures also impacted the social constructs of race relations. Originally race relations had been thought of in terms of a horizontal line where whites were on top and blacks were on the bottom. But when black industrial and professional classes developed, the line shifted from horizontal to vertical. Blacks were on a more even footing. Instead of being below whites, blacks found themselves parallel and social equals to whites. Thus a "bi-racial" organized society formed.[33]

Park's theories focused attention on a concrete analysis of the social and psychological meaning of race alienation, instead of simply justifying racial thoughts. By introducing data collection and measurements and making use of concepts like "attitudes, social distance, and mores" in addition to his race relations cycle, Park allowed researchers to conduct systematic investigations on the social problems of race. With this foundation, researchers found that racial antagonism in certain areas were increased by "exaggerated social distance between races" and that steps could be taken to reduce the social distance.[34]

Charles S. Johnson, the future organizer and director of the Fisk University Race Relations Institute, also believed that change played a critical role in racial conflict. In *Preface to Racial Understanding*, Johnson, a former student of Park, wrote

> The essence of the problem of race relations is change, and in this modern age change is constant, rapid and profound. Our physical world, our technological structure, our economic structure, our social institutions themselves are in constant process of change. Only in a stagnant society can we expect fixed and unalterable social relations, and a democracy is least of all political structures bound by unyielding conventions.[35]

In an undated memo in which he wanted to "examine the common and acute social phenomenon of race in light of the process of civilization itself," Johnson pointed out that racial conflict was necessary to the process of civilization. He wrote that although it's "frequently assumed that any kind of conflict is bad in itself and that racial conflict in particular can have only disastrous results for the weaker group," identifying "the role of racial conflict in the process of civilization...may offer a perspective that is at the same time more realistic and less racial in the instinctive and biological sense."[36]

Johnson took his theories of change a little further than Park in that Johnson believed that within the human relations process racially based prejudice was more than resistance to social change, and that race was the source of conflict. He explained that:

> Contact between different groups for whatever reason starts a reaction of forces which inevitably exert influence upon all groups involved. It's an elementary process of civilization—this hasn't changed, but what has changed is the concept of race and the increase in communication and commerce throughout world—problems stemming from conflict have become steadily acute.[37]

Throughout history, racial conflicts could be traced to the migration of certain races and their conquest of territories already inhabited by other races. As these societies were organized, the conquering race constituted the ruling class and the conquered made up the servant class, thus making race a factor of social superiority. The ruling race soon initiates philosophies that make their elevated status, which was acquired through conquest, seem to be based upon their moral and intellectual superiority. The ruling race then falls into the mind-set that they themselves are the only ones capable, "by nature or by the will of god, of providing political and social leadership in the interest of the lower races themselves." Because they are afraid of losing their economic and social status, they are likely to exploit or use other coercive measures to maintain their position. Eventually, these tactics incite rebellion from the oppressed races who wish to change their status.[38]

To support his theory, Johnson pointed to numerous societies throughout the world where significant changes in race relations had occurred since World Wars I and II. He cited areas throughout the East, the Bolshevik effort for racial minorities, the Republican regime in Spain, the Agrarian unrest in southeastern Europe, the Negroes in America, and the long-suffering Indians of Central and South America.[39]

Johnson also theorized that self-interest and group interest also contributed to tensions. He said that fear of "numerical domination...loss of status and prestige, largely social..the desire for security, largely economic...[and] sex-rivalry, largely biological" all played a role in racial conflict. Fueling these fears were factors inherent in the notion of culture, which Johnson defined as "the whole round of life; the total of acquired behavior patterns transmitted by imitation or instruction."⁴⁰ Because some cultures had different types of material objects, such as houses and clothing, other cultures took this to mean that they also differed in beliefs, ideals, and ethics. They believed these differences also meant different mental capabilities and supported racial superiority and dominance.⁴¹

Johnson was not the only social scientist building on theories of change. Sociologist Brewton Berry took Park's basic theory of change and applied it to economics. Berry's economic theories held that feelings of antipathy were natural developments for rivals if the groups felt like their economic or social positions were threatened. Reluctance to welcome those who would compete for the same desired things is common, as is efforts to exclude, eliminate, or cripple those who would deprive us of those things. Although economic factors may not be the sole reason for racial prejudice and conflict, prejudice develops and remains because something can be gained by it. That gain is clearly economic.⁴²

In 1944 sociologist Gunnar Myrdal shocked the country when he squarely blamed white America for America's racial tensions. In *An American Dilemma*, Myrdal argued that America experienced racial violence because the country had not resolved its contradictory behavior towards blacks. He pointed out that America professed one thing based on the ideals of democracy, but when it came to blacks, practiced something totally different.⁴³ In his book, an analysis of numerous studies and available information from the period, Myrdal analyzed American attitudes and actions towards blacks and the "disparity between American ideals and behaviors."⁴⁴ In his introduction Myrdal clearly blamed white America for the situations that caused the "Negro problem."⁴⁵ He wrote:

> The more important fact, however, is that practically all the economic, social, and political power is held by whites. The Negroes do not by far have anything approaching a tenth of the things worth having in America. It is thus the white majority group that naturally determines the Negroe's "place." All our attempts to reach scientific explanation of why the Negroes are what they are and why they live as they do have regularly led to determinants on the white side of the race line.... The Negroe's entire life, and, consequently, also his opinions on the Negro problem, are, in the main, to be considered as secondary reactions to more primary pressures from the side of the dominant white majority.⁴⁶

Myrdal also predicted that World War II would be crucial to the future of blacks as it would redefine the group's status. He wrote:

> This War is crucial for the future of the Negro, and the Negro problem is crucial in the War. There is bound to be a redefinition of the Negro's status in America as a result of this War. The exact nature of this structural change in American society cannot yet be foreseen.⁴⁷

He was right. Blacks increasingly questioned and challenged America's racially oppressive system as they were well aware that the country had gone abroad to fight a war to uphold the virtues of democracy over fascism and racism. The tensions stemming from racial unrest on American soil had become increasingly difficult for blacks to ignore. Blacks were growing tired of being reminded of their second-class citizenship. They were tired of being relegated to rundown homes, unskilled jobs, and the negative assumptions whites held about them. This ever-growing anxiousness became more pronounced as highly publicized individual black accomplishments inspired group pride and confidence. Hattie McDaniel became the first black actress to win an Academy Award in 1940 for her role in *Gone With the Wind*, and Jackie Robinson became the first black to integrate Major League Baseball when he joined the Brooklyn Dodgers in 1947.

The emerging black empowerment was not only reflected in black efforts to secure economic opportunities, it was also seen in literary and scholarly pieces written by blacks. For example, the magazine *Ebony*, which was compared to the white mainstream's *Life*, brought issues that were important and applicable to blacks into the homes of blacks. Scholarly pieces by blacks and white authors also reflected concern for black-white relations in America. John Hope Franklin's *From Slavery to Freedom*, and Charles S. Johnson's *Into the Main Stream* appeared in 1947, while Richard Wright's *Black Boy* and *Native Son* also appeared during the decade.[48] It's clear that black-white relations were also on the minds of whites as well as they also challenged the contradictions in American ideology. In addition to *An American Dilemma*, which appeared in 1944, *Color and Conscience: The Irrepressible Conflict* by Buell Gallagher appeared in 1946 and highlighted the contradictions of racial inequality that the author believed would keep the South permanently disadvantaged.[49] Organizations advancing racial equality also formed during the decade. Blacks and whites organized the Congress of Racial Equality (CORE) in Chicago in 1942. The national CORE was founded in 1943.

This emerging black empowerment did not go unnoticed. White philanthropic organizations who had a history of supporting the educational and medical needs of blacks were concerned that blacks' developing resistance to the standard practices of social injustices could be misdirected. In a June 27, 1942, conference memo from the Julius Rosenwald Foundation, a program that played an instrumental role in race relations and will be discussed in closer detail later in this chapter, it is evident that whites feared the growing black consciousness could be misdirected.

> The characteristic movements among Negroes are now for the first time becoming proletarian, as contrasted to the upper class or intellectual influence that was typical of previous movements. This present proletarian direction grows out of the increasing power of Negroes in labor and increasing general feelings of protest against discrimination, especially in the armed forces and in war activities

generally. The present movements are led in part by such established leaders as A. Philip Randolph, Walter White, etc. There is likelihood (and danger) that the movement may be seized upon by some much more picturesque figure who may be less responsible and less interested in actual improvement in conditions.[50]

Whereas black intellectuals had traditionally voiced the concerns of black America, whites feared the latest movements were ripe for other leaders who were not as educationally or culturally astute. Many remembered Marcus Garvey's militant critiques of white racism during the first quarter of the twentieth century and wanted to avoid the rise of others like him. Others feared the lack of intellectually savvy leaders would lead to more racial eruptions.

Resolving Tensions

Besides the riots; social, economic, and political conditions; and literary and scholarly works that concentrated on tensions during the 1940s, the number of national organizations that were working to address racial issues mirrored the country's concern with race relations. In a handbook compiled by the Julius Rosenwald Fund in 1945, some 123 national organizations were listed as working directly or indirectly in the field of race relations. The number still remained impressive at 75 organizations when church and international relations groups, special agencies like FEPC, and individual labor unions were excluded.[51] Among the groups primarily concerned with black-white relations were the National Urban League, the National Association for the Advancement of Colored People, Congress of Racial Equality, Julius Rosenwald Fund, Phelps Stokes Fund, the Carnegie Corporation, the General Education Board, American Council on Race Relations, and the Bureau for Intercultural Education.

One such organization that would end up having a significant impact on the development of the Fisk University Race Relation Institute was the American Missionary Association (AMA). The AMA, incorporated in 1846, consisted of several abolitionary societies. The AMA's purpose, as stated in their original charter, was to assist in ending "sins of caste" because they believed the practice of slavery to be "inhuman, immoral, and unchristian." Immediately following the Civil War, the AMA worked to bring the freedmen education and full citizenship by opening primary and secondary schools for the former bondsmen and their children. The schools, which at one time numbered 500, served as the forerunners to free public schools and specialized in the preparation of public school teachers. Some of these schools like Hampton, Fisk, Atlanta, Talledega, Lemoyne, Dillard, Tougaloo, and Tillotson, became colleges and universities.[52] As racial situations stemming from population mobility, industrial adjustments, housing shortages, military training programs, and general war hysteria became more violent and frequent during the 1940s, the AMA set its sights on directly impacting race relations. Inspired also by Myrdal's *An American Dilemma*, the AMA focused its attention on showing the ironic hypocrisy in ideology to those who professed a belief in brotherhood while simultaneously supporting racial segregation.[53] In 1942 the AMA set up the Race Relations Department at Fisk University. The department's goal was to establish "non-institutional ministries of reconciliation in communities of acute Negro-white tension in the United States."[54] Confident of Charles S. Johnson's ability in the area of race relations, the AMA selected Johnson to direct their endeavor.

The AMA's race relations program would essentially be an action program related to and based largely on the research program at the Department of Social Sciences at Fisk University. The AMA's general objectives for their Race Relations Division centered around identifying racially tense areas; developing courses that taught constructive ways to deal with tensions, developing leaders who could deal with racial tensions in "an acceptable manner"; developing educational resources and community resources to "avert or prevent overt racial clashes"; "assisting communities in addressing anticipated racial problems and developing new areas of racial appreciation, understanding, and common responsibility. This would complement developing programs of racial democracy within churches, labor organizations and youth groups."[55]

The work of the AMA's Race Relations Department began formally in January 1943. Johnson cautioned supporters not to expect sudden miracles just because their program was grounded in Christian ideals. He pointed out that as a group they were still dealing with the "same slow moving elements of custom and tradition and problems of human behavior that [had] resisted the high principles of Christian democracy since the founding of the nation." Rather, Johnson envisioned the program allowing participants to understand the problems and utilize the best experience of the social sciences in programs of constructive action. The program would maintain its Christian base.[56] Johnson would hold this same philosophy at the Fisk Institute.

Two factors helped determine the direction of the AMA's Race Relations Department: 1) the Department of Social Sciences at Fisk University upon which the AMA's program was based, and 2) the Julius Rosenwald Fund, with whom Johnson was also associated and which had an interest and program in race relations.[57] Like the AMA the Julius Rosenwald Fund (Rosenwald Fund) also had a long-running relationship with blacks. The Rosenwald Fund, established by Julius Rosenwald, president of Sears, Roebuck and Company, was incorporated on 30 October 1917 in Illinois as a nonprofit organization. Its broad chartered purpose was "the well-being of mankind."[58] The first Rosenwald school was built in 1913 near Tuskegee. The school, a one-room frame building, was funded in part by Rosenwald, local African Americans, and local white citizens. The school was maintained by public authorities. By the Rosenwald Fund's end, Rosenwald-supported schools numbered 5,000.[59] From 1928 to 1948 the Rosenwald Fund had also donated $1,832,820 for 1,537 fellows, of which 999 were African American.[60]

In the beginning the Rosenwald Fund was under the personal control of Julius Rosenwald himself, but he changed it from private to corporate control. When he did this, Rosenwald named Edwin R. Embree, who had served as director and vice president of the Rockefeller Foundation, as president of the Rosenwald Fund. In addition to changing the trust from private to corporate giving, Rosenwald, who believed that ongoing endowments could actually hinder progress, stipulated that all the money in the fund be spent within 25 years of his death.[61]

Although the Rosenwald Fund had been contributing to education, health and medical services, and fellowships for blacks, its first attempt at influencing race relations didn't come until the Depression era. During the 1930s the Rosenwald Fund believed that the best chance blacks had at making any real progress relied upon the New Deal administration. But as the new administration came into power, the Rosenwald Fund, realizing that the new administration had not made provisions for black affairs, became concerned. This concern prompted the Rosenwald Fund officers to suggest to the administration that an office within the Department of Interior be added that would be responsible for handling black interest in all national recovery acts. To show the Rosenwald Fund's commitment to this office, the group offered and paid the salary for the office head's position.[62]

In 1942, towards the end of the Rosenwald Fund's life, Embree sought ways to continue the Rosenwald Fund's contributions in the area of race relations. Johnson had previously worked with Embree on the Chicago Commission on Race. In a letter dated May 29, 1942, Edwin Embree let Johnson know that the Rosenwald Fund was interested in actively participating in efforts to show the American people that racial problems were a national concern. He wrote:

> I am thinking very seriously about the active implementing of our program in race relations ... I should like very much to have a thorough talk with you and with several others about the kinds of things that we might do.... [and ask] "what are the things that a foundation might do during the next two to five years to bring home to the American people most effectively the color problem in America and in the new world order"? I have in mind the possibility of the making of some really good movies, the use of the radio, as well as an aggressive program of writing and speaking and whatever other means can be used to crystallize thinking on this most important of present-day problems.[63]

Johnson and Rosenwald Fund representatives outlined the objectives of the Rosenwald Fund in the area of race relations during their last years as an organization. They realized that priority had to be given to monitoring black-white relations across the country and that conditions in the South affected conditions throughout the country. Their plan to improve relations included organizing and disseminating literature, sensitizing people who directed federal agencies throughout the South, and supporting new liberal leadership.[64]

Alexander, Johnson, and Embree were concerned not only with black-white relations, but also with developing a well-rounded program that addressed other American minorities. An October 15, 1942, letter written by Embree also shows this concern:

> ...I am convinced that we must think of race and color from now on as a national and world problem. I do not want to keep bogged down by the reaction and stodginess of the South, but I do recognize the special problems that exist there and I know that special machinery must be set up to deal with them.[65]

The Rosenwald Fund's efforts in the area of race relations were also not going unnoticed. In an August 10, 1942, letter from Pearl S. Buck to Embree, Buck states her support of the Rosenwald Fund's efforts. She wrote:

> ...I am delighted that the Julius Rosenwald Fund is considering the question of extending its field of work. The problem of the Negro in America is simply a local example of a world-wide problem and to my thinking, the greatest one that human beings have at the moment....[66]

As the issue of race was heating up, numerous social scientists were working to come up with possible strategies and activities to resolve racial tensions. In *Black Americans in the Roosevelt Era*, John B. Kirby writes that Will W. Alexander, a Methodist minister active in race relations during the Depression era, also had several thoughts on addressing racial prejudices. His suggestions would include political, social, and economic efforts. Alexander felt that many of the "special problems" of African Americans could be eased by economic and other types of governmental reform.[67] Alexander also felt that if whites were to truly develop new attitudes towards African Americans, they would first have to get rid of their old thoughts, which were constantly being disproved by modern scientists.[68] Like Johnson, Alexander noted that African Americans would have to play a role in changing the attitudes of whites. He pointed out that whites talking about the intelligence of African Americans were not as persuasive as educated African Americans who could serve as living examples.[69] Racial prejudices would be eased because not only would these educated African Americans change the minds of whites, they would also build the confidence of other African Americans.

Ruth Benedict, another social scientist, also offered suggestions for dealing with racial prejudice in *Race and Racism*. Like Johnson, Benedict valued education as a major weapon in combating racial prejudice. She felt that education could be the foundation to end racism if it would offer facts about race and different racial groups, and teach about the mutual interdependence of different groups. Students could learn facts about race and racial differences during regular social studies classes. The differences in groups that they found to be unsatisfactory, and had been told were natural to the groups, could be rectified through concerted efforts.[70]

Although Benedict saw education as a key component to ending racism and racial tensions, she believed that simply teaching about the contributions from different groups was not enough to end racism. She wrote:

> ...to avert racism we must "strongly resolve" that all men shall have the basic opportunity to work and earn a living wage, that education and health and decent shelter shall be available to all, that regardless of race, creed, or colour, civil liberties shall be protected.[71]

Benedict maintained that government investment in rebuilding America would allow the country to become the democracy it claimed to be. Investments in housing, health care, and education for America's minorities and poor would make democracy work and therefore end racism.[72]

In *An American Dilemma*, Myrdal agreed with Benedict. Myrdal wrote that racial problems in America could be solved or rectified to a certain degree by actually improving blacks' social position. He wrote:

> Assuming as our value premise that we want to reduce the bias in white people's racial beliefs concerning Negroes, our first practical conclusion is that we can effect this result to a degree by actually improving Negro status, Negro behavior, Negro characteristics. The impediment in the way of this strategy is, of course, that white beliefs, directly and indirectly, are active forces in keeping the Negro low....[73]

Myrdal conceived two other strategies would also contribute to improving whites' perceptions of blacks. First, he held educational efforts would be more beneficial once additional research about blacks by black scholars could be offered to the masses. Myrdal pointed out that whites—out of a need to justify the caste order that operated within America—developed and maintained negative images about blacks. As the research advanced and misconceptions eradicated, Myrdal held whites would reconstruct their beliefs about blacks. Second, Myrdal deemed attacking the "valuations for the rationalization of which false beliefs are employed" would also lower the apprehension whites felt toward blacks.[74] The American caste system had not been predicated upon a society that promoted political, economic, and social equality to all groups. Black opportunity had been denied. To lower the resistance whites felt toward blacks, Mydral suggested efforts be made to change white people's minds toward equalitarianism.[75]

In *Race Relations: The Interaction of Ethnic and Racial Groups*, sociologist Brewton Berry suggested that a full-scale concerted effort be employed by numerous organizations utilizing education and propaganda as principal weapons.[76] Schools, churches, radio stations, movie and stage theaters, the press, billboards, labor unions, and service clubs—all the places where people gather—could be used to disseminate facts about differing races and racial prejudices.[77] Johnson agreed with this.

Believing that blacks were just as responsible for improving race relations as whites, Johnson suggested that blacks participate in social organizations that were making efforts in the field of race relations. He encouraged blacks to work with local administrative officials to make sure blacks shared in funding reserved for education, health care, recreation, and employment. This type of participation would also bring black needs to the forefront of committee discussions and would allow blacks to equitably share in measures that were developed to help the underprivileged. Johnson also encouraged blacks to work on labor policy by getting involved with the labor unions to ensure the inclusion of blacks in labor organizations.[78] Realizing the impact education could have on race relations, Johnson encouraged high schools to offer courses in sociology and colleges to broaden their studies of race problems. He recommended the use of field work projects with an interracial focus for college students, and black guest lecturers for high school students.[79]

Johnson's educational strategies were not limited to schoolchildren and college students. He noted that the general public could benefit from massive dissemination of literature aimed at listing correctable actions and thoughts held against blacks, along with works that would point to their cultural development. Local librarians could get involved by offering and promoting books by black poets and authors for general reading. Local communities could include blacks in forums, musical programs, poetry readings, folk plays, or lecturers that would highlight their talent and give their racial experience.[80] Local newspapers could also get involved by correcting false and harmful statements about blacks. They could publicly condemn public crimes such as mob violence and lynchings, economic exploitation, and the unfair treatment of blacks in courts based on racial prejudice.[81] Johnson also recommended that blacks and whites organize meetings on public affairs where racial problems were not the primary focus.[82]

Arnold M. Rose, another University of Chicago trained sociologist, was also concerned about combating racial prejudices. Like Benedict and Myrdal, Rose found that the basic problems of race relations were buried within the ideal of American democracy, which had not been completed. Rose believed that regardless of how racism and racial prejudices started, they persisted because they were so well entrenched in everyday life that people really didn't know that they were being racists or prejudiced.[83]

Because people didn't realize when they were being prejudiced, Rose doubted that simply asking people to get along would stop them from being prejudiced. Racial prejudice could only end if all existing forms of discrimination were uprooted, and this could only be done through a "militant campaign" to extend to many, for the first time, the rights that they had already been theoretically guaranteed but never enjoyed. Rose also pointed out that democracy was achieved when "freedom from fear and freedom from want have been securely established."[84]

Rose also offered suggestions utilizing education and legislation for improving race relations. First he called for defined objectives. The ideals of tolerance and brotherly love were vague in his opinion and did not work well in a society that was built upon well-defined objectives. After establishing the defined objectives, Rose suggested that proponents of racial tolerance obtain the needed facts about the conditions that they would fight and the resources to be used so that they could gain mass participation.[85] With the specific objectives, facts, and mass organization, the next step would be to utilize all resources that were available. Rose suggested that the ballot box, legislation, judicial precedent, administrative regulation and enforcement, the powers of state and municipal governments, mass pressure on public officials, technology and communication—films, radio and other mass communications—all be used in conjunction with each other. He argued that although it was true that prejudice could not be legislated out of existence, fair practice legislation to establish practices that violated democratic rights could be. Fair practice legislation would hinder and make illegal the development of reinforced prejudice. New norms and patterns of social conduct could then develop without the influence of prejudicial stimuli. A strong proponent of legislative strategies, Rose felt that educational plans to avert racism had to be practical and needed to concentrate on a specific issue. He desired the organization of a campaign for the passage of a state fair educational practices bill that would involve the active participation of numerous people working for a receptive legislation and the general support for future enforcement.[86]

The federal government also showed increased concern over racial tensions and inequality. Numerous violent racial attacks in the South during 1946 and 1947 prodded President Harry S Truman, who had been cautiously seeking political equality for blacks, to take more direct action. In 1947 he formed the President's Committee on Civil Rights. The committee's job was to study and recommend new legislation that would guard against discrimination. In its October 1947 report, "To Secure These Rights," the committee reported that "separate but equal" was a failure. In accepting and endorsing its findings, Truman formally placed the executive branch in opposition to segregation and publicly declared that America could not wait another decade to address its racial hate. Although this action went virtually unnoticed by many Americans, it was the first time a president had officially taken a stand against segregation.[87] This act laid the foundation for the political context of black-white relations that would follow in later decades in that it signaled the possibility of federal intervention in the race relations arena.

Obviously, Johnson was not alone in the thought that education and legislative action were the key components to changing oppressive societal conditions. Johnson would draw upon his affiliation with Fisk University supporters, the AMA, the Rosenwald Fund, and noted scholars throughout the country to further develop and implement his ideas. The end product, which was the Fisk University Race Relations Institute, would be "a laboratory of social action" dedicated to training and research.[88]

CHAPTER TWO

"Intelligent and Effective Direction": The Fisk University Race Relations Institute

In 1942 Charles S. Johnson set out to address the decade's racial hostilities through the Fisk University Race Relations Institute. Johnson proposed the RRI as an arena where social scientists, educators, and community leaders could come together and work to build racial tolerance. Johnson did not initially envision the RRI, which first ran for three weeks during the summer of 1944, to be a recurring event. Response, however, dictated otherwise. The RRI would end up running uninterrupted each summer until 1969. During those 25 years the RRI stood firm in its belief that education was the key to dealing with racial strife. Specifically, the RRI, which was the first of its kind in the South, sought to integrate training, research, and social action.

Johnson and his supporters believed that providing trained personnel to lead efforts in improving race relations, a space where research on issues of race and race relations could be presented and critiqued; and a space where "intelligent and effective direction of social action" could be conceptualized would prove most effective in efforts to resolve the nation's racial tensions. These components needed to be closely integrated because Johnson and his supporters believed that "[t]raining, to be adequate, need[ed] to be carried on in an environment of active research; and research, to be effective, need[ed] to be constantly tested in the laboratory of social action."[1]

Prior experience and work in the field of race relations made Johnson adamant about the valuable role he saw education and the social sciences playing in addressing the country's racial quagmire. Johnson specifically sought to have scholars utilize research to provide facts about blacks and other minorities that would offset the negative stereotypes whites held about the groups. Once whites understood those facts and the atrocities practiced against blacks in particular, Johnson hoped moral whites would work to implement changes in social policies that would, in turn, promote democratic treatment for subordinated groups. With policies in place that reflected America's democratic ideals, Johnson hoped that racial groups would deal with one another in a tolerant manner.

Without a doubt, Johnson's strategy for dealing with racial tensions was a top-down approach that might seem peculiar in light of more well known bottom-up, grassroots civil rights efforts and activities. But Johnson was part of a generation of people who experienced life before and after the implementation of racial segregation in America. That shift, in and of itself, must have produced a surreal disorientation that would be unknown to later generations born under the oppressive rules. Considering Johnson's positioning within this unique generation of people who saw legislation alter the patterns of black-white relations situates his ideas within a context that is less intellectually elite. Thus, understanding Johnson's life experiences and work in race relations lends context to the structure and ideologies behind the RRI.

Discovery and Awakening:
Charles S. Johnson and Race Relations

In large part, the RRI reflected the various lived experiences and learned lessons of its founder and director Charles S. Johnson. Reflecting on his life in "A Spiritual Autobiography," Johnson noted how difficult it was to separate his intellectual and spiritual growth from his early life experiences. He wrote:

> ... it is impossible to disentangle the threads of my own intellectual and spiritual growth from the realities of this early environment. No one lives in a social vacuum, or in his family alone. Ideas, impressions, feelings about life and people and things all seemed rooted in this period, and all my life I have been working with the problems, social, intellectual and spiritual that were generated there and then.[2]

Johnson was seven years old when the onset of legalized segregation changed life as he knew it. After an ordinary day of Saturday shopping in his hometown of Bristol, Virginia, Johnson and his mother stopped by their favorite drugstore to buy ice cream sodas. Just as he had done on numerous occasions, Johnson placed his order and took his regular seat at the lunch counter. The clerk, who had always been friendly and often piled extra ice cream into Johnson's glass, nervously dallied with the fountain gadgets for several minutes before dashing to the back of the store in search of the owner. When the owner, "an old family friend, in a sort of way" appeared, he told Mrs. Johnson he could no longer serve them at the counter. "[E]xtravagant in his expressions of respect" for the Johnson family and other blacks who frequented his business, the owner "never discussed the law or the policy directly" and "had no defense" to Johnson's mother's "obvious dismay and sense of humiliating embarrassment." Johnson and his mother "simply went home in silence."[3]

In *Having Our Say: The Delaney Sisters' First 100 Years*, Sadie and Bessie Delaney also share memories of the dismay they felt when legalized segregation made its way to their town, Raleigh, North Carolina. Sadie reflects:

> We encountered Jim Crow laws for the first time on a summer Sunday afternoon. We were about five and seven years old at the time. Mama and Papa used to take us to Pullen Park in Raleigh for picnics, and that particular day, the trolley driver told us to go to the back. We children objected loudly, because we always liked to sit in front, where the breeze would blow your hair. That had been part of the fun for us. But Mama and Papa just gently told us to hush and took us to the back without making a fuss.[4]

Racial segregation had long been practiced in many places throughout the South since Emancipation. In *The Strange Career of Jim Crow*, C. Vann Woodward shares:

> In the early years of the twentieth century, it was becoming clear that the Negro would be effectively disfranchised throughout the South, that he would be firmly relegated to the lower rungs of the economic ladder, and that neither equality nor aspirations for equality in any department of life were for him.[5]

The custom of racial segregation was legalized with the Supreme Court ruling in *Plessy v. Ferguson* in 1896. The case revolved around Homer Plessy, a fair-skinned man, who appeared white but also had black ancestry. Plessy had been arrested for refusing to sit in the "colored" railroad car on a trip from New Orleans to Covington, Louisiana. Plessy lost on his appeal to the Supreme Court, which sanctioned "separate but equal" facilities for black and whites. Woodward goes on to share that "The public symbols and constant reminders of [black] inferior position were the segregation statutes, or 'Jim Crow' laws. They constituted the most elaborate and formal expression of sovereign white opinion upon the subject."[6] Sadie Delaney agrees, noting "We knew we were already second-class citizens,... but those Jim Crow laws set it in stone."[7]

Johnson's early understanding of human relations and social action played a crucial element in the development of the Fisk University Race Relations Institute. Johnson was born in Bristol, Virginia, on July 24, 1893, to a college-educated father and homemaker with notable "social graces." Johnson's father, Charles Henry, was the son of a slave and had grown up in the home of a "quiet" Greek scholar and theologian, who was "so lost in the richness and other timeliness of the classics, and so aloof from the burning political controversies of his time" that he educated Johnson's father alongside his own son "without apology."[8] Johnson's father later attended college and theological school in Richmond, Virginia, and became a Baptist minister. Johnson's mother, Winifred Branch Johnson, was a homemaker who had the "poor best that the public schools of Lynchburg, Virginia" offered combined with the social graces that were passed along from her mother, who had been a "privileged" servant for some of Virginia's old and prominent families.[9]

Bristol reflected the intricate patterns of day-to-day southern black-white relations. Located in the southern range of the Cumberland Mountains, Bristol's main street divided Virginia and Tennessee.[10] Johnson described Bristol as a "rough, frontier town not far from the Appalachian coal mines; Southern in its racial mores, but relaxed enough by other preoccupations, to permit a few fairly normal relationships" between blacks and whites.[11] For example, Bristol had the typical racial distinctions like black churches, neighborhoods, and business areas, but the town's atmosphere also allowed a black butcher at the largest meat market, and for the Johnsons to have a white wash lady. This, however, did not mean that a person's color did not matter. Although blacks and whites lived in terms that ranged from "tolerant indifference to restrained cordiality,"[12] race was an ever-present factor that had to be negotiated on a daily basis. Johnson wrote:

> The problem was always one of finding a reasonable state of personal equilibrium in the intimate community. Overshadowing every conceivable prospect of growing up was the ever present danger of difference and dispute with forces that emerged from the social and racial customs of the time and place. Custom and habit can, under normal conditions, support normal behavior thus remove the strain and tension of new or hostile situations. The customs to which I refer were patterned on race and occasionally exercised force, without benefit of reason, logic, morals or simple fair play.[13]

Johnson watched his parents negotiate a reasonable state of personal equilibrium as they combined their Christian sense of responsibility with their sense of activism. As Johnson's parents worked jointly throughout the community ministering and addressing social concerns, he and his four younger siblings learned the value of social action early in life. Although black-white relations were for the most part cordial in Bristol, he noted his father's ability to translate religious convictions into "useful and pioneering social action" as his father often spoke out against racial injustice.[14] For example, Johnson's father was the lone voice of dissent when a white lynch mob set out to kill a black man. Edwin Embree writes about Johnson's father and that particular incident in *13 Against the Odds*.

> The little man was as fearless of white toughs as of black. Once as a lynch mob came roaring up his street, he reared his five feet four inches of moral courage right in their path. While the gang threatened to hang him beside the victim they were dragging along, he stood his ground so that the men had to shuffle around him to get past, while he cursed their evil, quoted Scripture against their violence and prayed for their change of heart. This mob was too far gone in blood lust to be stopped. But the whole town was so shamed by the orgy and by the preacher's rebukes, which echoed in white churches as well as colored, that no lynching has ever again threatened Bristol.[15]

Johnson's father's church "became the rallying ground for the whole colored community."[16] Johnson recalled with "pride and affection" in *13 Against the Odds* "the burdens his father willingly took on: spiritual advisor, legal and business counsel, guardian and banker, nurse and doctor, tutor and social worker."[17] Johnson's parents also helped facilitate art in the community as they often opened their home to notable artists and invited the black community.[18]

Johnson learned other crucial lessons about human relations while growing up in Bristol. He witnessed the physical and psychological impact that segregation had on black-white relations. The implementation of Jim Crow laws taught young Johnson that segregation not only physically separated the races but also eroded existing cordial and tolerant relations between groups. Just as the drugstore incident gave life to the "remote and abstract character" Jim Crow, more incidents followed as legalized segregation became a way of life in Bristol.[19] The "familiar friendly face" of the trolley conductor, for example, "took on strange grimness and determination." The man who now told blacks to sit in designated areas was the same man who used to assist black women and children onto the car.[20] The black community was shocked and dismayed that "these friendly old men were now the agents of a new and obnoxious policy."[21] Johnson realized that the policy allowed whites to know less about blacks and blacks to "care less and less about their opinions."[22]

Upon completing the black elementary school, Johnson, then fourteen years old, left Bristol to attend secondary school at Wayland Academy in Richmond. There was no black secondary school in Bristol. Wayland was the preparatory school of the private Baptist black college Virginia Union University. Johnson stayed on at Virginia Union after completing Wayland, and earned his AB degree in 1917.[23] Johnson learned another important lesson about human relations and social action while a student in Virginia. Johnson met Dr. Joshua Simpson, a black professor who taught Greek. Johnson highly respected Simpson "who was able to convey the full and rich meaning of a wholesome life, through an exacting, but never oppressive discipline." Simpson, "with all his surface austerity, came closest to understanding the art and meaning of human relations" and helped Johnson articulate the "deepest and most real questions about people and the meaning of life." During one of Simpson's class service projects in a needy black community, Johnson discovered the "core" of what would become his personal social philosophy: "no man can be justly judged until you have looked at the world through his eyes."[24] Embree shares

> In the Christmas vacation of [Johnson's] last year in college, he had an experience so stark that it sealed his interest in social problems. Checking applicants for Christmas baskets for the Richmond Welfare Association, he stumbled one afternoon into a basement room of a tumble-down shack and found a girl alone, on a pile of rags, groaning in labor. He rushed out for a doctor, but those he found "had no time to attend." He finally got a midwife who saw the girl through. Then

he set to have the girl cared for on some lasting basis. He went first to her family, and was shocked at their cold refusal to take her home or even to speak to her. He tried to get other families to take her in, only to meet the same scorn. He tried institutions and found obstacles, sometimes because she was colored, other times "because she had sinned." In the midst of his earnest crusade the girl vanished. He never saw her again, nor heard of her. But he has never been able to get out of his mind that Christmas tragedy, nor to cease pondering the anger of people at a human catastrophe while they calmly accept conditions that cause it.[25]

That incident led to Johnson's interest in social work. In 1916 Johnson enrolled at the University of Chicago as a graduate fellow in sociology. Johnson carried his life lessons with him to the university where mentor Robert Park "linked" Johnson's "deep and moving human concern with science and human understanding."[26] Park had advanced the study of race relations beyond conversations of the inferiority and criminality of African Americans by introducing conceptual tools that led to the objective study of race relations. By introducing data collection and measurements and making use of concepts like attitudes, social distance, and mores and social tools like cycles of contact, conflict, assimilation, and accommodation, Park's work enabled social scientists like Johnson to conduct systematic and empirical investigations on the social problems of race. Richard Robbins shares that Park enabled Johnson and other students, including Everett and Helen Hughes, Louis Wirth, Robert Redfield, and E. Franklin Frazier, to "synthesize the European-based 'working concepts' of sociology and the social facts of life in real communities, producing a unique genre that came to bear the stamp 'Chicago school.'"[27]

Park was also president of the Chicago Urban League, where he organized a bureau of research and investigations. In 1917 he had Johnson hired as the director of research and investigations. Johnson utilized his social science skills and human convictions and concentrated on race relations at the Chicago Urban League. He began "interpreting colored people to whites and white people to Negroes, Southerners to Northerners, rustics to city dwellers; analyzing people's problems so that they can understand themselves."[28] Johnson worked on numerous projects concerning the social and economic conditions of blacks in Chicago and around the country, and conducted several surveys of housing conditions for blacks in Chicago while directing the bureau. Johnson later wrote of the profound impact the Chicago Urban League had on his development as a social scientist:

> Out of this early period came my own first deep interest in social research and it was the Chicago Urban League that first initiated a thorough-going program of basic research as the touchstone of realistic work primarily with Negroes. It was the original emphasis of the Chicago Urban League on fundamental studies as the basis for action that found emphasis in the study by the Chicago Commission on Race Relations.[29]

World War I interrupted Johnson's graduate studies and work at the Chicago Urban League for a year. Although he was apprehensive about the concept of war, Johnson entered the military in 1918 and served as a regimental sergeant major. He wrote of war: "I cannot say that I regard this type of resolution of human conflict as being as effective for its purpose as it is wildly destructive and inconclusive." Although he was under fire for twenty-two consecutive days, he noted that "No deep hatred of the Germans was generated in me at any time of the war."[30]

After serving in World War I, Johnson returned to Chicago assuming he would continue his graduate studies at the University of Chicago and work at the Chicago Urban League. Little did Johnson know that his arrival in Chicago would precede a violent race riot by one week. The death of seventeen-year-old Eugene Williams, a black man, sparked a four-day riot that would become one of the country's largest and most violent. While swimming in Lake Michigan on Sunday, July 27, 1919, Williams accidentally floated into the "whites only" section of the Lake Michigan beach. Whites on the beach began throwing stones at Williams and he drowned. When police refused to arrest the young white man black witnesses accused of throwing the fatal stone, tensions flared. "Within two hours the riot was in full sway, had scored its second fatality, and was spreading throughout the south and southwest parts of the city. Before the end came it reached out to a section of the West side and even invaded the 'Loop,' the heart of Chicago's downtown business district."[31]

On the second day of the riot, Johnson experienced firsthand the intense and violent manifestations of racial tensions. While making his way to his job at the Urban League on Wabash Avenue, Johnson witnessed the stabbing death of a man on the steps of a building and narrowly escaped bullets himself.[32] After making his way back to his University of Chicago room, Johnson speculated about the violence. In a manner that was somewhat stream of consciousness, Johnson speculated that a variety of urban realities collided and ignited the tensions. He wrote:

> Mass migration, like unto the flight of the children of Israel out of Egypt, half a million black folk pouring up from the poverty and persecution of the southern rurals, hungry for the wages and freedom of the Promised Land, northern cities overrun by black migrants fresh from the cotton and tobacco fields, lost in the frenzy of city slums, noisy factories, freezing winters.
> The new Negro newspapers of the North whooping it up for the exodus, "I beg of you, my brethren, to leave that benighted land. You are free men... Your neck has been in the yoke...To die from the bite of frost is more glorious than to die from the rope and faggots of the mob."
> A hundred thousand Negroes swarming into the single city of Chicago, "God's country" to the masses along the Mississippi bottoms, houses overflowing, rents soaring, black hordes pouring into forbidden territory, swarming over yesterday's fashionable boulevards of the South Side, Prairie Avenue, Grand

> Boulevard, South Parkway, and everywhere no repairs, bad plumbing, no gas, no heat, no water.
> Grumbling and jostling as white soldiers back from the war clamor for jobs now filled by Negroes, guerilla warfare, gangs of young hoodlums chasing Negroes down back alleys feeling the thrill of battle and the joy of duty well done for their race.[33]

After further gathering his thoughts, Johnson realized the widespread impact of the riot. He realized that the riots were not isolated, but part and parcel of the conflicts he had also witnessed on the East Coast while traveling home from the war. "Without washing the blood stains off his clothes, he sat down and wrote out a detailed plan for a study of the Chicago riots as a symptom of the social and economic conflicts of the time."[34]

On the fourth day of the riot, the local National Association for the Advancement of Colored People (NAACP) hurriedly assembled a committee and asked the governor of Illinois to appoint a commission to study Chicago's race relations and devise ways of addressing issues. Two days later, another group of influential Chicagoans also asked the governor to create an emergency state committee that would research the causes of the riots and make recommendations to curtail future outbreaks.[35] Illinois Governor Frank O. Lowden finally called on the state militia to assist police in restoring order to several affected sections of Chicago, including the "Loop," the heart of the downtown business district. The four-day riot, which ran intermittently July 27 through August 2, left 38 dead—15 white and 23 black—and 537 injured. Of the injured, 178 were white, 342 were black. The race of 17 injured was not recorded.[36] Approximately 1000 were rendered "homeless and destitute."[37] The state of actual calm was not restored until August 6.[38]

The Chicago riot gave Johnson the opportunity to focus on the social and economic reasons for negative relations between blacks and whites. In October 1919 Lowden, familiar with Johnson's work in race relations, and fearing more riots would occur, sought out Johnson as a "routine witness." It's important to note that Johnson's academic advisor, Robert E. Park, had supported Johnson's interests in race relations and had introduced Johnson to some of Chicago's notables. Johnson also became the investigator of black migration for the Carnegie Foundation. The commission was "staggered—and delighted" however, when instead of a testimony, Johnson presented a plan of study he had prepared.[39] The governor accepted the plan and appointed Johnson as Associate Executive Secretary of the Governor's Commission on Race Relations. The governor was justified in thinking additional riots could erupt. Although the death of Williams had sparked the Chicago riot, Chicago was not the only city to experience interracial violence following the war. The summer of 1919 became known as "Red Summer" because twenty-six riots erupted across the country.[40] Red Summer's largest and most violent riots included Chicago; Charleston, South Carolina; Longview, Texas;

Omaha, Nebraska; Washington, DC; Elaine, Arkansas; Tulsa, Oklahoma; and Knoxville, Tennessee.[41] The racial conflicts were not confined to the summer of 1919. Numerous other race riots erupted during the first half of the twentieth century.[42] The Governor's Commission was comprised of Johnson and an interracial group of researchers who investigated the social and economic reasons for the riots. Reflecting on the riot and its causes, Johnson noted

> Hates and angers and confusions touched off to wild explosion by a single incident at a South Side bathing beach on that historic Sunday, July 27, 1919, a seventeen-year-old colored boy swimming into the area used by whites, a shower of stones, the boy sinking to his death, angry Negroes collecting on the beach, police refusing to arrest the white offenders and beating up the Negroes, a colored man firing at the police and being himself shot down, terror spreading as night came, mobs of blacks and whites meeting, fighting with fists, shooting, stabbing.
> Sporadic fighting all day Monday, roaring into rioting and killing as darkness of the second day came on, the whole phantasmagoria turning into a nightmare in a car strike Monday midnight, tying up all traffic on surface and elevated lines, men walking to work and stopping to fight, automobiles speeding through the hot dusty streets of the black belt, armed hoodlums firing through windows and doors and into the milling crowds on the streets.
> Negro homes burning, mobs everywhere, chasing their victims even into the downtown business streets, the police helpless, a city seized with panic, twenty-five Negroes slain, fifteen white people killed, 538 persons, white and black, wounded before state troops and a lucky rainstorm quelled the rioters.[43]

Johnson served on the Commission until 1921 and made lasting friendships with such figures as Julius Rosenwald. Rosenwald would later play a pivotal role in Johnson's race relations projects. The results of the study were published in 1922 by the Chicago Commission in *The Negro in Chicago: A Study of Race Relations and a Race Riot*. Johnson found that Chicago was ripe for a racial outbreak as a massive wave of blacks, who migrated to the area from the South in search of industrial jobs, began competing with whites for those positions. Embree notes that "[c]alls poured in upon this brilliant student to make study after study of the migrating Negroes, their clashes and adjustments, in a score of cities into which they were still swarming." Johnson wanted to see his studies "result in action" and "gladly tied his work" to the Urban League. Johnson conducted surveys in "Baltimore, Trenton, Hartford, East St. Louis, Fort Wayne, Buffalo, and Los Angeles." He "stated the problem and outlined the programs that branches of the Urban League should tackle in those cities to help Negroes get employment, find houses, make their way through the maze of hurdles that were being thrown up in the new northern settings."[44] In 1919, Johnson earned a Ph.B. (Bachelor of Philosophy) from the University of Chicago.[45]

Although busily working in the field of race relations, Johnson married Marie Antoinette Burgette (1891–1965) of Milwaukee in 1920. Johnson described Marie as "an unusually sensitive young woman, richly endowed mentally and spiritually, with a rare capacity for sensing and seeing the beautiful good in people, and drawing out these qualities into a self-respecting grace."[46] In 1921 Johnson and Marie moved to New York so that he could become head of the National Urban League's research department. Johnson started the organization's monthly publication, *Opportunity*, which published issues concerning race relations and showcased the literary works of blacks. *Opportunity* became a vehicle by which Johnson and other social scientists could address the racist scientific notions that permeated the subject of race relations.

Research by such scientists as Park and Franz Boas had expanded conversation on race relations beyond theories of the inferiority and criminality of blacks, but attempts to catagorize races by either intelligence or brain size and structure continued to promote ideas of racial superiority and inferiority well into the mid-1900s. Johnson took special interest in refuting attempts to classify blacks as subhumans because he believed the "scientific" findings about black inferiority contributed to the negative myths and beliefs European Americans held about blacks, and thereby increased the social distance between the two groups. In two separate articles published in *Opportunity* Johnson criticized "scientific" findings that classified blacks as subhuman. One study conducted in 1906 by Johns Hopkins professor R. B. Bean concluded that racial groups had different-shaped brains that not only reflected racial differences, but also indicated differences in intelligence between the groups. This study, based on Bean's observation of 150 African American brains and 150 European American brains, reported blacks were intellectually inferior to European Americans and was widely accepted as scientific evidence.[47]

Rejecting Bean's findings and noting Bean's bias against blacks, Johnson argued in a 1923 *Opportunity* article how "absurdly easy" it was to "prove almost anything where there exists a *will to believe.*" Johnson referred to a follow-up study by Franklin P. Mall, another Johns Hopkins professor, who replicated Bean's study to determine its accuracy. When Mall measured the brains, he excluded his own "personal equation...to insure objectivity" by covering the labels indicating race.[48] Mall found no difference in the brain structure of blacks and European Americans.[49]

Besides challenging the idea that blacks were mentally inferior to European Americans, Johnson also refuted popular beliefs that blacks were immoral and criminal by nature. The stigma that blacks were immoral was based largely on the high illegitimacy rate in the black community.[50] In another article published in *Opportunity*, Johnson countered that although the rates may have been factual, the records used to support the claims were scarce and only told one side of the story. He argued that among other things, the records did not reflect figures for the dominant white population who had "greater means of secrecy and knowledge of birth control...."[51]

Johnson also challenged the popular belief that blacks were criminal by nature. This belief hung on allegations that a "peculiar emotional instability" predisposed blacks to commit violent crimes, especially sex crimes, and a "constitutional character weakness addict[ed] them to petty thefts."[52] Those who held this belief pointed to the fact that crime rates for blacks were disproportionately high in cities with large black populations. On this point, Johnson conceded that although some blacks were actually criminals who deserved punishment, the whole "bugaboo of the 'criminal nature of Negroes' [was] unnecessarily severe."[53] Johnson argued that if anything, blacks' supposed predisposed "criminal nature" was caused by the European American controlled and operated legal and penal systems which had an "invarying [sic] tendency" to arrest and convict blacks more readily, on less evidence, with harsher sentences than whites. The fact that blacks had "less money to fight their cases, to escape detection, to pay fines or even, so far as records go, to bribe officials" also played a role in the high figures.[54]

Johnson's efforts to critique the negative and widespread research on blacks can be linked to the philosophies of Jean-Jacques Rousseau. Although Johnson's race relations philosophies are traditionally linked to Park's ideas, Johnson credited Rousseau as the "one that contributed most of the basic slant" of his attitude towards life. Born in Geneva, Switzerland, in 1712, Rousseau's early writings and general philosophy revealed his belief that man is basically a "noble savage" when in the "state of nature," but is corrupted by society which he viewed as "artificial" and "corrupt." Mankind was at its best when untouched by the civilization of society. Thus, man's continuing unhappiness was inextricably linked to society's advancements.[55]

Explaining his connection to Rousseau's philosophies, Johnson wrote:

> If I were called upon to select from the streams of ideas to which I have been exposed, one that contributed most to the basic slant of my attitude toward life, I would probably begin with Rousseau. I have been impressed with the tremendous influence which he has exerted on modern society. His ideas, in the first place, contributed profoundly to the divorce of morals from pure theology, to reinterpret life in terms of what might broadly be termed humanitarianism, and this humanitarianism is probably nothing more than the much abused term, service. I have not followed him the full distance, but he seems to me to have touched the key that released some of the present forces shaping the modern world, and shaping much of the thought which controls the most effective work in the field which I have selected for my working life.[56]

Johnson's belief that education could be used to positively influence human interactions can arguably be directly linked to Rousseau's basic theory that man is naturally good and that institutions make man evil. Johnson somewhat modified Rousseau's theory and held that institutions had both negative and positive impacts on man. He wrote:

> I am certain, however, that man is made both good and bad by his institutions; that these institutions are responsible for the shaping of personalities, our morals,

and the patterns of our social relations; and that the re-shaping of our institutions are our responsibility. This is not only a function of formal education, but of all our social concerns.[57]

Johnson's belief in institutions being able to positively influence human interactions was obvious in his attempt to use the RRI as an educative mode to addressing the country's racial problems. After all, if legislation created the tensions that sparked the racial eruptions, then legislation could rectify those tensions. The institution of education could be utilized to positively influence that legislation.

Johnson's efforts to critique negative research on blacks by whites were also in keeping with the attempts of other black scholars to refute the faulty findings at the beginning of the twentieth century. Studies by noted white scientists such as psychologist Robert Yerkes, Carl Brigham, Joseph Peterson, and Horace Mann Bond all reported blacks intellectually inferior to whites.[58] Some scientists like Johnson and his Chicago classmate E. Franklin Frazier utilized the "subdued protest"method[59] of research that reflected Park's teachings to counter the claims of black inferiority. Others like W.E.B. Du Bois and Oliver C. Cox, both described as "forgotten sociologist" by Charles U. Smith and Lewis Killian, abandoned the ideas of utilizing research for social action and started supporting "propaganda and social action" as the first steps to social change.[60]

Whatever the tactic, historian Vincent P. Franklin shares that black social scientists between 1920 and 1940 "challenged many of the findings and conclusions of the 'mental testers'" and "not only pointed out the flaws in the methodologies, test procedures, samplings, and other aspects of mental testing, but also contributed to our general knowledge of what the so-called 'intelligence tests' were actually measuring."[61] *The Atlanta University Studies of Negro Life* (1897–1914), edited by W.E.B. Du Bois, and *The Crisis* magazine, published by the National Association for the Advancement of Colored people and also edited by Du Bois, regularly published works that analyzed and critiqued the findings on blacks by European researchers.[62]

Johnson left the National Urban League in 1928 to establish and head the Social Science Department at Fisk University. In addition to performing several jobs at Fisk, which included professor of sociology, director of the Social Science Department, and head of the Social Science Institute (later to become the Race Relations Department), Johnson continued to build a name for himself in race relations through solid sociological research. He wrote widely on race relations during the 1930s and into the 1940s. In 1930 Johnson depicted a contemporary view of black life and relationships with whites in *The Negro in American Civilization*. He combined information gathered from national organizations engaged in working for the improvement in social conditions for blacks. He continued on this path with his 1932 work *Negro Housing: Report of the Committee on Negro Housing* and again in 1933 with *The Economic Status of Negroes*. In 1934 *Shadow of the Plantation* offered a look at the folk culture of the "peasants" of the Southern plantations by analyzing information gained from interviews with 600 families. That same year Johnson also co-authored *Race Relations: Adjustments of Whites and Negroes in the United States* in which he shared his views on race relations. In 1936 Johnson offered a glimpse of his theories and beliefs on race relations in *Preface to Racial Understanding*. In 1941 Johnson showed how race relations impacts the personality development of Southern black youth in *Growing Up in the Black Belt*.

Besides being busy writing scholarly works which gave insight into his theories on race relations, Johnson also found time to put some of those theories into practice. During the summers from 1934 to 1938 Johnson co-directed the Swarthmore College Institute of Race Relations in Swarthmore, Pennsylvania. At Swarthmore Johnson further developed some of his ideas on the causes of racial tensions, as well as possible ways to educate those working to find solutions to racial tensions. This project ran during the summer months from 1933 to 1938.[63]

The first Swarthmore College Race Relations Institute was organized by the Society of Friends in July 1933 for "mature men and women" who wanted to "study and discuss the world problem of race and the factors which constitute[d] the American inter-racial situation, with emphasis upon Negro-white relations."[64] Basically, the Society of Friends and Johnson wanted the Swarthmore Institute to provide a framework so that participants would have the opportunity to study race relations, especially black-white relationships, scientifically and in more detail. By doing this, participants could examine specific and factual data on racial and cultural problems, as well as evaluate the techniques that were being utilized to address those problems.[65]

The Swarthmore Institute's purpose was not to prescribe a cure for the racial ills that plagued America, or make specific conclusions or recommendations; but rather to "aid in the develop[ment] of essential personnel" that was needed during this time of "racial and cultural confusion, where intelligence rather than indignation [was] the test of ability to meet and control these relations."[66] To achieve these things, the Society of Friends and Johnson believed that those working in the field of race relations needed to be exposed to the "complex social phenomena" that make race relations intricate and emotional.[67] Like Johnson, the Society of Friends believed that racial tensions exist throughout the world because civilized groups do not have planned methods to meet interracial needs and tensions. So the aim of the Swarthmore Institute was to assist in planning methods and developing strategies for interracial activity based on "background of fact" and "impartial analysis."[68]

In order to execute his plan for Swarthmore, Johnson assembled a group of noted leaders from various fields to share their research and insights on race relations. These figures were not only prominent for their work on race and race relation theories, many were personally acquainted with Johnson through either foundations and organizations like the American Missionary Association, The Urban League, The Rosenwald Foundation, and the NAACP, or through Johnson's graduate school experience. Among those who were either faculty or lecturers at the five year summer program were: W.W. Alexander from the Southern Interracial Commission and President of Dillard University; Franz Boas from the Department of Anthropology, Columbia University; Ralph Bunche from the Department of Education, Howard University; Ambrose Caliver, from the United States Office of Education; W.E.B. DuBois from Atlanta University; E. Franklin Frazier, from the Department of Social Science, Fisk University; Melville Herskovits from Northwestern University; Charles A. Houston Dean of Howard Law School; anthropologist Otto Klineberg; Howard Odum from the University of North Carolina; Robert E. Park, sociologist and Johnson's professor from the University of Chicago; Ira DeA. Reid of the National Urban League; and E.B. Reuter from the Department of Sociology, University of Iowa and President of American Sociological Society.[69]

Swarthmore's intellectually elite speakers and workshop leaders lectured to an educated audience basically consisting of educators, social workers, labor leaders, employers, and journalists. Participants paid one hundred dollars for tuition, and room and board at the monthlong program.[70] The course of study for the Swarthmore Institute was divided into five major sections: race and culture; world race problems; cultural and historical factors in the American Negro-white race problem; sociological factors in the American race problem; and techniques and methods.[71] Formal classroom lectures were offered during the morning sessions, with more informal lectures and discussions offered in the afternoon. Some evening lectures were also provided for those not registered at the Institute.[72] The Swarthmore Institute gave Johnson the opportunity to actively utilize his training and research as a sociologist in the field of race relations and implement some of his ideas. Although Swarthmore organizers tried to secure Johnson's participation in future race relations programs, in 1938 his focus turned to the racial tensions in the South. Johnson would however, continue to draw upon his previous experiences and connections during the 1940s as he worked to identify causes of racial tensions and find ways to address those problems at the Fisk University Race Relations Department and Institute.

Johnson gained additional experience in the field of race relations and further developed his theories by working with well-known organizations like the American Missionary Association of the Congregational Church and the Julius Rosenwald Foundation of the Sears Roebuck Corporation. Johnson continued building a name for himself as he assisted the United States Department of Agriculture and served on the Federal Children's Bureau on War-time Care and Post-war Planning for Children, and the Department of Labor's

Committee on Fair Labor Standards. Johnson did all this while maintaining his positions as director of the AMA's Race Relations Department at Fisk and co-director of the Department of Race Relations at the Julius Rosenwald Fund. During 1943 Johnson also published two more books, *To Stem This Tide*, which described acute racial tension areas throughout the United States, and *Patterns of Negro Segregation* which described different types of segregation and discrimination and how African Americans responded to it. With the Rosenwald Fund he distributed the monthly "Summary of Events and Trends in Race Relations."[73]

Charles Spurgeon Johnson learned numerous lessons about human relations throughout his life. From the first time he was denied service because of the color of his skin, to nearly being shot during the Chicago race riots, to conducting numerous sociological research projects on segregation and discrimination, Johnson was steadily building an arsenal of information that would be instrumental in refuting information that supported and promoted social distance between the races.

THE FISK UNIVERSITY RACE RELATIONS INSTITUTE

When the RRI opened its doors on July 3, 1944, it was armed with noted professors of anthropology, sociology, economics, and education as well as white and black professional workers and students from various fields including social welfare, labor, religion, education, industry, and government. Although the RRI was the first of its kind in the South, the experimental project was not a new concept for Johnson. It was grounded in a "lineal and logical outgrowth of research and educational work" that had been ongoing for many years at Fisk's Department of Sociology and Anthropology and the Social Science Institute and similar work done for Swarthmore College in Swarthmore, Pennsylvania, during the summer months from 1933 to 1938.[74]

As discussed earlier, during the 1920s Robert E. Park, a sociologist at the University of Chicago and a former professor of Johnson, framed a reference for race relations which marked the beginning of the scientific study of race relations as we know it. Park noted that race relations could be broken down into a cycle of contact, competition, accommodation, and eventual assimilation.[75] As different racial groups come into contact with each other, they compete for available resources. Through time, although the competition may remain, the different groups learn to accommodate each others' differences. This accommodation eventually leads to assimilation. This cycle is progressive and irreversible.[76]

Johnson felt that because racial tensions were brewing across the country, America needed a unified knowledge of the status of racial and cultural minority groups. Basically concerned with competition between groups and accommodation of minority groups, Johnson utilized Park's frame of reference to shape the general theoretical structure of the Fisk Institute. This frame of reference would accommodate training and research and deal with the distinctive character of national cultures, migrations, statuses of minority and dependent groups in culturally advanced as well as culturally backward areas, and the effects of local customs and social and political restrictions as barriers to effective intergroup relations.[77] Johnson believed that a separate black culture could not exist in the United States even though the thought may have appealed to many blacks. The above frame of reference was useful because as Johnson saw it, the goal for blacks was equal opportunity and assimilation.

The RRI's foundation in a research-based perspective for social action can first be seen in its initial incorporation into the framework of Fisk University as a nonprofit organization.[78] Fisk was considered a logical location for two primary reasons. First, the university's Department of Sociology and Anthropology and the Social Science Institute had conducted years of research and educational work on race relations.[79] The department was geared to provide a systematic foundation in the social sciences and reflected an interest in race and culture. For example, the introductory survey course for undergraduates dealt with the racial and cultural consequences of migration of peoples in the modern world, while a seminar course provided the conceptual framework for the study of actual problems in their cultural and racial settings. Other courses included: The Negro in America, The Negro Rural Community, Human Geography, Population Problems, Geopolitics, Clinical Sociology, and Anthropology and Modern Life.[80] The Departmental Research Library also provided the RRI with extensive resources on race relations, including the Robert E. Park collection consisting of some 1,000 volumes of work dealing with problems of race and culture throughout the world, as well as collections from other race researchers such as C. Luther Fry and Edward B. Reuter.[81]

Johnson's presence at Fisk was the second reason the AMA selected the university to house the RRI. His expertise was highly sought after and highly regarded in the field of sociology. The AMA felt comfortable with and confident in Johnson's work. They noted themselves as being "fortunate" that Johnson, who had led a "busy and charmed" life in "rendering valuable counsellor service" to authorities in areas of racial tension would be joining them in their efforts.[82]

The 1942 prospectus for the project specified that the program be headed by the president of Fisk University; however, at the RRI's inception Johnson was a department head. Johnson did however become the president of the university in 1947. Apparently, in organizing plans for the RRI, the AMA, which had long been financial supporters of Johnson's work, had foreseen Johnson's role as president of the university they had helped establish. A "self perpetuating" board of trustees composed of leaders in public affairs and education would have the final say on policies and program work. The AMA and Fisk were to be permanently represented on the board, which also had the responsibility of safeguarding the RRI against the influence of any political, social, or economic special interest groups.[83]

Key to the RRI's conception was the belief that while technological advances in trade, communication, and transportation contributed to race and culture consciousness throughout the world, America, or the "Great Society,"[84] lacked the "social and moral unity" which Institute organizers felt could only come through "intelligent direction by specialists trained in the social science of human relations." Thus, the RRI's focus on research and training as methods of constructive social action can also be seen in several program announcements representing each decade the program was in existence. From a 1946 program:

> The central purpose of the Institute is to advance the all-important science of human relationships by providing knowledge about the complex factors of race and race relations, leading to insight and understanding, intelligent behavior and constructive social action. The incidental, yet perhaps most important value of the Institute is the experience of common fellowship itself.[85]

A 1956 program states that the Institute was designed to promote:

> ...statesmanship which [could] preserve the integrity of the law, substitute reason for hysteria, maintain communication and free discussion, pursue the steady course of justice founded in religious conviction....[86]

A 1965 program states that the Institute's purpose was:

> ...to orient these actual and potential community leaders to the problems, processes, and methods of implementing better intergroup relations...the participants learn to evaluate techniques and strategies for advancing the cause of civil rights and equal opportunities for all Americans.[87]

The Institute would accomplish this by

> ...[attempting] to relate the knowledge and theoretical insights developed by the social sciences to practical programs for breaking down the barriers and removing the inequities which have so long kept Americans of different backgrounds strangers to each other.[88]

The Institute's underlying belief that social change could be fostered by using research to appeal to the morality of the dominant white culture can also be seen in statements and announcements made about the program. In a 24 June 1964 article announcing the start of the '64 program, Institute director Herman H. Long stated that the program's purpose was to:

> ...help preserve the integrity of law, to substitute reason for hysteria, to maintain communications between groups and to pursue the steady course of justice founded on religious conviction.[89]

The 1965 program also points out the underlying belief in morality:

> ...sought to look beyond the significant events in the current racial scene to see their implications for a society which cherishes the political ideals of the Declaration of Independence and the religious ideals of the Judeo-Christian tradition.[90]

The Institute's format also indicates its commitment to a research-based agenda for social change. Patrick Gilpin shares that Johnson first saw the RRI as a type of professional conference where some 30 persons would read papers and facilitate discussions; however, because Johnson received such favorable and enthusiastic feedback to his invitations, he decided to expand the program.[91] To do this, Johnson organized the RRI into three major operating sections. The first section concentrated on training in the social sciences. Here, provisions were made to ensure that undergraduate and graduate students would be a part of the cooperative program. Advanced graduates who already had a Master's degree were encouraged to spend a year at the Institute as research fellows. This year was spent gaining training and research experience and working on doctoral dissertations under the supervision of the staff. Those graduate students without a Master's would receive Training Fellowships that would enable them to conduct research on various minority group relationships within the United States and abroad. This work would culminate in a Master's theses. Undergraduate students would be encouraged to enter the field through tuition waivers and honor's courses. This coordinated approach was intended to provide an extensive body of knowledge in the field of race relations and a reservoir of trained personnel.[92]

The second major operating section focused on research in the social sciences. Here, current research was exchanged and provided to participants of the Institute. The third major operating section of the RRI concerned social action. Methods and techniques in dealing with racial tensions as well as community planning was covered in this section. This section was also responsible for the Race Relations Field staff, the Institute program, the Fisk University Social Center, and the *Monthly Summary of Trends and Events in Race Relations*. The director of the Institute would name representatives from each section to serve on an executive committee which would be responsible for integrating the policy and work of the program. The head of each section would be a specialist with university faculty status. This was required so that the developing information would be related to Fisk's program. The director of the Institute would coordinate the policies affecting all three sections and would appoint prominent specialists in the field of race and culture to serve as an Advisory

Committee. The Advisory Committee, which served a one-year term, was the Institute's reviewing agency and offered technical advice on specific topics.[93]

Four basic areas would be addressed in the research and social action areas of the Institute: (1) race and racial theories, which included anthropological and psychological aspects of race and race relations, and comparative race relations throughout the world; (2) racial aspects of social problems, which covered racially tense areas in the United States, problems of racial adjustment and integrations in industry, labor, housing, educational institutions and the church, social planning, and postwar problems of readjustment; (3) methods, techniques, and community planning, which focused on the review and analysis of methods and practices useful for improving racial situations; and (4) the role of personal religion in human relations and democratic practices.[94] In essence, in order to address America's problems, the Institute was divided into areas that correlated with them. Obviously, the program was designed to practice Johnson's theories of education and interracial contact in informal settings. The four areas would be covered during the daily eight hours of lectures, seminars, and discussion groups led by 36 resident lecturers and consultants. The program would run for three weeks on the Fisk campus and was designed to promote interracial contact and group exchange.

There were five basic types of sessions at the Institute, which were called "methods of study": panel round-tables, seminars, cross-topical round-tables, consultations hours, and evening lectures. In the panel round-table sessions experts in a particular area would first present basic statements dealing with different aspects of a stated problem. Following their presentations, the members of the panel would engage in a round-table discussion examining all positions. The seminar sessions concentrated on problems and techniques in particular areas of concern like employment and labor, education, and housing. Within the seminars were workshops where topics raised in the panel round-table sessions could be further explored.

Cross-topical round-tables sessions differed from panel round-table sessions in that specialists from a variety of areas would discuss their views on a general topic. The consultation hours sessions allowed for individuals or small groups to discuss immediate problems they were facing with consultants and resource persons. This was done in an effort to translate the theory that was provided by the Institute into constructive social action. As participants desired more hands-on sessions, in 1949 at the 6th Institute, the consultation hours were further developed into individual scheduled clinics so that interested persons could discuss local problems of immediate concern with specialists. The evening lectures were a special feature of the program offered in the Fisk Chapel and open to local people who couldn't attend the entire Institute.[95]

The first few years of the Institute had an average of 90 lectures[96] by leading scholars and specialists invited by Johnson and the board of directors per workshop. Later programs would average 40 lectures.[97] Lectures, consultants, and discussion leaders who regularly attended the Institute included Will W. Alexander, the former director of the Farm Security Administration, director of the Southern Regional Council and vice-president of the Julius Rosenwald Fund; psychologist Gordon W. Allport, chairman of the Department of Psychology at Harvard University and editor of *Journal of Abnormal and Social Psychology of Radio;* psychologist Smiley Blanton, an associate professor of clinical psychology at Vanderbilt University; Horace Mann Bond, President of Lincoln University in Pennsylvania and author of *The Eduction of the Negro in the American Social Order;* race relations specialist Ina C. Brown, professor of social anthropology at Scarritt College for Christian Workers in Nashville and the author of *National Survey of the Higher Education of Negroes;* Fred Brownlee, the general secretary of the American Missionary Association Division of the Board of Home Missions of the Congregational and Christian Churches; and Ambrose Caliver, a specialist in Negro Education for the U.S. Office of Education.[98]

Others who attended included: Kenneth Clark of Queens College and the Northside Testing and Consultation Center in New York City; Lester B. Granger, first the executive secretary of the National Urban League and later its director; Edwin R. Embree, president of the Julius Rosenwald Fund, chairman of the Chicago Mayor's Committee on Race Relations, and author of *Brown Americans* and *13 Against the Odds*; John Hope (II), specialist on industrial relations and social science instructor at Fisk; Charles H. Houston, vice-president and consultant for the American Council on Race Relations, and legal counsel for the NAACP; Thurgood Marshall, chief counsel for the NAACP, who along with Houston, prepared the *Brown* case; M.F. Ashley Montagu, anthropologist and author of *Man's Most Dangerous Myth: The Fallacy of Race;* sociologist Ira DeA. Reid from Atlanta University and author of *In a Minor Key, Sharecroppers All, the Urban Negro in the United States;* Arnold Rose, race relations specialist from Bennington College, Bennington, Vermont; and Hilda Taba, intercultural education specialist, professor of education at the University of Chicago, and director of Intergroup Education in Cooperating Schools.[99]

Richard Robbins shares that other noted lecturers and consultants attending the program included historian Henry Steele Commager; white southern liberals Frank Graham and Representative Brooks Hays; race relations specialist Rev. John La Farge; labor movement leader Willard Townsend; historian Eric Williams, who later became prime minister of Trinidad-Tobago; race relations specialist Louis Wirth; and historian C. Vann Woodward.[100] Martin Luther King Jr. attended the 1956 Institute and spoke on the Montgomery bus boycott, which was then going into its ninth month.[101]

The scholars, specialists, and legal minds present at the RRI during the 1940s, 1950s, and 1960s were without a doubt among America's who's who.

One notable figure, however, did not participate at the RRI. Although early in his career W.E.B. Du Bois had supported the notion that social science could provide information to combat the social injustices practiced in the United States and had participated in Johnson's northern-based Swarthmore Institute, he did not attend the Fisk program. It's safe to speculate that Du Bois' 1942 call for Southern Black land-grant colleges to take the lead in studying black-life by conducting ongoing, in-depth studies through social science programs at the schools did not go over well with the dominant white power structure. Du Bois made this call after charging that the study of blacks was being dominated by southern whites. Apparently, Du Bois' charges hit the nerves of several people as he was "retired" as professor and head of the sociology department at Atlanta University in 1944.[102] With the Institute in its first year at Fisk and not yet an established annual event, there's little doubt that Johnson wanted to avoid the added pressure of dealing with a controversy between Du Bois and Fisk supporters. Robbins also notes that Johnson felt it too risky to invite W.E.B. DuBois to Fisk.[103]

The first RRI, held on July 3–21, had 137 registered participants from nearly all the southern states, with whites outnumbering blacks about 8 to 5.[104] Evidence shows that by 1951, over 800 participants from 200 communities in 36 states and 6 foreign countries had attended the Institute.[105] On average, 125 participants attended the program each summer.[106] Full participation in the 3-week workshop carried 3 semester hours of credit at Fisk and was priced at $61.75: $25 for tuition, $10.50 for room, and $26.25 for board. Those participants who could not be in attendance for the full 3 weeks could attend sessions at their convenience. Those in attendance for 2 weeks paid a total of $47.50, and those in attendance for 1 week paid a total of $27.50. Those attending less than a week paid a $2.00 registration fee, $1 per night for room, and around $1.50 per day for board. Evening lectures were also offered for those who could not attend because of jobs. Participants lived in an integrated setting on campus in the residence halls and university houses.[107] These figures show that the RRI may not have been financially accessible to those who were not scholars, professionals or students as most blacks were restricted to working menial jobs that paid little.

The RRI's incorporation into Fisk University, its utilization of the scientific method and eminent scholars and leaders, its operating sections and structured formats, its ability to offer college credit to participants, and its summer scheduling all reflected its research-based methods for social action. Robbins writes that a close friend and former student of Johnson's described Johnson's methods as "indirection" because Johnson's intent was not to show others that the black man was angry about his position in society, but to make others so angry about the black man's situation that they would seek to change things.[108]

While Johnson relied on research and methods of "indirection" to provide social change, blacks in the South were increasingly relying upon the power of the oppressed to facilitate those changes for themselves. The growing philosophy was that "strong people [didn't] need strong leaders."[109] Although the RRI was the first interracial project of its kind in the South to be incorporated within a university, it was not the only organization operating in the South where interested persons met to discuss issues of social change in an integrated environment. Highlander Folk School had been established in Monteagle, Tennessee, by Myles Horton and Don West in the fall of 1932. Highlander originally concentrated on problems facing Appalachia's black and white laborers, but during the late 1940s and early 1950s, the program turned its attention toward strengthening its education programs and so that they could help educate the areas' poor and help them take control of their lives. Like the RRI, Highlander, gave participants a feel for an integrated society.[110] During the 1950s Highlander also became a meeting place and training center for civil rights leaders, including Septima Clark, Rosa Parks, and Martin Luther King Jr.

Highlander differed from the RRI in many ways. Whereas the RRI's basic philosophy held that research could be used as a social action method, Highlander's philosophy held that common oppressed people could produce that change for themselves; or as John Egerton puts it, "that ordinary working people, no less privileged, could find within themselves and their neighbors the solutions to whatever problems they faced."[111] Because of its strong belief in the oppressed, Highlander was big on developing the leadership and often brought in leaders like Clark, Parks, and King to share their experiences with participants.[112] While the RRI was giving its participants factual information on the status of race relations, Highlander was acting in the true spirit of a movement halfway house, as it offered its participants a wide range of resources, including reading classes, protest methods classes, and a network base.[113]

The RRI also differed from Septima Clark's citizenship schools, which Highlander was responsible for spreading across the South. Although the citizenship schools used workshop formats, they concentrated on utilizing the culture of the oppressed to help them learn to read and write. For example, while the Institute held workshops on theories of race and race relations, the citizenship schools held workshops on teaching people to write money orders, or fill out voter registration forms, or use sewing machines. Again, like Highlander, the goal of the citizenship schools was to empower the oppressed so that they could in turn help themselves. As Charles M. Payne points out the schools often discussed what he called the "big" ideas like "citizenship, democracy, and the powers of elected officials."[114]

Although the RRI differed from Highlander and the citizenship schools in its tactics, there was an exchange between the programs. In a 6 January 1958 letter from Septima P. Clark to Herman Long, who became director of the RRI in 1950, Clark asked for Long's assistance in finding leaders for four summer workshops at Highlander. She wrote:

> Highlander will have four workshops during the summer...the staff needs your assistance in helping to recruit civic-minded community leaders and also your contribution gained from your experience in the field of leadership....The People in many communities are waiting for a boost from a person like you....Won't you let us know if you can serve as a consultant during one of these months?....[115]

Highlander also provided scholarships so that people could attend the RRI, as shown in this 23 May 1967 letter from Septima P. Clark to the Institute's 1967 director, Clifton H. Johnson:

> The Highlander Research and Education Center is giving a scholarship to a worthy young person to the Race Relations Institute this summer...in memory of George Mitchell, who was Highlander's Chairman for many years. I've found a very proficient young man from St. Helena Island, Frogmore, South Carolina who is receiving the Associate of Arts Degree May 28, 1967 from Mather Junior College in Beaufort, South Carolina.... His name is Roland Al Gardner.... He plans to attend A. & T. College in Greensboro, North Carolina.... He will major in physical education and physical therapy....[116]

In this same letter, Clark requested the RRI's assistance in providing an additional scholarship to another young man from Mather Junior College, Alphonso L. Scott. Although the RRI did not match the full Mitchell scholarship, they did cover all expenses and the $5.00 registration fee.[117]

Even though Johnson felt that the RRI's format was the most effective way to address social injustice, he realized that improving race relations would not be an easy task and that definitive methods of calming tensions might not be possible. He did feel, however, as noted below, that there were principles that could be followed to dealing with racial tensions. He wrote:

> In the field of race relations, it is not so important that there should be envisaged exact solutions, for there will inevitably be differences of opinions.... But it is important that there should be principles guiding these relationships, and that these principles should be high.[118]

In Johnson's eyes, the RRI provided those principles as it utilized trained researchers and specialists in a laboratory of human relations to disseminate factual information to those working in the field of race relations so that those workers could in turn utilize the material to address racial tensions in their prospective areas.

CHAPTER THREE

Closing Social Distance, Building Racial Tolerance

At a first glance the RRI might appear to be little more than an academic conference where scholars met to present their research. However, a deeper look reveals a vehicle that sought to secure allies—whites in particular—to assist in the fight against racial oppression in the United States. As noted in the previous chapters, Johnson believed refuting racist scientific notions was critical to improving black-white relations. He hoped providing whites with accurate information about blacks would lead to less white resistance toward blacks. Previous experiences had shown Johnson that there were whites who were sympathetic to black issues, but he also knew that these whites needed more than concern and good intent if they were to effectively assist efforts to dismantle racially divisive practices. Thus he designed the RRI to be an arena that was both academic and personal. The RRI would be a place where whites could not only access research that dispelled myths about blacks and other minorities, they could also learn how the segregated system impacted blacks and other minority groups while interacting with those groups on a personal level. Whites would then be better prepared to go out and counter negative perceptions in their communities. In *Sidelines Activist: Charles S. Johnson and the Struggle for Civil Rights*, Richard Robbins notes Johnson's belief in scholarship as social action and utilizing whites as allies in the struggle for civil rights. He writes:

> Johnson firmly believed in the scholarly role in itself as a powerful instrument of advocacy. the more thorough the work on the scope and depth of the problem of lynching or desperate farm poverty, the more the majority community, the white community would be stirred to anger, outrage, and—what counted most—action in the form of public policy. Lewis W. Jones, first Johnson's brilliant student and then his close friend, had the most apt term for this—a strategy of "indirection."

the young Jones, when student editor of the Fisk paper, showed Johnson a furious editorial he had just written. "This piece says you are angry," Johnson told him, "that is not what you are after; you want to make other people angry."[1]

Scholarship

One way the RRI sought to educate whites and close the social distance that existed between the groups was through the use of a cadre of social scientists whose research challenged and refuted the ideas of racial superiority and inferiority. During the first seven years of the project, lecturers including anthropologists Ina C. Brown,[2] Gordon W. Allport,[3] and M.F. Ashley Montague; and psychologist Smiley Blanton[4] utilized their research to argue fervently for human equality and against the claims that blacks were intellectually inferior to whites. All of their presentations acknowledged three major racial groups, but promoted the idea of one human race. They attacked the widely held idea that the races could be classified by intelligence and noted that physical characteristics, such as the size and shape of the brain, did not determine intelligence and were of "no significance" to a person's thoughts, feelings, or actions.[5] Human behavior, they argued, was determined by "individual potentialities, plus the influence of the environment."[6] The researchers also countered myths of some races having more primitive traits than others. Anthropologist Ethel Alpenfels presented research that concluded all races had "developed equally" and "developed according to geographical areas" in which they lived.[7] For those who maintained that blacks were more primitive than whites, Alpenfels argued that she could provide 212 traits that all peoples had that could be considered "primitive."[8]

The RRI maintained a heavy focus on theories of race and racial prejudice because organizers realized the program's participants had probably been exposed to arguments that attributed the decade's overt racial hostilities to biological differences between the groups. RRI scholars also offered explanations on why racial tensions existed. In 1945, psychiatrist Helen V. McLean presented research concluding that unconscious fear hinders the development of positive race relations. McLean theorized that America's racial conflicts were rooted in the "unconscious fears of both Negroes and Whites living under the stress of racial prejudice."[9] This fear, which she identified as "[c]ertain irrational forces operating between races," had to be realized before steps could be made toward positive relations.[10] She noted:

> Fear, a partially conscious and a partially unconscious emotion, is ever disturbing human performance and plan. Conscious fears, if not too intense, may be mastered by the average person. However, the human animal early in life finds frank expression of fear incompatible with pride and self respect, and throughout life develops techniques for disguising feelings of anxiety which may arise under stress...In lower animals fear is often expressed by flight or fight.[11]

McLean held that whites internalize this fear and told participants that "[m]ost white fear stems from within, rather than from any direct external cause." She went on to say "the feelings of shame and guilt" which accompany fear "may take a dangerous outlet in the form of new aggressions against the Negro, or the projection of faults onto him, in an effort to escape the feelings of guilt."[12]

McLean also theorized that the unconscious fear whites had about blacks had sexual undertones with whites believing "in the greater sexual potency of the Negro male." This widespread belief, she argued, contributed to "the white southerner unconsciously fear[ing] competition with the Negro."[13] This unconscious fear then manifested itself in scapegoating.

> The Negro is used by the white man as a scapegoat for hostilities which might otherwise be directed against those near to him in his own social group. The preservation of his own group is in the interests of his own security. His own self love and prestige are also saved.[14]

Whereas McLean's ideas on racial intolerance were more in keeping with symbolic theories that held people see in certain racial and ethnic groups something to be despised, feared, or envied, writer Margaret Halsey's perspectives were more in line with theories that the basic problems of race relations were buried within the American ideology and entrenched in everyday life. Halsey maintained that in order to understand the roots of racial tensions in America, one had to first understand the real nature of American life, which was built around a business culture that ultimately left Americans unhappy. She wrote:

> If we view Americans freshly, as if we had never till this moment seen them, the first and most obvious thing that strikes us is how unhappy they are. They have not been bombed. Their citizens [sic] are not rubble. Their food is not rationed. But out of the newspapers and the radio arises daily a huge, swollen chorus of complaint. Hundreds of times a day, Americans describe themselves as confused, baffled and afraid. It is not necessary to look up statistics on the mounting use of alcohol, cigarettes and other escape mechanisms...The point must be made, in parenthesis, that the American unhappiness under discussion is the white man's unhappiness. Negro Americans are unhappy, too, but in quite a different way. Negro unhappiness has a rational basis and is not neurotic. The Negroes know their enemy.[15]

Halsey attributed this unhappiness of white America to the business culture.

> The first and most obvious truth about the United States is that it is a business civilization. It is not pastoral, not a military, not a clerical, but a business civilization. The point cannot be too strongly emphasized. Nor is there anything random, casual or accidental about the United States as a business culture. It is a throughly well-integrated business culture, organized from top to bottom for the maximum efficiency of commerce and industry. True, there are non-industrial pockets here and there in American lives, and they are sometimes yearned over

achingly by the prisoners of the machine. But these non-industrial pockets exert little or no influence on the prevailing moral and psychological climate, which is the climate of a business culture.[16]

Although Halsey pointed out that there are advantages to America's business culture such as the spread of "comforts, conveniences and material possessions" she noted that a business culture creates "aggression, competitiveness and skepticism" that can manifest itself as segregation and discrimination.[17]

> Aggression, competitiveness and skepticism—the sanctioned hostility of the business culture—cannot be turned off at five o'clock. These qualities can be repressed, after the business day is over—they usually are—but this simply means that they find their way to the surface in devious and twisted channels...The great problem of our era is the aggression, competitiveness and skepticism which have no place to go after five o'clock, and which spill out in all directions again....[18]

Halsey speculated that segregation and discrimination were "just one part of a national failure in human relations caused by the over-development of aggression, competitiveness and skepticism" in America's business culture.[19] Thus, this same culture needed to keep blacks disenfranchised and unequal because "it want[ed] a permanent low wage group and because it need[ed] helpless victims upon whom to expend its surplus hostility."[20] The role change played in racial intolerance also factored into the equation at this point because if blacks gained equality, it would modify the business culture. Although this modification would be "painful and stormy" Halsey felt it would serve a greater good.

> The extension of equality to Negro Americans is one part of the painful and stormy modification of the American business culture—a modification directed toward the end that Americans shall suffer only intermittent, not chronic unpahhiness [sic]. In that cultural transition, the breaking down of racial barriers is of primary importance. Every act or series of acts which leads toward full equality for Negro Americans takes that much of a load off the white man's bad conscience. Every development in the direction of equality produces a release of tension—a partial resolution of inner conflict—and brings into nearer view a more livable American life for all Americans.[21]

Anthropologist Ina C. Brown also presented research at the 1944 and 1946 RRI on the causes of racial intolerance. Brown offered "a lack of clear terms" about race contributed to the confusion surrounding race.[22] Although science had found no connection between race and innate capabilities, the social construct of race added to confusion. This confusion was magnified by an "over-shrinking world" which "force[d] peoples to live in close harmony."[23] She noted that "[m]echanical literacy" without "social literacy" was "fanning an explosive racial situation in a world where the majority of peoples are colored."[24]

Clearly, the RRI saw the repetitive use of similar types of anthropological, biological, and psychological arguments supporting the idea of racial equality as an effective way to counter racist scientific notions, but some RRI participants found the practice to be irritating and contriving. They criticized the program for "considerable overlapping"[25] and suggested lecturers compare notes to "avoid unnecessary reiteration."[26] One wrote:

> Our criticism is simply this: The audience seems already to have a very definite and pre-conceived point-of-view. The organizers of the institute seem to be not aware of this and they seem to have invited exclusively lecturers who share and encourage the opinions of members of the institute. 'The other side' never seems to be given a chance.[27]

Participants also noted the RRI's failure to include differing perspectives and labeled the project "propagandistic."[28] They charged the lack of diverse views

> ...diminishes greatly the value of the conference. It takes from it the label of an objective and scholarly meeting, and gives it the appearance of propagandistic and political event. It seems surprising to us that this very conference which stresses so much the value of democratic behavior applies so little the very essence of democratic procedure in its own proceedings namely to make progress by real discussion and by giving every point-of-view an equal chance.[29]

As RRI participants continued to criticize the race and racial theories lectures for redundancy and suggested other topics like social action methods be added to the program, the organizers eliminated the presentations from future programs.[30] This, however, does not mean that the ideas were eliminated from the project. A program listing activities from the 1951 RRI shows the ideas and research on race racial theories were integrated into keynote and public addresses. This was also true of subsequent institutes. Thus, the RRI continued to expose participants to research that countered ideas of racial inferiority and superiority in hopes participants would carry that message to the dominant masses.

People

The RRI knew its efforts to combat racial tensions and close social distance could not stop with scholarly research. Although white participants needed scientifically based information, they also needed opportunities to hear from groups whose day-to-day experiences under segregation differed greatly from the white experience. The RRI offered that opportunity by utilizing the personal accounts of blacks and other racially oppressed groups to give whites insight into how the apartheid system worked for subordinated groups. While these accounts also served as a way for blacks and other minorities to connect and work together, they also allowed whites insight into a world they did not know. For example, in order to illustrate the impact racism and segregation had on society and the general thinking of whites, Marie Jahoda, a sociologist with the American Jewish Congress in New York shared with 1944 RRI participants the results of an experiment she conducted in New York. Jahoda had passed out pictures to a small group of whites at a workshop. The pictures showed two scenes. In one scene a white man was shown holding a razor and threatening a "terror-stricken Negro on a subway platform."[31] Jahoda showed this picture to a white man and asked him to describe it to another man. The second man, without having seen the picture, described the details given to him by the first man to a third man. By the time the information got to the fourth man in the group, the razor had changed hands. The black man was the one with the knife, and the white man was terror-stricken. Jahoda had also circulated another picture to high school students attending the RRI. In the picture an overweight man "obviously non-Jewish" was shown smoking a cigar and crowding the other passengers in the elevator.[32] Next to him was another smaller man, "obviously a Jew," and "a model of good behavior."[33] High school students were asked to study the picture. When asked to describe what they saw, many students later recalled the Jewish man being the offensive passenger. Jahoda's experiments were meant to show how thoughts of minority groups' inferiority permeated the everyday thinking of the dominant culture.

Other sessions focused on the individual concerns of minority groups. For instance, Native Americans attending the 1953 RRI discussed the difficulty they were having reconciling a need for government financial support with maintaining their cultural identity. A panel of seven Native American leaders from tribal councils representing such groups as the Navaho, Sioux, Maricopa-Pima, and Cherokee told the RRI that proposals for the "withdrawal program"—taking away federal support for reservations and social services for Native Americans—would result in hardship for the masses of Native Americans. They noted that only 100,000 of approximately 400,000 Native Americans did not live on reservations. The Native American leaders felt the government should maintain federal funding because their people needed to develop the social and competitive skills critical to surviving American society before moving off the reservations.[34] Doing so would help the group be successful in adjusting to urban life off the reservation.

But maintaining those funds and developing the social skills needed to survive life off the reservation and in the dominant white culture came at a price. The Native American delegate noted it was difficult to teach American skills that emphasized competition and still maintain Native American culture which recognized the value of the group working as a whole. In *Education and the American Indian: The Road to Self-Determination Since 1928*, Margaret Connell Szasz also recognizes that difficulty. Szasz shares that the Bureau schools began utilizing a curriculum that stressed "elements on white cultural behavior,"[35] in order to "transform a reservation youth into an urban adult,"[36] they failed to incorporate Native American participation. Administrators and tribal leaders clashed in some schools over the policies as the "ultimate objective of Indian education" was "complete integration in the American way of life."[37]

Mexican Americans attending the 1951 RRI voiced their desire for the development of formal organizations and national advocacy groups for Mexican Americans. A Mexican American representative noted that although there was a "great need for it," Mexican-Americans had no formal organizational structure by which they could begin to address group concerns.[38] He went on to note that although Mexican Americans had the beginnings of an institutional framework, language differences, suspicions concerning organizational movements, and considerable differences between the Mexicans in California and the Mexicans in Texas hindered progress.[39] Perhaps the "beginnings of an institutional framework" about which the representative spoke was the League of United Latin American Citizens (LULAC). In *"Let All of Them Take Heed": Mexican Americans and the Campaign for Educational Equality in Texas, 1910–1981* Guadalupe San Miquel Jr. notes that in 1910 several Texas residents of Mexican descent held a conference "to organize an association to protect the rights and interest of all Mexicans in the state."[40] Although the group failed to establish a statewide organization at the time, their conference laid the foundation for the future development of the statewide LULAC in 1929.[41] LULAC concerned itself with "integrat[ing] the [Mexican American] community into the political and social institutions of American life."[42] According to LULAC's constitution a central concern of the organization was to "develop within the members of our race, the best, purest, and more perfect type of true and loyal citizen of the United States of America."[43]

Puerto Ricans attending the 1953 RRI noted the English language was the primary issue impacting their lives. The estimated 400,000 Puerto Ricans who migrated to New York during the 1940s and early 1950s moved into areas with existing poor housing. Failure to speak and understand the English language made Puerto Ricans ripe for exploitation. The language barrier also exasperated cultural conflicts as older residents were fearful of the newer residents.[44] The Puerto Rican immigrants were unique to other immigrants to the United States. Not only were Puerto Ricans the first group of minority newcomers to arrive as citizens, they seemed to maintain a stronger affiliation with their first language than other immigrants had. Sonia Nieto shares in *Puerto Rican Students in United States Schools* that since Puerto Ricans could travel freely between the United States and Puerto Rico, retaining knowledge of the Puerto Rican culture and Spanish language remained critical.[45]

Puerto Rican delegates were also concerned with the impact racial discrimination had on their intragroup relations. In Puerto Rico, the population was racially democratic; however, in the United States, the lighter the skin, the fewer restrictions placed on a person. "[T]he lighter complexioned" Puerto Ricans often found it to their advantage to "disassociate themselves from members of their own family who they felt would act as a factor in restricting their mobility."[46] This action caused "great psychological problems" for great numbers of Puerto Ricans residing in the city.[47]

Although conversations often centered around how white domination impacted the lives of minority groups, fiery conversations on the relationships between minority groups also occurred at the workshops. For example, Jewish-black relationships took center stage as several RRIs Jewish leaders noted that Jews were often criticized on one hand for participating in civil rights efforts, and on the other hand for not doing enough. One rabbi acknowledged that although the Jewish memory of a long history of suffering enabled them to identify with the black struggle for social change, Jews often resisted the identification because their relationships were in the white community—a community of which they were members. He noted that Jews living in the South were often made an "honorary white Christian" in their communities, but still lived in fear of white neighbors.[48] That same rabbi intimated that black antipathy toward Jews might stem from the fact that southern Jews tried to "skirt involvement in racial disputes," or reacted as if they were afraid to get involved with black struggles.[49] The rabbi maintained, however, that American Jews contributed more so than any other group to the civil rights movement through their philanthropic support of research projects and civil rights programs.[50]

Jewish representatives also voiced concerns about the hypocrisy America practiced when it championed the ideals of democracy to other countries, yet practiced unfair social, political, and economic policies toward its own minority and ethnic groups. They also saw hypocrisy among blacks who aligned themselves with anti-Semitics or whites who professed support for blacks, yet were anti-Semitics. These sentiments were reminiscent of others made during the 1944 RRI when blacks who were anti-Semitics were labeled "fools and traitors, sabotaging their own interests."[51] The Jewish leaders at that RRI warned blacks not to trust whites who professed support of blacks, but were anti-Semitics because "when expedient," whites could turn that same prejudice against blacks.[52]

The black-Jewish conversations at the RRI's workshops give insight into what VP Franklin refers to as "historical moments of both convergence and conflict in Black-Jewish relations."[53] In the introduction to *African Americans and Jews in the Twentieth Century: Studies in Convergence and Conflict,* Franklin notes that the chance of blacks and Jews forming an alliance was limited by "significant conflicts of interest between Jewish Americans and African Americans."[54] Franklin goes on to explain that the "entanglements" between blacks and Jews that Jack Salzman refers to in his work *Struggles in the Promised Land: Toward a History of Black-Jewish Relations in the United States* were really "examples of historical moments when the social, political, or ideological objectives of Jews and African Americans converged, or when they clashed for specific social, political ideological, or more recently, economic reason."[55]

The RRI offered presentations on issues facing minorities because few whites knew or had given much thought to how racism and domination actually impacted the groups. The RRI hoped that the exchange of knowledge would further close social distance and inspire whites to take action against oppressive measures. As one leader noted they wanted to "correlat[e] all of the people into a state of mind where they [wouldn't] accept leadership based on prejudice."[56]

COMMUNITIES

Closing social distance also depended on whites learning more about their own individual communities. The RRIs community clinic, sometimes called community action clinic workshops, challenged participants to learn more about their own communities. The clinics helped people "recognize and isolate problem areas, to discover community resources, and to devise some techniques for alleviating and eliminating these problems."[57] With participants from numerous states including Missouri, Massachusetts, Ohio, Alabama, Indiana, Kansas, Vermont, California, Pennsylvania, Illinois, Iowa, South Carolina, and Kentucky attending the clinics, the RRI encouraged people to examine their own communities. Some discovered that racial problems were not confined to southern or distant communities. They learned that problems often existed at home. For example, informal case histories alerted attendees to problems of segregated eating facilities in Wichita, Kansas. One RRI participant noted:

> This clinic discussion while failing to evolve simple solutions to the pressing problems of our world, did present so well-delineated a challenge that many of us feel compelled to look more carefully at our communities, more critically at the issues arising there, more humanely becoming able to work more wisely, justly and courageously toward the development of the great society in our own sphere of action.[58]

Area Institutes picked up where the community clinics left off. Born out of the desire to "deal helpfully with specific and concrete issues and problems at the local level in light of available resources," the Area Institutes were spin-offs of the RRI.[59] Area Institutes targeted two distinct groups within a designated community. The first group consisted of race relations workers who wanted to learn the latest developments in the field. Those in this group would register for the conference and represent organizations concerned with improving relations. Their goal would likely be to gather resources and attend the sessions and meetings to hear national and local experts discuss problems impacting race relations. The second group would consist of the general public. Included in this group would be those who might attend one or all of a variety of public meetings or who might hear of the Area Institutes discussions via the media.[60]

Area Institutes were held between 1946 and 1947 in numerous cities, including Richmond, New Orleans, St. Louis, and Baltimore. Cities that wanted to hold an Area Institute had to secure community support for the project. To ensure local issues remained "the entire focus" of the Area Institute, local agencies had to assume the main responsibility of sponsoring the project and securing the assistance of other local groups.[61] Representatives from the groups generally formed a council of community agencies, which acted as the general steering committee for the project.[62] For example, the Baltimore Institute of Race Relations was held in conjunction with 18 local sponsoring organizations and at least 36 cooperating civic organizations. The Baltimore project, held in 1947, ran for 3 days and registered 475 participants. The program had an average daily attendance of 400 persons per session with approximately 1200 people attending the evening public meeting.[63]

The Baltimore Institute of Race Relations began with a bang as chairman H. Milton Wagner, trustee of Morgan College, declared at the opening meeting "no city needed an institute on race relations more than Baltimore." Wagner noted that "whereas some cities are proud of racial discrimination, and others are ashamed of it, 'Baltimore simply tries to ignore it.'" He hoped "that the dyed-in-the-wool Baltimoreans [would] be shocked into some of the new ideal" of ridding the city of racial prejudices.[64] Perhaps the racial prejudices to which Wagner eluded were things like the substandard living conditions in Baltimore's slums referenced in the *Baltimore Evening Sun*. The newspaper noted that Baltimore Institute of Race Relations representatives blamed the slums for Maryland's "high tuberculosis death rates."[65] One health official charged the "primary cause" of the death rate in Baltimore was "the low economic status of Negroes, which coupled with 'prejudice,' forces them to live in the 'worst conditions' in overcrowded areas."[66] He charged that "because of their color" blacks "found themselves deprived of jobs and compelled to live in overpopulated areas of the city."[67]

Like the parent RRI, Area Institute lecturers and presenters also believed education and social contact improved race relations. Just as she had championed intergroup education at the RRI, Hilda Taba, director of Intergroup Education Project, American Council on Education, also championed the ideology to the Baltimore Institute. Goodwin Watson, professor of education at Teachers College, Columbia University, also supported the idea and added "in numerous instances" he had found "that where Negroes and whites were permitted to mix naturally—at work, recreation centers, summer camp or the like—even the most prejudiced persons lose their stanch dislike for the other race."[68]

After the Baltimore Institute concluded, residents wondered about the next steps in improving relations. One editorial charged those who attended the project were "democratic persons of many faiths from many walks of life who hardly needed exposure to the democratizing effects of the institute."[69]

It noted the people who attended the conference were already "convinced of the senselessness of racial bigotry."⁷⁰ The editorial argued more would be needed to improve conditions than a three-day discussion. Relations would not change simply because a few "top drawer individuals already convinced of the need" supported the idea.⁷¹ Whereas W.H. Grayson Jr., the representative for the RRI, noted the institute did not "seek to inspire action on racial problems" nor "approach legislators or operate on a plan of action" but rather "to stimulate discussion and encourage the general public to think racial problems through," the questions posed in the editorial illustrates that there were individuals at the Area Institutes who were looking for more than conversations on race.⁷²

School and Church

Formal structures could also help close social distance and build tolerance between whites and minorities. The RRI looked to the schools and churches, pillars in every community, to build racial tolerance. While schools could educate the minds of children and could champion social justice through a democratic ideology, churches could target adults and appeal to their moral and spiritual values. Intercultural education was the primary method championed by schools during the 1940s and 1950s to help teach students to be democratic citizens. Intercultural education had developed in the early 1900s in response to the anxiety created when some thirteen million southern and eastern Europeans immigrated to America. Ethnic groups leaders seeking positive relations supported the idea of cultural integration and first used the term "intercultural education" to reflect "the study of history and cultural contributions of ethnic groups to American society." As it sought to "1) raise minority self-esteem, 2) build attitudes of mutual appreciation among groups and promote intergroup harmony, and 3) stimulate a 'renaissance' of American culture," intercultural education sought to promote positive group images and assimilation.⁷³

In 1944 Theodore Brameld, an associate professor of education at the University of Minnesota, conducted a study of seven key school districts in order to look at educational practices toward minorities. The study would give school districts a snapshot of themselves—allowing them to see their policies and practices toward minority groups.⁷⁴ Brameld's findings, which were discussed at the 1945 Institute, were significant because they showed how schools, which idealistically were seen as vehicles for transmitting democratic ideologies, chose to avoid issues concerning minorities, social equality, and democratic living. Even though 6 of the 7 schools had established intercultural education committees, they did nothing to actively implement intercultural ideas or practices. The teachers mirrored the schools' indifferent attitudes, and many of them were no more abreast on topics of social inequities in education than any other professional group. Some teachers were found to be prejudiced, others avoided the issues of race and equality, and most didn't have the skills or knowledge for handling intercultural problems.[75]

RRI participants were particularly interested in this information because the education workshop promoted intercultural education as a solution to social inequalities.[76] From 1946 to 1953, the seminars and clinics on education focused on the problems that hindered intergroup education and methods that advanced intergroup education. Hilda Taba, a professor of education at the University of Chicago and an intercultural education specialist, led seminars at the 1946 Institute that concentrated on numerous issues that fostered successful programs. Successful programs had systematic and consistent efforts instead of brief attempts like studying a certain book, or attending a certain play, meeting, programs, or institutes. Research, however, was needed in a variety of areas. First, researchers needed to examine the materials and techniques utilized to train teachers to see if they were actually effective. Second, researchers needed to see if facts alone could combat emotional feelings or if prejudice could be solely addressed through intellect. Third, methods of translating anthropological and psychological facts into the realm of social status were needed along with ways of transferring the knowledge of cultural process to the educational process. Finally, teachers needed to be trained to utilize intercultural techniques.[77]

Another education session at that same 1946 Institute highlighted types of intercultural education activities that were being utilized around the country. The "contributions" activities stressed the contributions of noted individuals and group contributions in certain areas like music and dance. Activities in this category were the most popular, although specialists agreed and warned improper emphasis had the potential of perpetuating false ideas about a group or maintaining associations that the group wanted to drop. The "American Dilemma" activities took into account that students were mature enough to handle some of the actual facts and contradictions of American life at early ages as long as the facts were taught in such a way that they did not undermine the child's respect for law and order. Examples of facts that could be addressed were the Ku Klux Klan, segregated housing, and segregated swimming pools.[78]

Teachers who had incorporated intercultural education in their classrooms shared with RRI participants examples of actual classroom activities. One teacher facilitated a class discussion on minority groups by having students do library research to find fictitious and factual material on the groups. Another teacher had students trace religious tensions from colonial to modern times. Still, a history teacher had students analyze the labor tensions between whites and blacks while they studied the Civil War and Reconstruction.[79]

Intercultural education efforts were not confined to the North. An Amarillo, Texas, teacher offered examples of her lesson plans for her American Problems course. The teacher told participants that the objectives of unit II in her course were to 1) strengthen the American democracy, 2) develop national unity, and 3) provide individual understanding. To do this, students were separated into groups and focused on minority groups classified as 1) the socioeconomic groups; 2) the religious groups; 3) the ethnic groups; and 4) the racial groups. The groups concentrating on racial groups could not study the blacks as that group was reserved for a larger class discussion. Within these groups, students would look at their groups history, population, treatment, and living conditions. After analyzing the information, students purposed changes for positive treatment. The teacher supplemented her course with pamphlets, magazine articles, current material, and books. She also organized field trips to black homes, schools, and doctor's offices, as well as Catholic churches and Jewish synagogues. After the trips the teacher would utilize the Socratic Method to facilitate student discussions and observations about their experiences.[80] One Carbondale, Illinois, teacher was inspired to incorporate a unit on blacks into her English class when she found that students at an all-black school knew little about their own race. The teacher had her students write letters and request material on blacks from people in different sections of the country. The students received about 500 responses and arranged their information in several rooms at the school along with an exhibit on "the Negro" from the New York–based Council Against Intolerance in America. The city-based paper carried daily articles to promote the project, which was open 3 nights a week for 2 weeks, to the public.[81] Although the teacher could not measure exactly how much the students learned, she did see an increase of interest in blacks as indicated by students continuing to gather information after the project was complete. She also saw an increase of public interest on blacks as indicated by the public library's increased demand for material on blacks and the local university's request to have her speak on black music and art. The university subsequently invited black artists to their campus.[82]

Intergroup education became so popular throughout the United States that the 1951 Institute had a separate clinic dedicated to it.[83] The clinic was offered especially for teachers and those people who dealt with children on a regular basis. Regular consultants included Hilda Taba; Helen Ammerman, Research Assistant, Committee on Educational Training and Research in Race Relations, University of Chicago; Dr. Barbara MacKenzie, Department of Education, Brooklyn College; and Grace C. Jones, Race Relations Department of American Missionaries Association, Congregational Christian Churches.

The RRI realized churches could also play a significant role in facilitating and building racial tolerance as they could be utilized to educate adults on democratic and moral behavior. In 1946, the Federal Council of Churches issued a statement professing commitment to a "non-segregated church in a non-segregated community."[84] Although this may have been the desire, the RRI realized many ministers and religious leaders did not know how or where to begin. The Church and Race component of the RRI provided those interested in creating nonsegregated churches a place to identify issues and strategies critical to achieving their goals.

Presenters conducting the Church and Race sessions at the RRI told participants that one of the first things that needed to be addressed when trying to create a nonsegregated church was the reality that some congregations contained people who supported segregation and saw nothing wrong with the practice.[85] Although encouraged that most of the major denominations had taken a stand against segregation, presenters charged "changing the climate of opinion within our churches and enlisting Christian men and women individually and as organized groups in eliminating discriminatory practices" would be difficult because "so many in America belong to the privileged section of our society and therefore do not appreciate the humiliations, frustrations, and inequalities imposed upon those who suffer from discrimination and segregation."[86]

Presenters felt it was imperative that the ministers and churches address the issue of segregation because "segregation [was] a critical reason why the church's message of Christian living [was] largely neutralized." They charged that ministers were not saying enough "from the pulpit" and what they were saying was "too generalized" or fell on "indifferent ears." They noted that few interracial churches existed because the "beliefs and truths the people profess are frequently not applied in practical everyday Christian living."[87] Presenters also warned participants that change would not come quickly. They noted it would take a "definite and deliberate plan of perhaps two to four years in scope," but argued it was worth the effort because "[c]ompulsive segregation degrades human beings on both sides of the lines" and "created bitterness, false feelings of superiority and inferiority, and a host of other pathological conditions."[88]

The repercussions that ministers and churches could face because of their efforts to desegregate churches were also addressed. Presenters noted that some members might leave the church. If ministers were to find that happening they were encouraged not to disown the former members, but to "keep the door open for their return." Presenters knew that a declining membership meant fewer dollars and possible financial difficulties, but insisted ministers stand firm in their efforts. They advised minsters to develop a "broad base of democratic financial support" to offset declining contributions. Presenters also offered hope to the ministers when they noted that experience had shown that "1) few members actually withdraw when the local church takes a stand on this issue, and 2) a certain number of other people who have been previously alienated by the seemingly evasive attitudes of the church will become new adherents."[89]

Again, the RRI saw churches as a viable vehicle for educating adults. They especially wanted predominately white churches to educate their members because those members were also the "real estate dealers, bankers, contractors, architects...as well as homeowners" who prevented minority groups from obtaining valuable resources.[90] Presenters suggested churches "take a look at their basic nature, their limitations and their strengths" before attempting change because "the people in the so-called white institutional churches are generally the same people as those who constitute the problem."[91] Presenters felt churches needed to truly assess their situations and potential support because it was "not realistic" to suppose those people would be "in the vanguard" where supporting nonsegregated churches were concerned.[92]

At first glance the RRI may have appeared to be just another academic endeavor where scholars met to present their research. But a second and more in-depth examination shows the RRI was actually doing much more. From the 1940s throughout the 1960s, the RRI provided whites a safe academic setting where they could access information that could help them become effective allies in fighting racial oppression. The lectures, presentations, workshops, community clinics, and area race institutes provided by the RRI exposed whites to a world they had taken little time to examine.

CHAPTER FOUR

Leaning on Legislation

While the RRI focused on educating whites about the ills of a segregated society, it simultaneously worked on providing blacks with valuable information on legislative measures designed to promote social and economic opportunities. The RRI enabled the foremost legal minds, scholars, and leaders to sift through the red tape and legal jargon and explain to participants what the legislation meant, how it could be utilized, and what had been the results. In doing so, the RRI was able to demystify efforts and provide blacks with information that was paramount to the group being able to take advantage of the emerging opportunities.

EMPLOYMENT LEGISLATIVE EFFORTS

As employment opportunities were a major concern for blacks, Executive Order 8802 was the first legislative effort the RRI monitored. As discussed in Chapter 1, A. Philip Randolph, president of the Brotherhood of Sleeping Car Porters, and his supporters threatened to have 100,000 blacks march on Washington during June 1941 to demand the rectification of unfair employment practices. Several factors contributed to the limited job opportunities blacks faced during the decade. First, in efforts to secure jobs for whites, between 1880 and 1907 the southern states enacted laws to separate the races and limit the privilege of franchise to whites. Commenting on this legislation in a 1932 article for *Opportunity*, Charles S. Johnson wrote:

> In effect this legislation, backed by a solid sentiment, threw up an economic breastwork of protection for white workers against the free competition of the blacks who had the sole advantage of actual possession of the trades as a heritage of three hundred years of slavery.[1]

Second, by 1880 southern European immigrants dominated jobs in industrial areas. This domination also relegated black workers to menial labor where they were unable to acquire the skills needed to compete in the industrial market. The skills that blacks had maintained since enslavement, like carpentry, were not in demand as the building trade had turned to steel instead of lumber.[2] The Great Depression, which devastated the country, served as the final blow that limited black economic success. After the 1929 crash, whites took over the menial jobs that blacks had typically dominated.[3]

The New Deal liberals and World War II, however, offered hope to blacks. Since the New Dealers saw the "Negro problem," discussed in Chapter 1, as basically one of economics, upon his election in 1932, President Franklin D. Roosevelt and supporters began their push for reforms they felt would benefit all Americans.[4] The New Deal reformers promised programs that would get the country back on its feet and promised to prohibit discrimination in public service jobs. In *TVA and Black Americans: Planning for the Status Quo*, Nancy L. Grant shares that Roosevelt's New Deal not only expanded the government's role by making it a source of public services and relief for Americans, it also became important as both employer and service supplier. Grant writes:

> Under Roosevelt, moreover, the federal government expanded in size and became important as an employer as well as a supplier of services. In order to fulfill its expanded role, the government bureaucracy increased the number of civilian federal employees from 580,000 in 1929 to 1,042,000 in 1940. The federal budget increased from 3.0 percent of the gross national product to 9.1 percent.[5]

Like the New Deal, World War II offered blacks the hope of securing war-related jobs. The group would, however, face difficulty. Across the board, blacks faced the same discrimination they had in the past in numerous areas of war-related industrial employment. Those blacks who did obtain war-related jobs often found themselves omitted from training programs or confined to training for unskilled positions like industrial cooks or blacksmiths. Blacks were seldom promoted or upgraded if it meant that they would supervise white workers. Promotions involving blacks supervising other blacks were more common. Blacks were also subjected to lower pay and poorer working conditions than white coworkers.[6] On average, 75 percent of southern black men in any given city would work as common laborers in unskilled jobs. This compared to only 25 percent of white men. Fifty percent of black women worked as domestics, compared to slightly less than 1 percent of white women. Another 20 percent of black women worked as service workers, compared to less than 10 percent of white women. Nationally, minority families earned only 54 percent of the median income of white families.[7]

In 1940 a special office was set up within the National Defense Advisory Commission to promote the training and employment of black workers who, as a group, had been confined to the "hot, heavy, and hard" jobs better known as "H" jobs.[8] However, because the National Defense Advisory Commission made little progress, Randolph and supporters, in response to the growing unrest in the black community about the lack of jobs, threatened the March on Washington Movement in 1941. Randolph's actions led Roosevelt to issue Executive Order No. 8802 on 25 June 1941. Basically, Executive Order 8802 said that employers and labor unions were responsible for providing fair employment opportunities to all men in defense industries.[9] In part it read:

> ...that there shall be no discrimination in the employment of workers in defense industries or Government because of race, creed, color, or national origin, and ...that it is the duty of employers and of labor organizations, in furtherance of said policy and of this order, to provide for the full and equitable participation of all workers in defense industries, without discrimination because of race, creed, color, or national origin.[10]

Executive Order 8802 also authorized the establishment of the federal Fair Employment Practices Committee (FEPC). At first glance, the FEPC seemed to be the ammunition that blacks and other minorities needed to access employment opportunities; but, the committee, designed to "receive and investigate complaints of discrimination" in violation of the provision and take "appropriate steps" to address complaints as well as "recommend further measures to the government and the President necessary to carry out the order," had no legal repercussions for violators. At best, the war contracting and regulatory agencies could punish offenders by canceling their government contracts or, in some cases, referring them to the president. The FEPC could only hear complaints and hope to persuade companies to voluntarily comply with the regulations.[11]

Although the FEPC technically had no recourse for discriminatory complaints, the RRI viewed Executive Order 8802 as a positive step taken by the federal government toward equalized employment opportunities. Charles Houston, attorney and member of the President's Committee on Fair Employment Practices, compared the federal wartime FEPC to the Emancipation Proclamation. He told the 1945 Institute participants that both documents were "definite turning points in American history" in that they both went beyond their original purposes to become "declarations of national morality." The FEPC had made African Americans and other minorities "front page news" by showing the unfair labor issues they faced across the country.[12] The RRI hoped this exposure would prompt moral whites in influential positions to act to rectify the situation.

It's obvious from newspaper reports that RRI organizers were not alone in thinking legislative measures like the FEPC could actually bring about social change. When the FEPC established regional offices in the southern states during late 1943 to keep abreast on employment discrimination in the area, southern FEPC opponents cried foul. This excerpt from a 1945 editorial which appeared in the *Nashville Banner* on 3 July 1945 shows this.

> It is clear for all to see...the SOUTH is the target of the FEPC. In the eyes of the FEPC it is the criminal to be prosecuted—or in the bright allegories of broad and non-discriminating sociological minds, the patient upon whom this witchdoctor must perform a major operation.[13]

The same article proclaimed that the South had been "TRIED by the FEPC, CONVICTED by the FEPC, and subjected to whatever penalties the judgment (FEPC's) entail[ed]." The article further blasted the FEPC by stating, rather colorfully, that the agency was counterproductive and could not control race relations.

> As a healer, the FEPC is approximately as effective as a lighted fire-cracker in the bed of a heart patient; or an arsonist on the fire department. Assigning to it the responsibility of race relations is like assigning Typhoid Mary to oversee a health camp, with the possible exception that Mary would not deliberately inject a germ for the simple joy of seeing the fever rage. But comparisons are not necessary, inasmuch as most Southerners of both races are aware of the FEPC's record as a social insurrectionist, and its fight for dictatorial power in this field has been opposed by right-thinking, intelligent, able leadership irrespective of race....[14]

Such colorful attention given to the FEPC shows that the program with essentially no bite was indeed threatening. The fear of legislative correctives bringing about social change was at the root of the controversy surrounding Executive Order 8802 and the FEPC. Robert Weaver, director of community services for the American Counsel on Race Relations in Chicago, told Institute participants that the opponents of FEPC were fighting a symbol of federal racial policy rather than the agency itself. He said:

> The fight against FEPC is not so much a fight against the agency itself as it is a fight against a symbol of federal racial policy. Although a trend toward local determination of policy will come during the period of reconversion to peacetime living, some measure of federal determination of racial policy needs to be retained wherever federal funds and services are used in local areas for social welfare services to all the people.[15]

The fight over FEPC continued as supporters saw the efforts as more than an advancement for minorities, but as an opportunity to show opponents of democracy that the democratic ideology professed by Americans was actually practiced by Americans. Isidore Dollinger, a New York Congressional Representative, told the 81st Congress that because the United States was struggling against communism, it couldn't afford to allow discrimination to continue. He said:

> Our obligations as a signatory of the United Nations Charter, "to promote universal respect for, and observance of, human rights and fundamental freedoms for all without distinctions as to race, sex, language, or religion" are sacred. We should fulfill those obligations willingly and at once, and not be forced to observe them.[16]

In its five-year tenure, the federal FEPC "satisfactorily" settled nearly 5,000 cases in "peaceful negotiation," including 40 strikes caused by racial tensions. During the last year of the war the FEPC held 15 public hearings and docketed 3,485 cases, settling 1,191 of them. Although Truman issued Executive Order 9664 on December 20, 1945, to continue the work of the federal FEPC, strong southern opposition and a lack of funding caused the agency to close on June 28, 1946.[17] The efforts started by the agency, however, continued.

Although the RRI and FEPC proponents saw the FEPC as making major strides for African Americans, its effectiveness remains questionable since the individual states determined if they would have FEPC legislation and to what extent those laws could be enforced. Eleven states followed the federal FEPC and established their own Fair Employment Practices (FEP) legislation. New York, Indiana, New Jersey, and Wisconsin had passed FEP legislation in 1945, but the laws were nonenforceable in Wisconsin and Indiana. Massachusetts passed FEP legislation in 1946; Connecticut and Oregon in 1947; New Mexico, Rhode Island, and Washington in 1949; and Colorado in 1951. Attempts to pass FEP laws were unsuccessful in Arizona, Illinois, Kansas, Minnesota, Montana, Nebraska, Utah, West Virginia, Michigan, Ohio, Delaware, Iowa, Wisconsin, and California. Bills were pending in Missouri and Pennsylvania.[18]

The RRI continued to decipher employment legislation for participants. The federal government took additional steps to initiate fair practices on 26 July 1948 when Executive Order 9980 set up a Fair Employment Board in the Civil Service Commission. The order authorized the appointment of a Fair Employment Officer in each executive department. This officer was empowered and directed to carry out 9980's order, which was to:

1. Appraise the personnel actions of the department relative to conformity to the Order
2. Receive complaints and appeals concerning alleged discrimination because of race, color, religion, or national origin
3. Appoint central or regional deputies within the particular department to investigate or receive complaints
4. Take necessary corrective, or disciplinary action, upon authority of the head of the department[19]

The Fair Employment Board reviewed decisions made by department heads, devised rules and regulations relating to the order, advised departments on fair employment policies and disseminated the information, coordinated departmental programs, and made recommendations to the President via reports to the Civil Service Commission.[20]

A 1951 Race Relations Department memo outlined and explained how the federal legislation impacted employment. The federal FEP would:

1. Bar employer from refusing to hire, from discharging, or discriminating in advance because of race religion, color, national origin or ancestry.
2. Prohibit discriminatory job advertising.
3. Ban questioning job applicants about race or creed.
4. Provide more or less tight job protection for so-called "Minority Groups" members: Catholics, Negroes, foreign-born residents, Jews, Mexican and Spanish-Speaking people, etc.[21]

Legislative efforts for fair employment practices continued on December 3, 1951, when the president issued Executive Order 10308 with the intent of "improving the means for obtaining compliance with the nondiscrimination provisions of Federal contracts."[22] The order provided the appointment of the Committee on Government Contract Compliance, which was authorized to assist federal government departments and agencies in complying with the nondiscriminatory provisions required in all government contracts.[23]

The RRI paid close attention to these latest federal efforts to address unfair employment practices. John Hope II, an industrial relations consultant to the Institute and the workshop's Labor and Industry Clinic leader, noted the "significant though gradual shift" in the way policy-making employers, labor leaders, government agencies, the National Labor Relations Board, the railroad boards and the courts viewed minority workers. Minority workers were increasingly changing from a "secondary and peripheral position to one of central and integral importance."[24] In noting the changes in thought, Hope pointed out that during the previous decade the "mere recognition" of discrimination and admitting its importance through statements of nondiscriminatory policies hailed accolades and "deep gratitude."[25] The RRI attributed the changes in employment practices to various things. Hope credited changes to "the more alert" who wanted to preserve and strengthen democratic institutions by making fair employment practices a daily occurrence. The "more alert" were part of a society that was increasingly demanding improvement in the status of minorities throughout the world and challenging the American democracy to uphold its professed tenets and treat its minorities as true citizens. This challenge from the national and international communities forced the government and individual employers to acknowledge the existing relationship between fair employment practices and production, and the market, and profits. Hope noted that "[p]aternalism in dealing with industrial minorities is giving way gradually to fair play based upon self-interest and the quest for survival in a war-torn world split sharply along ideological lines."[26]

In a July 1, 1952, article that appeared in the *Nashville Banner*, Charles S. Johnson credited five things for the changes that were occurring. All of his reasons basically stemmed from the changing forces of ideology and not from the grassroots types of efforts that were developing in the South.

1. A cultural revolution in which the minorities are benefitting and have found a sure basis of incorporation into the national mentality and political state.
2. A modification of the old concept of common law in which the emphasis has been on liberty rather than equality or fraternity.
3. The rapid spread of a dynamic doctrine of human rights which condemns discrimination based on race, nationality, religion, or social origin.
4. The appearance of new nations of colored peoples with a present and potential power in determining the course of world events.
5. A conflict with Soviet ideology that has deepened faith and comprehension of our own values and prompted measures to correct weaknesses in our own system of life.[27]

The RRI believed the FEPC was a "vital, necessary, and desirable" program and held firm to its position that legislative measures were effective tools in addressing social injustices.[28] Some participants at the 1954 RRI, however, disagreed. Since the FEPC had no enforceable laws, they viewed the program as more of an educational project that helped disseminate information on labor conditions and the discrimination and the employment status of minorities. They felt other tactics were needed to secure jobs. This view could be attributed to the changing mood in the southern black communities where a rich tradition of protest was growing steadily as people increasingly took notice of the efforts by organizations like the national Congress on Racial Equality (CORE) and the Southern Christian Leadership Conference (SCLC).

Amid the growing mobilization of grassroots efforts, the RRI maintained its optimism in top-down legal and legislative methods of change. It continued on its path of demystifying legislative efforts and showing participants how those efforts were being utilized. For example, to support its position that a change in policies could stimulate a change in social justice, the RRI often invited company executives to share stories of how their companies adhered to fair employment practices. This occurred at the 1949 Institute during an Employment and Industry clinic meeting. Joseph J. Morrow, a personnel manager for Pitney-Bowes, Inc. in Stamford, Connecticut, gave participants an insiders view of his company's nondiscriminatory employment policy and how the employees reacted to it. Morrow told participants that preventing trouble associated with integration relied on the company's position on minority workers, employer-employee relationships, top management, and black workers.[29]

According to Morrow a company's position on minority workers was crucial to combating the negative feelings of workers. Once a company said it was going to activate a nondiscriminatory employment policy, it had to make it "crystal-clear" to employees that that's the way it would be. The company couldn't be "sheepish" about its stand because employees would detect it and agitators would try to revolt. The process would thus be destined for failure.[30] By establishing solid employer-employee relationships with white workers before introducing minorities, white workers would feel valued and secure and would be less anxious about the new arrivals. Morrow found that many Pitney-Bowes workers tried to prove to the company that they were not prejudiced and could accept the black worker in a friendly manner. Morrow believed that integration went relatively smoothly at Pitney-Bowes not because their white personnel were any better than other whites, but because their employees' desire to meet the company's expectations overruled their thoughts of acting on their prejudices.

Top management's support of the nondiscriminatory policy was also critical for success. When Pitney-Bowes started hiring blacks for positions other than maintenance workers and truckers, many whites feared that the company was planning to eliminate them for cheaper labor. Instead of addressing the rumors, Pitney-Bowes management continued to add other skilled blacks from time to time and maintained their wages at above-average rates. Eventually the rumors died out.

Where a sense of fair play could not be legislated, Morrow noted that black workers had to prepare themselves for personal attacks from those who couldn't handle working together on an equal basis. Calling to mind a black female employee, Morrow said:

> I stressed to her, and to each Negro office employee who was hired later on, the fact that she was a real missionary for her race; and that her own self-restraint in the face of possible embarrassment, and her poise, tact, and diplomacy, would be the best means through which she could defeat prejudice among her working associates—who, more often than not, would probably need very little selling.[31]

Other strategies included identifying potential agitators and using them to the company's advantage. Morrow suggested, rather tongue in cheek, that these people be taken aside and told that they were being asked to help offset expected trouble because they were known not to be prejudiced. Confiding in them that the company wanted to avoid harsh and unpleasant repercussions helped by letting them know in a nonconfrontational way that their negative actions would not be tolerated.

Maintaining its position that legislation was a key vehicle in promoting social justice and that scholars could provide information needed to initiate such measures, the RRI continued to bring in representatives like Morrow to show the employment advancements being made through legislation. Participants, however, sought more practical and immediate strategies for addressing tensions.[32] The RRI tried to respond to these desires, but their offerings still held to indirect methods. For example, civil rights attorneys Thurgood Marshall and Loren Miller advised participants wishing to promote equal opportunities to identify symbolic places where large groups of blacks and whites could intermingle and get to know one another. This intermingling could lead to employment opportunities. Whites might become less hesitant to hire blacks in clerical and professional positions and blacks would be more prone to seek the job training required for those jobs.[33]

The second practical suggestion was born out of the philosophy that "[s]uccessful demonstrations, beget other successes and maintain the morale of the participants."[34] With this approach efforts would begin in a place where there was low resistance. For example, the black who did well on a job as a janitor or typist could be used as examples when companies were urged to integrate. The third practical suggestion was to find areas in need of labor and have large groups of qualified minority applicants apply for the jobs. To do this, participants suggested looking through the want ads or utilizing employment offices.[35]

But labor and industry participants realized that before successful manipulation could be achieved from a practical approach that a few basic things had to be considered. First, since each community was different, each community had to be evaluated on an individual basis. Second, the industries also had to be evaluated to find the policy-maker and determine the policy-maker's power relationship to other parties involved, i.e., administrative management, labor, consumer, government and civic groups. Third, the local companies had to be evaluated a second time to see their position on fair employment. Participants noted that some companies or unions may be hesitant to practice fair employment strategies because they were afraid of repercussions. In being the "pioneer" for fair play, they might experience backlash from competitors. So in these cases, unions and companies would also need fair employment legislation to protect them from unfair competition.[36]

Although the RRI overwhelmingly supported research-based, indirect social action, some time was set aside to discuss what individual blacks could do to obtain jobs. Specifically, labor and industry clinic members discussed examples of how other blacks had used practical "push tactics" to secure their jobs. In one case "ability and imagination pushed [the] process of integration." A black window decorator who had been rejected by an employer presented the employer with a sketch of the window as it was and then as he would have created it. The employer hired the decorator after seeing his work.[37] In another case "sheer numbers...pushed [the] process of integration." When 200 qualified applicants went to apply for a typist job, the employer could do nothing more than administer the personnel test. Out of the 200, the employer could find no valid reason to disqualify eight applicants who passed the personnel test. Those eight were hired. Numbers pushed integration again when the Minneapolis Joint Committee for Employment Opportunity circulated petitions and gained 10,000 consumer signatures on petitions in favor of integrating their retail stores.[38]

A black machinist used legislation to push integration. The machinist was a member of a segregated local and was fired from his job when he applied for membership in the white local. After filing a complaint with the National Labor Relations Board, the union reinstated him and paid him $3,000 in backpay.[39] Finally, "...unquestionably high qualifications for the job and ... courage in applying" worked for a black veteran who passed 18 out of the 20 fields on the United States Employment Service's (USES) General Aptitude Battery Tests. Encouraged to apply for a job listed in the local paper, the veteran did. The manager was shocked by the black applicant, but upon seeing his qualifications, hired him.[40]

The committee suggested that RRI participants who wanted to try "push" tactics start by having a qualified person apply for a job. If the qualified applicant was rejected, tactics similar to the one the window decorator used should be tried next. They also encouraged participants to take an aptitude test and use the scores to support their applications.[41]

As years passed, the RRI maintained its position of utilizing "intelligent" methods for social change, but it increasingly offered concrete strategies on how to secure jobs. The 1954 Employment Clinic, formerly the Labor and Industry Clinic, told participants that before tackling fair employment, they needed to assess the situation and determine the following:

1. Who is the responsible official?
2. Does the firm have a policy?
3. If firm is a multi-plant company, are the individual plant minority practices determined locally or nationally?
4. Is there a union?
5. Does it have a policy? (Courts are now taking the position that unions have a responsibility to protect the minority within their jurisdictions, whether union-members or not.)
6. Ascertain and understand the grievance machinery of the plant (whether determined by the employer in an "open shop" situation or by a union-management contract).[42]

Once the situation was assessed, the next step was to determine the type of corrective action to be taken: legislative, executive, or administrative. Either federal, state, or local government enacted legislative efforts. Company or union policy-makers initiated executive correctives through the form of a policy. A "responsible" company or union official administrator would initiate administrative efforts.[43] If people wanted to achieve legislative action, they could either direct their appeals to individual lawmakers or apply political pressure by way of voting. If people wanted to get policies changed at a particular company or union, they could alert the executive head of conditions and then appeal to his or her moral ethics. If this didn't work, they could enlist public condemnation and embarrassment through adverse publicity or adverse political consequences. If people couldn't get to the executive head they were advised to utilize an administrator. Questionable activities needed to be documented and then forwarded to the administrator. If this was not possible, workers should threaten to reveal the situation to either the public or executive head if the activities weren't discontinued. The next step was to utilize the press if needed.[44]

Once people decided on the type of corrective action they wanted to utilize, the RRI advised they decide on an approach. The RRI recognized four major ways of achieving changes in social policies: 1) the pressure approach, 2) the persuasive approach, 3) the coercive approach, and 4) the practical approach. The pressure approach utilized the political, legislative, and court litigations—executive orders and unions.[45] As for the persuasive approach, Institute Labor and Industry participants suggested that those interested in integrating minorities onto jobs should utilize the agencies like the United States Employment Service, the Urban League, Jewish Vocational Services, American Jewish Committee, and American Council on Race Relations. These agencies could assist in implementing fair employment policy; training personnel to effectively handle minority group problems on the job; keeping statistics for the public on minorities in the workplace; setting up advisory committees with labor, management, and public representatives to work toward fair employment practices; and providing counseling to minority group workers to aid in a smooth transition to the workplace.[46]

The coercive approach utilized the local, state, and national governments in promoting legislation for fair play by compelling contractors who provided services to government agencies to use fair employment practices. The unions also played a role in the coercion approach. They could design and implement a strong official union policies on all levels concerning minorities. These policies would include:

a) The detailed training of union officers and shop stewards as to methods of administering such a policy.
b) The education of rank-and-file members as to what the policy is, how to use it in their own interest, and the consequences for them of its failure.

c) The establishment and enforcement of penalties against members and/or local unions found guilty of discrimination because of race, creed, color, national origin, or sex.
d) The placement of responsibility for the enforcement of the non-discriminatory policy in the hands of a committee, preferably one having this as its sole responsibility, e.g., anti-discrimination committee, fair employment practices department or committee.[47]

The unions could also use their strength to bargain for clauses in all contracts with employers that would specifically prohibit discrimination, and force industries to utilize the grievance policies established in union-management agreements. The unions could also make sure that all members knew what the grievance policy said and how to utilize it.[48]

The RRI's efforts to disseminate information on how blacks had and could secure jobs shows that the project moved beyond discussions on legislative efforts. Although these methods were more in keeping with what Richard Robbins calls "sidelines activists" activities, the RRI did push for change. The RRI offered these strategies in addition to providing an arena to gain accurate and up-to-date information on other legislative measures that impacted equal employment practices. At the 1953 clinic John Hope II told participants that on August 13, 1953, President Eisenhower signed Executive Order 10479 with major provisions to champion "employment opportunity for all qualified persons employed or seeking employment on government contracts." The order also acknowledged that it was "in the interest of the nation's economy and security to promote the fullest utilization of all available manpower."[49] Apparently, blacks were taking advantage of the legislation efforts because Hope also reported that between July 1, 1958, and September 30, 1959, a total of 344 complaints had been filed by individuals and organizations. Blacks were involved in about 8 out of every 10 complaints filed by individuals. The total number of complaints filed through September 29, 1959, was 888.[50]

More legislative help came in 1961 when President Johnson established the President's Committee on Equal Employment Opportunity through Executive Order 10925. Dated 6 March 1961 the order created the "most powerful agency [then] concerned with job discrimination on account of race...."[51] The committee's primary function was to enforce the standard nondiscrimination clause required in most government contracts and had potential jurisdiction over some 50,000 U.S. companies with employees totaling more than 20 million not counting construction workers. Although the committee could only give orders to affected companies with government contracts, its presence was still significant because it set standards for other companies that would have to provide equal employment opportunities.[52]

The Employment Clinic maintained its focus on legislative correctives at the 1965 Institute as it concentrated on the new legislative advances in the area of civil rights. Specifically, they were concerned about Title VII of the Civil Rights Act, which prohibited discrimination based on an employee's race, color, religion, sex, or national origin. Title VII, which would be the most "all-inclusive source of employment rights,"[53] would apply to state and local governments and labor unions; however, it would not apply to the federal government, Native American tribes, certain agencies in the District of Columbia, clubs, and religious organizations. Executive orders would extend the legal principles to federal jobs.[54]

Although the Institute normally supported legislative measures geared towards equalizing opportunity, it did see weaknesses in Title VII. In its first year of existence, this complaint-oriented law only covered those firms with 100 or more employees, 75 in the second, 50 in the third, and 25 in the fourth. Individuals or groups acting as agents for individuals with local or state commissions could file complaints if they felt discrimination had taken place on the basis of race, color, religion, sex, or national origin.[55]

As grassroots movements like the Southern Christian Leadership Conference mobilized the common oppressed workers to take direct action for needed social change, the Institute held true to its basic belief that moral and democratic activity could be legislated. The RRI viewed its efforts as leading to direct action as it armed participants with information and encouraged them to put away their fears and file complaints.[56]

Education Legislative Efforts

When the 1954 Institute opened its doors on June 29, it opened them to the fight of public school desegregation. The U.S. Supreme Court had ruled on May 17, 1954, that laws requiring racial segregation in public elementary and high schools violated the equal protection clause of the Fourteenth Amendment of the Constitution. Although the RRI did not take any direct actions in efforts to support the desegregation process, it continued its role of interpreting legislative efforts and advancements to participants by inviting desegregation experts to the workshops. Thurgood Marshall, chief counsel for the NAACP, attended the RRI on a regular basis and discussed the case. At the 1954 Institute, Marshall discussed the landmark ruling. He told participants that although a favorable decision dismantling segregation was desirous, it was not the end of the struggle. He noted:

> ...a decision outlawing segregation, while momentus[sic] not be considered however as the conclusion of the efforts extended in behalf of full educational opportunity. Rather, a decision favorable to desegregation would only be a climax in the total effort which must ultimately end with integration.[57]

Marshall was realistic enough to know that in order to gain black support for desegregation, the group would want to know what could be expected of the whole process. Although Marshall offered the positive outcomes of the more popular desegregation cases like the University of Texas Law School and the Graduate School of the University of Oklahoma, which had a lot of controversy surrounding them, he realized more evidence based on research was needed to calm anxieties. Kenneth B. Clark, Associate Professor of Psychology at the College of the City of New York and associate director for the Northside Center for Child Development, offered that needed scholarship. Clark had conducted a large study on desegregation and presented his findings at the 1955 RRI.[58] Clark's findings gave way to principles that had practical implications as well as theoretical significance for social science. These principles were invaluable to desegregation proponents as they revealed that desired changes in individual and group behavior could be brought about directly by "changes in the social situations in which they are required to function."[59]

Clark started off telling the RRI that although the 1954 Supreme Court decision was both a "great social science document" as well as a "great legal document," it didn't make provisions for the particular procedures for desegregating schools.[60] This would be decided after more argument before the Court in the fall of 1954. The Court had recognized, though, upon further argument that the problem of implementing its decision couldn't be left to conflicting opinions that reflected the biases of those who preferred one type of desegregation to another. Clark argued that in order to assure maximum social stability during the process of complying with the Court's decision that the methods of implementing the decision be based as much as possible on concrete evidence rather than on speculation. He pointed out that there had been many cases of effective desegregation in schools and other social institutions within the past ten years that could be studied objectively to "provide a factual basis for future plans and procedures of desegregation."[61]

Clark had assumed that responsibility and collected and analyzed such instances of change, believing it would lead to the accumulation of evidence that would help answer concretely and factually the questions related to desegregation. He gathered information from numerous social institutions, including churches, colleges, universities, hospitals and health services, housing agencies, interstate transportation, public accommodations and recreational facilities, organized sports, labor unions and industrial employment, politics, and government.[62] Most of the desegregation cases in Clark's study took place in the northern and border states, but some were from the South.

Clark found that there was no one factor responsible for desegregation and that the "specific factor responsible for desegregation varied from situation to situation, institution to institution and from region to region."[63] He did find however that numerous factors could be involved in one way or another. These factors included:

a) Population Changes, b) Voluntary public opinion pressure, c) Referendum of electorate, d) Threat of publicity, e) Moral arguments, f) Activity of community action agencies, g) Personal decision of responsible authority, h) Non-judicial governmental action, i) Legislative action, j) Threat of court action, k) Pending court decision and l) Court action.[64]

Clark also found that "desegregation which resulted from litigation and judicial decision was just as effective as desegregation resulting from other causes."[65] This was important to those who maintained that court interference only hindered the process.

Clark identified numerous methods used in the desegregation process. These methods could basically be categorized as "gradual" and "immediate." The "gradual" methods of desegregation included:

a) "deadline"—where specified time for process was established
b) "time for preparation"—where the type of preparation is specified as well as time for completion of preparation before or during desegregation
c) "segmental progressive desegregation"—where the plan for progressive desegregation is in limited units of organization structure
d) "quota desegregation"—where a limit is placed on the number of Negroes to be introduced in a given unit at any one time[66]

"Immediate desegregation" methods included:

a) Abolishing segregated Negro facility and admitting Negroes to the previously all-white one
b) Opening all facilities without regard to race or color
c) Ruling a white facility can't exclude Negroes but letting Negroes decide if they want in or their own facility
d) Combining methods a) and b) and allowing specified time for necessary adjustments
e) Establishing a nonsegregation policy from the beginning/founding of an institution[67]

Several things held true about the methods desegregation. First, the time factor did not seem to be related to the effectiveness of the desegregation process. There was no evidence that gradual desegregation lessened the chance of confusion and disruption, nor did it guarantee effectiveness as prolonged intervals of time could be used for either positive preparation or to organize overt resistance. In fact, the evidence suggested that prolonged "preparation" time reflected "indecision, resistance and conflict" on the part of the controlling authorities. Even "segmentalized" gradual desegregation increased the chances of resistance and resentment as it seemed to prolong the period of opposition by whites immediately involved and supported their belief of being singled out to "bear the brunt of [the] 'affliction.'"[68] The anticipation of being involved in desegregation by whites only reinforced and intensified their opposition during the interval of waiting.

Again, in support of immediate desegregation, Clark found that the various types of the technique were no more likely to lead to nonviolent resistance or violence than were the varieties of "gradual" methods of desegregation. Some of the evidence suggested that a directive requiring desegregation was especially effective because it a) accomplished desegregation in a shorter amount of time, b) involved a larger number of whites and Negroes, and c) was accepted in a shorter time by the community with little overt resistance and controversy. Clark found that all of the relevant cases that were analyzed supported this principle.[69]

For those concerned with gauging the potential tensions associated with desegregation, Clark reported that it couldn't be done. The degree of active resistance or violence that was associated with desegregation could not be determined by the degree of expressed racial prejudice among whites prior to desegregation. Prejudiced whites adjusted just as well to the socially changed situations of desegregation as did less-prejudiced whites. There was even some evidence that a change in social situation brought about by desegregation tended to decrease the intensity of expressed racial prejudice and that in general those whites who had expressed the more negative racial attitudes had adjusted just as well as others and were considered likely to have their prejudices affected favorably by contact with blacks.[70]

On broader terms, Clark found that:

a) There was always some degree of opposition to desegregation.
b) A small group could precipitate overt resistance or violence to desegregation in spite of general acceptance or accommodation by the majority.
c) Overt resistance incidents had been quite rare.
d) Desegregation had been accomplished where there was strong opposition as well as where there has been minor opposition.
e) Opposition and overt resistance to desegregation were decreased, if not eliminated when the alternative for whites was the complete loss of the public facility or the imposition of a direct economic burden or some other important stigma.[71]

All the cases analyzed for Clark's survey revealed that there was always some initial opposition to attempted desegregation, and it varied in intensity, form, methods, and sources, from situation to situation and institution to institution. Although active resistance and violence were rare[72] when it did occur it was related to "ambiguous or inconsistent policy; ineffective policy action; and conflict between competing governmental authorities or officials."⁷³ Evidence also showed that violence was more likely to occur with lower-class and lower-middle-class whites who felt threatened socially and economically by contact with African Americans, or whites who were competing with blacks for limited facilities.⁷⁴

To accomplish desegregation with minimum social disturbance, Clark found numerous things were needed:

1) A clear and unequivocal statement of policy by leaders and other authorities with prestige
2) The firm enforcement of the policy by authorities and their persistence in executing the policy in the face of initial resistance
3) A willingness to use law enforcement action against violations, attempted violations, and incitement to violations
4) The refusal of authorities to "resort to, engage in, or tolerate subterfuges, gerrymandering" or other methods used to evade desegregation and its principles
5) The belief in the religious principles of brotherhood and the acceptance of the American ideal of fair play and equal justice of those concerned.⁷⁵

In addition, the reaction of local prominent leaders and figures significantly affected the mood and success of desegregation. When authorities and prestigious figures stood firm and supported the decision to desegregate, the transition occurred with minimum social disturbance.⁷⁶

Whenever desegregation occurred under the above conditions, for the most part, it was considered socially beneficial and successful. The size of the institution attempting desegregation didn't necessarily determine the success or failure of desegregation, although some evidence suggested that desegregating on larger scales increased the likelihood of general acceptance; and effective desegregation in one institution of a community or in one area of American life seemed to facilitate desegregation in other institutions and areas.⁷⁷

As local school boards were trying to prolong the desegregation process by saying that they needed more time to study the decision, Marshall told workshop participants that the NAACP would not give an inch in the fight for "full and complete desegregation of public schools in the south."⁷⁸ He reminded those in attendance that blacks were "not seeking handouts from state officials," but as "...full-fledged Americans citizens," would not be satisfied with anything less than complete fulfillment of constitution.⁷⁹ School boards asking for a longer period of time to "study" the Supreme Court's decision would be told that "the stage is over...now is the stage for action." The NAACP would tell boards that argued blacks were not ready for desegregation that "Negroes have been ready since they fought and died in wars for their country."[80]

"Anyone requiring segregation in public education" Marshall declared at the RRI, "is openly violating the Constitution...laying themselves open for prosecution"[81] as all the laws which supported public school segregation before the two court rulings were "not worth the paper they were written on."[82] Marshall, however, did caution participants that because a "frontal attack" on desegregation would be made by "pro-segregation boys" who "never follow[ed] the rules of the game," that desegregation proponents should not waste time in acting.[83] Pro-segregationists could be expected to use intimidation tactics against blacks. In fact, the school boards in some states had "reached a new low in their malicious and vindictive minds" by threatening the security of black teachers in efforts to hold back desegregation.[84] Marshall argued that any community that tolerated such actions by their school board had a "loss of morality" and that if blacks fell victim to the threats their past gains would be nullified. Marshall concluded the session saying that he didn't know how long it would take to desegregate schools in the South and that he didn't think anyone else knew.[85]

It is important to point out that opinions at the RRI did not always coincide. In fact, when that same 1955 RRI began, Marshall attacked predictions made by a fellow lecturer. Dr. George Mitchell, the Atlanta director of the Southern Regional Council, one of the largest research groups in the country, predicted during his education seminar that even with the Brown decision, it would still take six to eight years to implement. Mitchell told participants that his opinions were based on observations of "patterns of response" by people in the South who were questioned about desegregation prior to the 1955 Institute.[86]

When asked about Mitchell's comments, Marshall who "visibly became quite angry," countered "How does he [Mitchell] know?" In a newspaper interview, Marshall asked "Does he [Mitchell] know when I'm going to start a lawsuit? Do I know about his [Mitchell] field of operation?" Marshall said the obvious answer to both questions was "no."[87] The lawsuits Marshall referred to were future cases that would be brought about after the NAACP notified its local chapters to bring court action against local boards of education who didn't take definite action toward desegregating their schools by September 1955; but Marshall maintained that he had never set any special time limit for desegregation to be effected.[88] Kenneth Clark also addressed the time frames for desegregation during one of his 1955 lectures. Clark told participants that instead of debating when desegregation would be completed, they should be concerned with when the process would begin. "If time is used in good faith, desegregation will be realized," he said.[89]

Desegregation was again the focus of the 1956 Institute. Because the Supreme Court's decision didn't mean that "automatically integration, or even desegregation of schools [would] take place everywhere, or anywhere...even after the court [had] formulated and issued its decree" Marshall was once again on hand to clarify the legalities and the status of desegregation.[90] Marshall told participants that before they tried to address the objectives of implementing desegregation or how to desegregate, that they had to understand the basic facts of the Supreme Court's decision. The court had only "issued its decision" and had "deferred the formulation and issuance of its decree."[91] Marshall explained that, as he understood it:

> the differences between a decision and a decree [was] that the former indicates whether the court adjudges a practice as violative of the constitution not, and the decree sets forth the form and conditions of relief to be given the injured party.[92]

Although the Supreme Court decided unequivocally that legally enforced racial segregation in public schools was unconstitutional, as it stood, the decision did not automatically require integration, or even desegregation. The still-to-come decree would apply to specific cases. In addition, once the Court issued the decree, African Americans would still have to take the initiative and file cases in places that didn't comply with the mandate voluntarily and continued to practice segregation.[93]

Marshall also noted that the Supreme Court had not passed specifically upon the issue of segregation in public higher education, but it looked as if it too was banned under the broad scope of the decision. He told Institute participants that "if responsible officials could not be persuaded to comply voluntarily" cases would have to be brought to determine the issue.[94] Finally, Marshall pointed out that it wasn't clear if the decision applied to private schools or not. He said that if they didn't voluntarily desegregate the schools, suits would be needed to test it.[95]

With this clarified, Marshall told the participants that one of their "most important tasks" was to "define the major problems" that needed to be resolved so that implementation could be orderly and quick.[96] Defining objectives for the implementation of the Court's historic decision was also necessary as was answering the following questions:

> What do we expect or hope the Supreme Court's decision will do? When we persisted in our efforts to have the court declare legally enforced segregated schools unconstitutional what ends or objectives did we have in mind? Now that the court has spoken what would constitute a satisfactory implementation of the decision? Are or should our objectives be proximate and ultimate? If so, what are our proximate aims? Ultimate aims? To what ends should our next steps be directed?[97]

Marshall said that "unless and until we can answer these and similar questions with demonstrated validity, our task of implementation is going to be unnecessarily difficult to say the least."[98]

Besides defining desired objectives, implementation was also a problem. Marshall argued that the ultimate objective of the strategy had to be "the clear and unequivocal aim of eliminating all segregation and discrimination based on race, class, sex, natural origin, or what not from our national life."[99] Although blacks suffered the most from this "undemocratic practice," they had to realize that the problem was pertinent to building a democratic America.[100] Thus, blacks had to fight segregation not only for themselves but for democratic ideals, and they had to be interested in helping other oppressed groups, and vice versa. Like Clark, Marshall saw segregated schools as symbols of the inferior status of blacks in the American social order and felt the best way to effectively desegregate schools was to effect desegregation in other aspects of Negro life at the same time.[101] These other aspects, specifically employment, will be addressed in the next chapter.

Marshall argued that experience taught the first prerequisite for successful desegregation was a "clear, unequivocal policy from the top, and a willingness to back that policy with all the resources that can be commanded."[102] Where this happened there was little effective community opposition and less violence than was predicted. As encouragement, Marshall reminded participants that whether Clark found violence associated with desegregation wasn't dependent on the degree of expressed racial prejudice. He felt that their strategy should include a definite attempt to mobilize the large number of potential black voters in all Southern states.[103]

Another concern with implementation was the effect it would have on black educators. Marshall understood that there would be some apprehension on the part of black educators, but said efforts were being made to protect their vested interests. Numerous rumors circulated about reprisals for black teachers if the decision was implemented. Although the validity of the rumors were not known, they still disturbed black teachers. Marshall noted that the apprehension had to be considered in the overall strategies and tactics to desegregation.[104]

Marshall pointed out that past cases showed that desegregation had not resulted in the loss of black teachers in East St. Louis, Indianapolis, Phoenix, or even Cairo, Illinois. In fact in New Jersey, the number of black teachers had increased. Also promising was the fact that residential segregation, supply and demand, and the presence of tenure laws also acted as buffers to a major decrease in the black teaching population.[105] Principals and supervisors in particular, and some high school teachers who would most likely be displaced, would probably be reassigned to other jobs. Little was said about the problems black college instructors would face at black colleges when desegregation was fully implemented. To Marshall, their problem concerning integration was fairly simple in that they would have to make the colleges good enough so that there would be little trouble attracting white teachers and students. Private black colleges, like their public cohorts, would have to rethink their role in the scheme of higher education in the South. Land-grant colleges were expected to face more problems because they "directly duplicate[d] in many respects, the program of the white land-grant college, and that on a level inferior to white land grant college."[106]

Marshall did not attempt to give clear and final solutions at the 1955 Institute; he only made suggestions toward the aspects of the solutions as he was basically interested in getting people to understand the problem. The greatest problem that lied ahead was getting the Supreme Court's decision implemented in the "most expeditious and orderly manner."[107]

As public school desegregation gained national attention, some questioned the ability of the daily press to provide adequate information without bias. With the support of the Ford Foundation, a group of leading southern editors and educators established the Southern Education Reporting Service (SERS) in 1954 to act as an independent agency that would follow desegregation and provide impartial reports.[108] These reports could be utilized by the "interested educator or the conscientious layman" who wanted trustworthy and detailed information "all in one package."[109] The Ford Foundation believed that no matter what stance people took on the issue of school desegregation, impartial information was important because desegregation was a "vital problem" that "effect[ed] ...the future of education in America."[110]

Don Shoemaker, an SERS representative, went to update Institute participants on the regional status of public school desegregation. Shoemaker told participants that the border states from Delaware through Maryland, West Virginia, Kentucky, Missouri, and Oklahoma down into Texas were complying with desegregation. This pattern of "substantial compliance" was attributed to prominent figures in the areas who had accepted desegregation.[111] Kentucky, West Virginia, and Oklahoma in particular, had governors who "not only urged desegregation of schools but [had] taken pride in what they regard[ed] as the accomplishment of desegregation in large areas of their schools."[112] Most of the desegregated districts were in cities like Baltimore, St. Louis, Louisville, and Washington, D.C. South Delaware, however, was not complying. In fact, Shoemaker told participants that South Delaware residents were reacting like Mississippians.[113] The deep Southern states were still in "complete and utter resistance."[114] The only exception was "a very gradual breakthrough at the level of higher education...."[115] Shoemaker noted that the school districts that had begun or accomplished desegregation did so quietly months earlier without "announcement" or "fanfare." They just did it and people learned about it when the facts turned up "much later in reports from the county superintendent to the state superintendent or something of the sort."

But cases in places like Dallas, Little Rock, and Arlington County, Virginia, would be carefully watched as they were critical to the desegregation process. The Dallas school case was critical because its outcome was expected to greatly influence events in east Texas, Houston, and Forth Worth. The Dallas case could also impact changes in Louisiana where the Orleans Parish school board had refused for years a court order to desegregate.[116] Little Rock was critical because of its "profound effect on the situation in the South." Even Baltimore, where citizens thought they had handled their desegregation issues, felt Little Rock's repercussions. Arlington County was critical because it was one of a few Southern areas where a "substantial body" of white leaders favored school desegregation. This support, which was mostly inferred, was based on the white leaders' desire to keep the schools open.[117]

By the time the 1962 RRI opened, many of the desegregation cases that had been filed during the 1950s had been settled and were well into implementation. Preparations made in Atlanta, Dallas, and Chattanooga were all highlighted to show Institute participants how peaceful desegregation had been and could possibly be achieved. All three areas utilized community leaders, education, and law enforcement to facilitate their process.[118]

As reported at previous RRIs, prominent local figures who supported desegregation were vital to successful implementation. Community leaders in both Atlanta and Dallas "let it be known that no violence would be tolerated."[119] Atlanta utilized educational techniques in that they required their police officers to study literature on human relations, and both cities utilized the public media to offer factual information on desegregation and the process. In addition, Atlanta citizens were also required to fulfill their civic duties and "conduct themselves peaceably in obedience to the law."[120] Those that didn't behave peaceably were "promptly" arrested by police and quickly sentenced.

Dallas utilized their community leaders for educational purposes through a social organization called OASIS. OASIS was made of church, civic, business, and youth organization leaders who organized and sponsored meetings on school desegregation. The organization also sponsored a "law and order week-end" before school started to reaffirm their commitment to peaceful implementation. The Dallas news media was also utilized as news officials were consulted and helped plan a "systematic" presentation of information to the community.[121]

Unlike Atlanta and Dallas, who had already desegregated their schools, Chattanooga was planning to desegregate its schools that fall. Like Atlanta and Dallas, Chattanooga also planned to utilize community leaders and law enforcement, but their primary focus would be on educating their citizens about desegregation so that it could be peacefully facilitated. Chattanooga's educational plan consisted of educating teachers, the community, and children.[122]

Chattanooga "developed an educational technique to prepare teachers and other staff members for integrated classes."[123] These techniques consisted of meetings that were designed to allow teachers "to cope with anxieties and determine the best ways to teach."[124] Chattanooga used numerous techniques to addressed its community. Television programs were used to present citizens with information about desegregation issues discussed at both city and teachers' meetings. Historical and factual presentations concerning desegregation were offered, along with open discussions on the community's role in the process. A rumor clinic was held for anxious parents who were concerned about biological and cultural differences in the races. Once the community was addressed, Chattanooga could concentrate on the children who would be attending desegregated classes.[125]

Again, in dealing with desegregation the community was addressed first because its support was vital to peaceful desegregation. Participants were told that:

> If any school [was] to be desegregated peaceably the community [had to] be articulate in its assertions that no violence will be permitted and at no time must they lose sight of the child. The key to any peaceful desegregation program is a prepared and informed people at the grass roots.[126]

The 1963 Institute opened its door nine years after Brown, and the decision was still a concern of the Institute. Reed Sarratt offered participants an update and analysis of desegregation's status by utilizing statistical data from SERS. Sarratt told participants that during the 1962–63 school year 7.8 percent, approximately one out of every thirteen blacks enrolled in the public schools of the seventeen southern and border states, attended school with whites. In the 1960–61 school year, 6.9 percent of the black enrollment was in biracial schools. So, during the first seven years, the number of blacks in biracial schools increased at an average rate of about one percent each year. In the next two years the rate of increase declined to one half of one percent a year.[127]

At the beginning of the 1962–63 school year, there were 3,058 school districts in the region in which both white and Negro children of school age lived. Of these districts, 972 had desegregated their schools through mostly voluntary actions, and all but ninety-six were in the border states and Texas. Nine out of every ten black students in enrolled in desegregated schools lived in either D.C. or in the border states of Maryland, Missouri, West Virginia, and Kentucky. Adding Delaware and Oklahoma accounted for 97 percent of all the black children in the region who were enrolled in biracial schools. The remaining 3 percent lived in the eight states of Arkansas, Florida, Georgia, Louisiana, North Carolina, Tennessee, Texas, and Virginia. The six border states and D.C. had 14.3 percent of the areas black public school pupils, while 60 percent lived in the eight states that admitted relatively few black pupils to formerly all-white schools. The three completely segregated states—Alabama, Mississippi and South Carolina—had 25.7 percent of black pupils from their areas.[128]

Sarratt also told institute participants that there were three types of desegregation compliance:

1. "Compliance"—the border states
2. "Token compliance"—remaining six southern states
3. "Hard core"—five deep south states: Alabama, Georgia, Louisiana, Mississippi, South Carolina, make up this area.[129]

He pointed out that all eleven of the states in the last two categories belonged to the Confederacy during the Civil War and that the statistics showed that these states were successful in their resistance to desegregation. In the eleven states there were 2,283 school districts where both black and white kids of school age lived. At the end of the 1962–63 school term, 270, or about 12 percent, of the districts had some biracial schools. More significant, were the figures on the number of black kids enrolled in schools with white kids. During the 1962–63 school term the eleven states had a combined Negro student enrollment of 2,803,882. Of this number, 12,217 attended public schools with whites. That's only .004 percent of the total black enrollment. Almost 70 percent of the desegregated districts and 55 percent of the number of blacks in schools with whites in these states were in Texas.[130]

In Alabama, Mississippi, and South Carolina, all public schools were segregated. During the 1961–62 school year, 44 black kids were enrolled in white schools in Atlanta and 107 in New Orleans. With the exception of these two cities, the public schools in Georgia and Louisiana remained segregated. In Arkansas, Florida, North Carolina, Tennessee, Texas and Virginia, the number of blacks in schools with whites ranged downward from 2.16 percent of the total Black enrollment in Texas to .23 percent in Arkansas.[131]

Sarratt told participants that the figures showed resistance to desegregation in former Confederate states was stronger than desegregation forces. He went on to explain that the resistance was strongest near the Deep South, where the ratio of blacks to whites was highest. He used Texas as an example and said that almost all of the state's desegregated districts were in West Texas. All of East Texas, which bordered Louisiana, remained segregated. However, he pointed out that this was different in cities that had a high black population. The opposition was stronger in the rural areas than they were in the urban ones. In the "token compliance" and "compliance" states, desegregation was confined mainly to cities. For example, in Kentucky during the 1961–62 school year there were 24,300 blacks in desegregated schools. Out of that number, 15,300 were in Louisville. In Maryland 68,000 blacks attended biracial schools. Out of that number, 58,300 were in Baltimore.[132]

Sarratt went on to tell participants that the three patterns of compliance differed from place to place. Some of the school districts "simply removed race as a factor" in determining where kids would go to school.[133] Other states and districts devised complex and sophisticated plans that were actually meant to slow down the desegregation process. Some of the plans would begin in the lower grades and advance to the higher ones, or vice versa. For example, Nashville planned to begin desegregation in their first grade classes. They would then add another grade each year until all grades were desegregated.[134]

Little Rock was another good example. Whereas Nashville's plan started with first grade, Little Rock's plan started in the high school grades and worked its way down. Little Rock utilized a three-step plan where their high school would be affected first, followed by their middle school, and finally their elementary school. During the 1962–63 school year the middle school was desegregated. Georgia also utilized a twelve-step plan that started desegregation in twelfth grade and proceeded downward each year by one grade.[135]

Desegregation could also be slowed if states and school districts used administrative barriers to delay pupil transfers from the schools they were originally assigned. Sarratt told participants that this technique worked especially well against the mass movement of black students into white schools. State legislatures of some Southern states passed numerous laws that made desegregation difficult if not impossible. These laws, which were unconstitutional but assumed to be constitutional until exposed, were described by Sarratt as being "ingenious, in some instances, and reflect determination, imagination and resourcefulness on the part of their authors." They included pupil assignment plans, school closures, local option plans, tuition grant plans, private school plans, compulsory attendance laws repeal, and penalties against organizations and individuals who advocate desegregation.[136]

But Sarratt told participants that the federal courts were growing tired of the games states and districts played to delay compliance. He said the "clearest and most meaningful statement of this impatience" came from the Supreme Court in May 1963, in a ruling on a Memphis, Tennessee, public parks case.[137] Writing the unanimous decision, Justice Arthur J. Goldberg said that the Court:

> ...never contemplated that the concept of "deliberate speed" would countenance indefinite delay in elimination of racial barriers in schools... The basic guarantees of our Constitution are warrants for the here and now and, unless there is an overwhelmingly compelling reason, they are to be promptly fulfilled.[138]

Sarratt also told participants that desegregation among school personnel would also be pursued. He pointed out that although most of the efforts to desegregate public schooling concentrated on the student, segregated school personnel practices were also coming under fire. The courts were now turning their attention to cases in which the principle of desegregation also applied to school personnel. Referring to cases in Kentucky and Florida, Sarratt said a few decisions requiring desegregation of personnel had already been issued by federal courts. The districts in these states were ordered to "cease making racial distinctions among teaching, supervisory and administrative personnel in their school systems."[139]

Sarratt left the participants considering one other problem that was creeping up in light of desegregation: resegregation. Resegregation was appearing in areas where desegregation had already taken place. White schools that were desegregated were becoming all Black. Sarratt pointed out that Washington, D.C., Baltimore, St. Louis, and Miami were all going through this "cycle" because the residential areas surrounding the schools were changing from all white to all black. Although the Supreme Court's decision was directed toward states with laws requiring segregated schools, it mentioned nothing about "de facto" school segregation. Sarratt told participants that "de facto" segregation would soon gain attention because of a case in New Rochelle, New York, where the school board had established school district boundary lines that were racially discriminatory.[140]

Reflecting on the progress of desegregation since the 1954 decision and its future status, Sarratt noted:

> From all this it is clear that at the end of the ninth year after the Supreme Court decision, desegregation of the public schools has proceeded relatively rapidly and substantially in some areas, slowly in others, and not at all in still others. The easy part of implementing the Supreme Court's decision has been accomplished. What made it easy? The lack of resistance seems to have been the major factor. From this follows a second observation—the hard road lies ahead. Why? Because of the resistance in those areas that have not voluntarily complied. The realization is dawning that desegregation of schools may not be the panacea that some hoped and thought it would be. Desegregation of schools is a mechanical, legalistic process. Already full integration is being urged. What this protends [sic] is not clear, but it should give no comfort to those who seek to maintain the status quo.[141]

The RRI provided a valuable service to blacks and whites interested in implementing the Brown decision. By acting as a vehicle that disseminated information, rather than one which actively protested for equal educational opportunity, the RRI could keep participants abreast of the latest developments of the case. The RRI could tell participants about the communities that were implementing the ruling, how those places were implementing the ruling, and how the community was reacting. This information was important to participants who wanted to make an informed decision about how best to proceed with desegregation efforts in their own communities. Participants needed fears alleviated and questions addressed. They realized that just because *Brown* outlawed segregation, it didn't mean people were anxiously waiting to desegregate the schools.

CHAPTER FIVE

Community Reactions, Participant Evaluations

Perhaps one of the most striking characteristics about the RRI was that it was located in Nashville, Tennessee. Nashville during the 1940s seems like one of the least likeliest places to be home to a project designed to help improve social conditions for blacks and other racial minorities. After all, it was said to be "a place that could straighten Negroes out" because of all its racial restrictions.[1] Historian John Hope Franklin was a sixteen-year-old freshman at Fisk during the 1930s when he was "straightened out" in Nashville. After going downtown with "some other chaps," Franklin, a native of Tulsa, Oklahoma, needed to buy a transfer ticket for the streetcar.[2] After realizing he only had a twenty-dollar bill and no change, Franklin apologized to the white attendant. Franklin recalls:

> I went into this transfer point and I put down my money. And I apologized saying, "I'm sorry I only have a twenty dollar bill." I said, "I'm very sorry and you can give it to me in ones if you want to." He said—I thought he was going to jump through the cage – "No little Nigger's going to tell me how to make change!" And he proceeded to count my change in quarters and nickels and dimes." And I was shaken by it, I'd never been called a Nigger before. Not to my face...Talk about manners. That fixed me to the point that I must say that I can count the times I went to downtown Nashville after that.[3]

Nearly a decade later, future civil rights attorney and chief judge for the U.S. Court for the Southern District of New York Constance Baker Motley also avoided downtown Nashville because of its reputation. Motley arrived in Nashville in 1941 to attend Fisk University. In *Equal Justice Under Law*, she writes:

> In Nashville, I did not have a problem with local whites because I did not go off the campus. There was a movie theater for blacks across the street as well as a local drugstore. I had bought all my clothes and personal items in New Haven...so I had no need to go shopping.[4]

Johnson and the Fisk family worked hard to shield students as much as possible from that reality. For example, the dean of women worked with a few stores to allow students to try on clothing.[5] The "rawness of race,"[6] however, was embedded in the Nashville community and students could not escape most of the codified realities that existed. Those realities would even strike near the campus where students felt safest. Franklin recalls an incident that really shook the students. He had just been elected as student government president in 1934 when a young black man who lived about a block from the Fisk campus was lynched.[7] Seventeen-year-old Cordie Cheek was riding a bicycle when he hit a white girl. As was common with black-white altercations, rumors began to circulate until finally, the white community charged that Cordie molested the girl. One evening after the grand jury returned a "no bill" on the charge of molestation, a white mob seized Cordie, took him to the country, and lynched him.[8]

The racially charged environment between whites and blacks extended well beyond the Nashville city limits. In 1946 "colored folks stood together" in Columbia, Tennessee, when they exchanged gunfire with whites believed to be intent on attacking blacks in the community. Whites in Columbia, located in Maury County approximately 40 miles southwest of Nashville, were upset because blacks had prevented a public lynching of a black World War II veteran who had gotten into a fight with a white man.[9] The fight between the two men broke out after the black veteran, nineteen-year-old James Stephenson, defended his mother, Mrs. Gladys Stephenson, from the physical attacks of twenty-eight-year-old William Fleming. Fleming had repaired a radio for Mrs. Stephenson and became angry when she questioned him about his work. Fleming reportedly followed Mrs. Stephenson and her son out of the store where he finally slapped and kicked her. At that point, James went to his mother's defense, "struck Fleming and knocked him back through a plate glass window." A number of white men, including a police officer, went to Fleming's aid. The officer struck James with a nightstick and then Mrs. Stephenson after she protested the officer was attacking her son without knowing the circumstances. The policeman arrested Mrs. Stephenson and James on assault charges.[10]

Tensions surrounding the fight grew as rumors circulated around the community. Blacks, hearing the talks of a lynching, posted bond for the mother and son, and then began withdrawing to a two-block section of town where black businesses were located. The community had reason to believe the threats since residents could easily recall two lynchings of blacks in Maury County, within the previous two decades. Within a couple of hours of the Stephensons release, a mob of approximately seventy-five white men searching for the pair approached the jail. The sheriff, "leveling a submachine gun," ordered the crowd to disperse. Meanwhile, James had left the area after three county policemen told the black community of the growing white sentiment.[11]

Black businesses closed that day in an effort to avoid "trouble." By nightfall they were convinced that there would be either be an attempted lynching or and indiscriminate attack on the black community because Stephenson had left the area. According to reports, there was no disposition by the black community to "take it lying down." With "little faith in the ability or willingness of the city police to avert mob action, the Negroes settled down and prepared to defend themselves" as they could hear nearby gunfire and "wild yells." Accounts vary, but sometime "shortly after nightfall" city police entered the black area allegedly to investigate reports of gunfire. Blacks, already in a "state of apprehension" from the "lynching threats, mob activity, and gun-fire in adjacent streets" thought the attack was beginning when they saw white men enter the area. It's not known which group fired the first shots, but four policemen were wounded seriously.[12]

Such was the climate of the area the RRI called home. Although Nashville had the potential to be a racial hotbed, the first RRI stirred little emotions from the city's conservatives. Patrick J. Gilpin shares that Nashvilleans simply viewed the RRI as another one of Johnson's projects at the university. In fact, no accounts show threats of any kind against the program or its participants until the program's second year when Nashville conservatives took particular notice of Edwin R. Embree's speech which talked about the likelihood of the postwar world changing and the peoples of Asia rebelling against European dominance and gaining control of world power politics. The media portrayed Embree's speech as "a challenge to the region's racial etiquette."[13] The *Banner* and *Tennessean*, both local papers, ran editorials criticizing Embree's portrayal of the white race eventually being reprimanded for its actions. Gilpin observes that the local media contributed to that tension as many of their stories were written to incite violence against the program. Apparently, it worked as tensions ran so high that the Nashville police were dispatched to the Fisk campus during the second program.[14] Reflecting on the RRI Mrs. Haywood B. Johns, a Nashvillian who had attended the RRI for twenty-two consecutive years, noted threats of violence against the project were regularly made during the early years. In a 1965 article that appeared in *The Nashville Tennessean*, Johns noted, "People sent the fire department out, the police were alerted and we had to leave the building because of bomb scares."[15]

Throughout this storm, Johnson continued with his efforts. At the second RRI he urged the public to "view the Institute as a whole" and argued that Embree's lecture "was viewed out of context."[16] Nashville's *Globe-Independent*, the black newspaper, said Johnson was trying to pacify the white folks. It wrote

"Dr. Charles S. Johnson appears to have taken pains to say things calculated to lower the blood pressure of the discordant elements here that carried on daily trades against the institute and the truth telling that characterized the speeches."[17]

Besides criticizing the lectures being given at the RRI, conservative Nashville also reacted to the fact that blacks and whites were living together, eating together, and dancing together at the RRI. Apparently after visiting the RRI, prominent community leaders wanted to censure some of the lecturers but, Gilpin observes, Johnson "lost his cool" and threatened to leave Fisk and take the staff members who wanted to join him at another institution. The details of what happened after Johnson's ultimatum are sketchy, but apparently, as evidenced by subsequent RRI's and the speakers invited, Johnson established himself as head of the program.[18]

Like many educators and projects deemed liberal after World War II, the RRI had to confront the "Red Scare."[19] Headlines that ran with pictures taken at a 1945 RRI session labeled some participants as "communists." For example, one headline which ran in the July 30, 1945, issue of *The Nashville Banner* read "Communist Daily Worker Comes to Southern Conference for Human Welfare Here—And Workers Seem to Follow 'Line'."[20] Two years later the RRI would come under fire for being anti-communistic. In a story that ran in a July 12, 1947, edition of *The Nashville Tennessean*, a New York City councilman accused the RRI as being "a platform against communism" and not practicing the democratic roles to which it professed itself.[21] Councilman Benjamin J. Davis sent a telegram to Johnson requesting that a speaker from the Communist party be allowed time to speak at the 1947 RRI. Davis had accused the RRI of allowing two speakers to use their time for "the vicious red baiting campaign...." Johnson, however, ignored the request, telling an RRI audience that there was no time to answer the message. He said that the incident showed "how quickly stories on what we are doing here get around and how far."[22]

It's safe to assume that part of the reason Johnson refused to allow known Communist party representatives to speak at the RRI was that he wanted to avoided future attacks on the program that would detract from its mission. There's little doubt that Johnson also knew of the problems Highlander Folk School faced because of accusations tying it to communist activities. In *Highlander: No Ordinary School, 1932–1962* John Glen shares

> Highlander's attempts to promote a southern labor movement and its stated objective of a new social order meant that almost from the day it opened the school confronted charges that it was a breeding ground for 'radical social agitators whose baneful influence is felt throughout this section."[23]

Glen goes on to note that the attacks "often occupied an inordinate amount of the staff's time and occasionally affected its work."[24]

The RRI was again accused of being nondemocratic in 1949. In *The Nashville Banner's* article "'Next Voter' Criticizes Race Institute," the RRI was accused of having a monolithic point of view. "Next Voter" was a series of articles written by a group of northern preparatory school boys who were touring and writing their impressions of the South. After attending the RRI, the boys reported:

> Our criticism is simply this: The audience seems already to have a very definite and pre-conceived point-of-view. The organizers of the institute seem to be not unaware of this and they seem to have invited exclusively lecturers who share and encourage the opinions of the members of the institute. "The other side" never seems to be given a chance.[25]

The boys went on to say that the singular view devalued the program.

> This procedure diminishes greatly the value of the conference. It takes from it the label of an objective and scholarly meeting, and gives it the appearance of a propagandistic and political event. It seems surprising to us that this very conference which stresses so much the value of democratic behavior applies so little the very essence of democratic procedure in its own proceedings namely to make progress by real discussion and by giving every point-of-view an equal chance.[26]

Despite accusations of being either pro-communism or antidemocratic, the RRI maintained its course. Johnson continued to invite those speakers and researchers he felt would be most effective in building racial tolerance and addressing racial tensions.

Participant Evaluations of the RRI

Although Nashville did not welcome the RRI, participants who came from around the United States and other countries did. [27] As mentioned in Chapter 3, the RRI sought to provide information to whites who might have been either concerned about or inclined to improve race relations but were uncertain of where to begin. A housing manger for the Housing Authority of Atlanta noted that the RRI provided that information.

> ...the Institute, itself, fills a need that I have felt for a long time. It is my belief that there are many people in this country and abroad who are geniuiely [sic] interested in improving race relations but who do not have the time to search for the sources of information that would be necessary to improve their understanding of the problem.[28]

Still, another welcoming participant, a vocational counselor from Milwaukee, praised the program for using a scientific approach to deal with the issues of racial tensions.

> On the whole, your Institute served a most useful purpose, in my opinion, by exploring one social field objectively—using the problem-solving techniques which have long been urged upon the social sciences. For example, you made it possible for us to: 1. State the problem. 2. Make an analysis. 3. Form an hypothesis. The final step of course, had to take place in our own communities.[29]

Some comments showed that participants were actually surprised at what they found in Nashville. One minister from Bastrop, Louisiana, was amazed that such a program existed where people actually worked together. He wrote:

> A group drawn from so many parts of the country, and from such diverisifield [sic] backgrounds would inevitably bring conflict of opinion. Yet one of the surprises of the Institute was the prevailing tolerance and consideration. Perhaps one or two charged down from the Nroth [sic] to beat the 'bigot' into submission, and one or two from the South stood stalwart against outside interference: 'these affairs are private and sacred'. Yet even these found braod [sic] agreement on aims and objectives; they soon locked arms, not horns.[30]

Another respondent, a member of an intercultural education committee, and her friends were not so much surprised that the RRI existed as they were that it did in the South. She noted that her

> friends are "somewhat incredulous that such a thing could have been pulled off in the South, amid heat, and with such a notable galaxy of participants.[31]

Although most of the respondents made favorable remarks concerning the first Institute, many expressed concern about the overall organization. Their specific concerns centered around the program's length, speakers, material/topics, membership, and membership participation. Numerous people noted that the first RRI, which ran for three weeks, was too long. A minister from Louisiana was very candid in his critique of the program.

> But two weeks are sufficiently long. Few people can find more time. You overtaxed our energy and our brains. With professional absent-mindedness (or your own inexhaustible zeal) you forgot that it was Summer, and for most of us vacation time.[32]

However, not everyone agreed that the RRI's length should be reduced. Some people felt that the three-week period allowed more people to attend. A history teacher from Dillard University, New Orleans, noted that although the three-week project might "wilt those who remain for the entire period" it enabled a larger number of people to attend.[33]

Participants were also concerned about the speakers at the RRI, specifically the number who were present and their quality. Some participants like this YWCA volunteer from Tennessee were pleased with the numerous lecturers that were present at the first Institute.

> I am thankful for every one of the ninety lectures and the speakers who gave them...I treasure greatly the fellowship that we Americans, who live in the South, have been deprived of up to now.[34]

Others felt, however, that the number of lecturers needed to be reduced so that time could be made for discussing ideas presented during the lectures.

> I thought the program was well arranged and if there could be any improvement I should suggest that the lecturers be fewer and a little bit more time be given for questions and discussions or else that the time be lengthened in order to allow for a bit freer discussion of each presentation. I believe the best meetings that I have attended were those in which questions from the floor were brought out more clearly and the remarks made by the speaker in his presentation were much more explicit.[35]

Participants were also concerned with the representation of female scholars and speakers. One of the most striking critiques made on this subject came from a South Dakota professor of sociology who felt that some lecturers needed to be eliminated from future programs.

> It would be wise to eliminate some of the "weak sisters" from the speakers list... The feeling has been expressed by a number of Institute members that some of the speakers on the program were selected not because they had any contribution to make, but to serve some ulterior purpose.[36]

The professor's candid comments about some of the lecturers at the first RRI should not be taken as a lack of support for the program. Indeed, he found the RRI to be useful.

> The speakers, with the exception of a few minor figures, were well selected and rose to the occasion....It has been my privilege in other years to participate in race relations meetings, and in contrast with those this has been by far the most constructive and the more enlightening.
> ...Keep up the good work even if it is in the form of an experiment. An educational program of this kind, if kept up, will bear positive social fruits.[37]

Another participant from Louisiana was also concerned with a larger showing of female lecturers and wanted them "more prominently featured" at the RRI.[38]

Other evaluations about the RRI concerned the program's organization, specifically, the topics/material covered, those in attendance, and a lack of member participation. Many participants were concerned with the volume of material presented, the redundancy of material, and the absence of topics they found critical to race relations discussions. One participant from Gilbertsville, Kentucky, was concerned that, because such a large amount of information was presented at the institute, some of it would not be utilized.

> I may say that the volume of material was tremendous, which means that digestion had to take place after the Institute, and some of the implications thereby lost...Trim the volume of material.[39]

Others were concerned with either the redundancy or absence of topics. Participants seemed especially concerned with the repetitious discussion of race and racial theories. Upon reflection, one participant from Philadelphia who initially felt that the anthropological lectures overlapped, said that the redundancy could be useful for those unfamiliar with the area.

> To my biased thinking the anthropological contribution might have been condensed; there was considerable overlapping. But perhaps this was necessary for people who don't have the discipline of living with a sociologist.[40]

Another participant who was familiar with race relations and concerned with the overlapping material in the areas of race and racial theories made a suggestion as to how the repetition could be avoided. The Chicagoan noted

> I believe that if instead of three anthropologists covering the same material in three lectures each there could be one anthropologist giving six lectures, or two anthropologists who had made a division of material between them, some of the repetition of the anthropological material would be avoided.[41]

The absence of information was also an issue addressed by respondents. Although racial tensions were greatly impacted by the migration of blacks to urban areas in search of employment opportunities, housing and employment issues were not addressed at the first RRI. Many participants pointed this out in their critiques. An employee of the Rosenwald Fund expressed concern over housing issues because of his own "ignorance about the overall pattern and problems."[42] Another Rosenwald employee also concerned with housing wanted to know "...what the problems are, what has been done, and what might be done."[43] A representative from Chicago's committee on race relations expressed concern about the absence of information on labor. She wrote:

> ...I think that in view of the tremendous importance of organized labor in the field of race relations there was not enough weight given to this subject in the representation of speakers. I don't think necessarily that union leaders should be the speakers, since it is difficult for them to be objective (at least publicly), but I think that the possibilities that lie in labor organization and the tactics needed to make use of them should be very fully covered....[44]

Respondents also expressed a desire to have information presented on other minorities experiencing problems in the United States. Although the following comment shows that participants were basically satisfied with the information presented, it does show their interest in other racial groups. From Little Rock, Arkansas

> We feel that most of the important issues, conditions and situations that affect relations were entered into candidly and unbiasly [sic]. However, it appears to us that more time could have been given ti[sic] the discussion of common problems perhaps by group discussion in small units. Also, more attention might have been given to the discussion of problems affecting other minority groups as well as the Negroes.[45]

Another participant from Philadelphia also expressed her concern for information on other groups.

> I was sorry that there was so little room for the consideration of Anti-Semitism. In northern communities it is, as you know, enormously on the up-rise.[46]

A history teacher from New Orleans felt so strongly about the absence of information on other minority groups that he suggested that the RRI change its name.

> I believe that the Institute should be sub-titled. It should read: Institute on Race Relations with special attention to Negro-whote [sic] Relations in the United States. (During the Institute not a great deal was said about (1) the minorities problem in Europe and Asia and (2) about minorities problems, other than the Negro, in the U.S.).[47]

Other topics that members expressed interest in were the class status of blacks, patterns of racial prejudice among blacks, youth issues, and adult education.

The RRI did address concerns of other groups and even international issues during subsequent years. For example, conversations centered around the differences between English and French Canadians, the international role of the United States, and even issues of Appalachian poverty in 1967.[48]

Another critical area of comments focused on people attending the RRI. Several participants expressed concern over the first RRI being geared more towards the scholarly community rather than the community at large. One participant wrote:

> The attendance of young people of college age should be stimilated [sic]. Special effort should be made to provide 30 or 40 all-expense scholarships for a selected student from 30 or 40 white and Negro colleges..[49]

A Vanderbilt student also expressed his concern.

I wish to point out that I felt that the various audiences were composed of a very exclusive group. That is to say, the membership of the Institute was confined to a limited group of intellectuals who were all more or less familiar with the problems under discussion. Particularly noticeable was the absence of our business leaders and executives who indeed play a significant part in the process of interracial adjustment. May I suggest, therefore, that in future Institutes of this type the cooperation and attendance of these elements as well as other groups, such as for instance the clergy, be sought.[50]

The absence of the larger community caused a Kentucky participant to seemingly question the program's usefulness.

Such a program to my mind must reach a larger mass of people who are not professionals or who do not claim any scholastic standards, but who wield or could wield a tremendous influence in urban affairs. This means the barber shop, church and school room must be reached with the information.[51]

Although he readily admitted that he attended only three lectures during the first RRI, a Nashville teacher's comments echoed the sentiments that the program was geared more toward the scholarly community. He wrote:

My somewhat uninformed opinion is that two groups should first be reached—those who are working in the field of race relations and the general public, particularly people who are in position to exert some influence on attitudes of young people. The program of the Institute seemed adequate for the first group mentioned.[52]

Even a Rosenwald employee expressed concerns about the practicality of the RRI and suggested ways of achieving it.

...I should like to ask, in these rather vague paragraphs about "emphasis," for as much time as possible to be given to practical techniques for achieving better race relations; descriptions of what is being done and how it is working in local areas, perhaps divided half and half between North and South. Possibly there might be seminars toward the end of the Institute in which groups in specific fields like social work, teaching, the ministry, or those in local committees could discuss with experts in their respective fields concrete, practical action programs possible for them.[53]

There's little doubt that calls for reaching a larger mass of people came because some of the RRI's participants were familiar with the grassroots project Highlander Folk School where organizers like Septima Clark worked with "sharecroppers, common folk, black men and women who had little or no schooling...."[54]

The lack of member participation was another critical area of response that would impact the organization of future workshops. The overall thought was that the RRI did not allow time for participants to discuss the information that was presented to them, exchange information that they themselves had, or get to know one another. Johnson's Rosenwald secretary wrote:

> ...I heard one other suggestion, which seemed good, and that was that some opportunity might be provided for a discussion period which would not follow a lecture, but which would be more in the nature of an exchange of experience and ideas among the members of the Institute themselves.[55]

A future social worker from Nashville agreed.

> ...More time should be put on seminar organization. There should be, perhaps, more time for actual discussion.[56]

Another Rosenwald employee added:

> ...I think also that it would be helpful to members of the Institute to have some means of identifying the persons present. Perhaps it would be possible to include in the program booklet a list of the members, where they come from, their professional field or the institutions with which they are connected, etc. to help those with similar (or diverse) interests to get acquainted more quickly. A slightly reduced schedule of meetings would also give the members of the Institute more time to learn from, and about, each other.[57]

A graduate student from Pembroke State College in Pembroke, North Carolina, agreed:

> In planning another such Institute I am only able to suggest that more adequate provision be made for the institute members to become acquainted with each other.[58]

NAACP attorney Charles Houston also expressed his desire to see more input from the RRI's participants and suggested that adding panel discussion to the current lecture-only format would promote group discussion. He suggested:

> If you are going to hold the Institute next year, I would suggest the possibility of using panel discussions on some of the evening meetings....a panel on the issue of separate schools would have provoked a great deal of interest. My idea would be for you to distribute before the meeting prepared forms for those attending the Institute on which they could write their own answers and reactions to the topic of the evening. They would then be given about ten minutes after the close of the evening session to set down their opinions and the papers would be taken up thereafter, read and correlated. In that way, you would get a sense of feeling of the Institute and its current thinking. I am afraid that you do not always get the sense of the membership by the questions raised in open meetings. Frequently, it happesn [sic] that the empty tub makes the most noise.—Charles Houston, Institute Lecturer, Attorney at Law, Washington[59]

In addition to suggestions for improving future RRI meetings, participants shared their thoughts on what they gained from the program. One participant from Nashville shared that her own prejudices had been impacted.

> To me, the Institute was a great stimulus. It served to modify, to a large extent, my class prejudice. There are too many interfering variables for me to determine just how great a value it was in the modification of my racial prejudices.[60]

She added that the Institute would be beneficial to other areas experiencing tensions.

> I am convinced that the Institute is valuable and that it should be held in the South whenever and wherever it is expedient. I hope someday to see the institute held at LeMoyne College. Memphis is a "hot bed," but the college, at least, is not under control of the political machine. These people need it desperately.[61]

Other participants shared that the RRI gave them hope that race relations could be improved. One participant wrote:

> This experience renewed my optimism. If human beings, young and old, as varied in colour as in creed and background, can live together so smoothly and so friendly even in the synthetic society of a university campus, somehow they will find a way to live together at home.[62]

Another wrote:

> By next years conference, if some of us are big enough to broaden the scope of our meager vision by sweeping all bigotry from our hearts—perhaps the stinted vision of other dwarfted souls can be adjusted to focus properly.[63]

Although the first RRI had offered several scholarly lectures which provided the latest research on race relations, human interaction made a lasting impression. A participant from Newport, Tennessee, noted:

> ...For me, the meals were a significant feature. Not only were they appetizing, but I liked the informal social contact they offered.[64]

Participants from the 1945 RRI also shared their thoughts about the project.[65] The respondents gave favorable comments about the RRI, and many made references to personal gains and their desire to see the RRI continue. A couple of people noted that the RRI was a reality check for them. A Berea College student from Chicago wrote that the RRI helped her see the reality of problems facing minorities. She wrote:

> The growth I've felt within myself, and the more mature outlook upon the minority groups' problems as a whole has been quite profound [sic] deepened.

COMMUNITY REACTIONS, PARTICIPANT EVALUATIONS 101

> It is no longer a localized thing, but vast and very real—no longer remote and intangible, or purely theoretical, but challenging, and factual.[66]

An educator from Montgomery, Alabama, agreed and wrote:

> Many of the contributors are helping us face realistically the situation confronting us at this time.[67]

Even a captain from the army agreed:

> The awareness which I had of the problems under discussion at the Institute of Race Relations was intensified greatly by my visit to Fisk this week. The few days I was able to spend there helped me visualize far more clearly than I had before the situations and problems which constitute such a challenge to the present and future welfare of this country...I sincerely appreciate the opportunity you gave me to participate in the informative and excellent discussion periods.[68]

Others wrote of the inspiration they found at the Institute. From Cleveland:

> The lively and pertinent discussions, the association with persons of like ideals, the interchange of thinking and experience have certainly broadened my perspective of racial horizons. I received inspiration which I have been attempting to pass on to others in my day to day contacts.[69]

From Richmond, Virginia:

> The Institute far exceeded my expectation both from the view point of giving valuable information, as well as providing inspiration to carry on in a field where the going sometimes—often—gets tough.[70]

From Atlanta:

> I found it stimulating and hopeful that the people are willing to gather in such numbers to discuss the pressing problems ahead.[71]

One editor from Tuskegee, Alabama, wrote:

> The wealth of helpful material placed in our hands; the opportunity to meet at close range so many fine people who are doing something to add to the world's happiness; the magnificent [sic] array of brain power present; the well-balanced, thoroughly discussed, nationally needed programs; the beautiful hospitality of Fisk University; the warm, friendly atmosphere created by Americans of different racial groups meeting, sharing experiences, exchanging ideas, trying sincerely and honestly to thrash out problems the solution of which is bound to mean a better world—all of these will be of lasting benefit to all of us who had the privilege of attending this Institute.[72]

Noted anthropologist M.F. Ashley Montagu noted the RRI was "destined to be a considerable success and I am glad to have been given the opportunity to be associated with it."[73] University of Chicago sociologist Allison Davis noted "It usually happens that the second year of such ventures is not so good as the first. In your case, however, I felt that the same high level had been attained."[74]

A June 16, 1945, memorandum to Johnson outlined other participant concerns. First, they were interested in having more diversity among speakers and issues. One suggestion was that there be "[m]ore participation in panels by competent Negro women."[75] Another suggested:

> Presentation and representation of other American minorities—especially Oriental-American, and Indian-American possibly also of foreign-born, and of religious minorities with information and discussion in ethnic groups, population trends, immigration policies, etc.[76]

Still, someone else suggested at least one panel on world problems of race—with various races represented from places like China, India, Britain, member countries of the United Nations, the Philippines, Puerto Rico, and Hawaii.[77]

Participants also felt that the lectures, panels, and seminars should include a wider variation of timely and urgent themes such as:

a) Domestic service
b) Agriculture and rural organization
c) Segregation in transportation
d) The role of the private Negro college both in leadership training and as a focus of social action on issues involving race (several felt the need for more emphasis here)
e) Specific race relations organizations, their programs and methods e.g., Urban League, NAACP, Southern Regional Council, AMA's American Council, etc.
f) Positive reports of church programs of action in race relations from leading denominations[78]

The memo also pointed out that participants were interested in seeing the RRI take a more active role in the area of race relations. Their suggestions for more active participation, however, were not confrontational as they called for developing "anti-segregation comics like Donald Duck," "simple Bible-based books for southern white [sic] on Christianity and Negro-white dealings," and "good songs like those developed by unions to sing Jim Crow off the scene."[79]

It's important to point out that as suggested in evaluations from the 1944 RRI, organizers did make variations in the program's general plan. Lectures, panel discussions, and seminars were added to subsequent RRI programs; however, a memo discussing general evaluations for the 1948 RRI showed that some participants still found too much information being covered at the program and too little time for interacting with other participants. The memo stated that:

> The program seemed to most if not all present much too crowded. One person proposed that Wendesday [sic] be a free day to catch up with the notes, to talk with the leaders and with other members, to sight see, and to rest.[80]

The memo also pointed out that participants were apparently still interested in issues facing other minority groups:

> Several felt that the inclusion of the race relations problems and situations in other countries and in the world as a whole was excellent and that not less but more of this might well be done.[81]

Evaluations of the RRI did more than suggest changes for the program's organizational structure; they also showed the program's impact on participants. An analysis of several comments shows that the RRI's plan to educate the influential so that they could in turn stimulate changes might have worked on smaller scales. Some participants said they returned to their homes and made changes in their communities. An Episcopal minister in Louisiana obtained a resolution through the Bishop and Episcopal Council of his diocese stating that blacks could attend white Episcopal churches "without restriction" in areas that didn't have black Episcopal churches.[82] Another RRI participant from Tennessee temporarily withdrew her family's funding from a hospital until the hospital changed its policy about not accepting or treating blacks. Three YWCA workers from St. Louis went home after attending an RRI and organized a local Institute on Race Relations during March of 1945. Their program focused on issues that were critical to their area such as segregation in their schools, housing, and employment.[83] The RRI also inspired one former participant to build a hospital in memory of black soldiers in Canton, Mississippi. He wrote:

> I am trying to build a hospital in memory of Negro soldiers that were in service in World War II. We have around $10,000 in the bank. The directors are of both races, meeting and working together in the Negro high school. We have a better spirit in Mississippi for the improvement of the Negro people.[84]

It must be mentioned that verifying these statements has been difficult. Even the RRI noted that participant accounts were only "anecdotal" since the project didn't pass any resolutions or take action as a conference body that would make it easier to document activity.[85]

But evaluations also show that RRI participants were not trained to handle direct confrontations. Another participant who obviously felt empowered by the RRI returned to her home in Decatur, Georgia, and sought justice for a local black woman who had been raped by a white man. The man had not been convicted by an all-white jury. The former RRI participant had tried to gain support for the victim, but was not successful. She wrote of her one accomplishment on the case:

> Recently she [victim] wrote me that she needed her coat, which had been held as evidence, but the authorities would not give it to her father. Through the county probation officer, who, thank heaven, really believes in justice, I was able to get the coat. So far, one coat returned to its owner seems to be the sum total of my accomplishments in the case.[86]

Others found that the RRI gave the opportunity to learn about different groups with whom they might not have otherwise come into contact. One participant from Milwaukee said:

> The Institute gave me my first opportunity to know Negroes. I was much impressed by the charm and culture of those with whom I came in contact.
> —Milwaukee, Wisconsin[87]

Although Nashville may not have welcomed the RRI, available evaluations from the project show that participants were generally impressed with their experiences and felt that the RRI was a valuable tool in developing positive race relations. The majority of participants wanted less of the theoretical and scholarly lectures and more of the practical information and direct action techniques which they could use in everyday interactions. Annual newspaper coverage around the country also reflects that there was a larger interest in and support for the project. Events at the RRI were covered in the *New York Times*, *The New York Amsterdam News*, *The Los Angeles Times*, and *The Philadelphia Tribune*, among other news sources.

CHAPTER SIX

Winds of Change

The RRI closed its doors on July 11, 1969, after 26 years of working to achieve positive race relations and civil rights. Within that time the RRI and the country had witnessed the murders of Emit Till, Medgar Evers, Martin Luther King Jr., and Malcolm X; race-related bombings of homes and churches; boycotts of buses and lunch counters; desegregation of schools; the passage of civil rights legislation; and growing cries of "Black Power." Within that time the RRI had also known three directors. Johnson, the founding director, became the first black president of Fisk University in 1947. He continued to direct the RRI until 1950, when Herman Long took the helm.[1] The RRI, however, remained under the watchful eye of Johnson until his sudden death in 1956. While traveling from Louisville, Kentucky, on October 27 to a New York meeting, Johnson collapsed and died of heart failure at a train station.[2] Long continued to direct the RRI until 1964 when he left Nashville to become president at Talladega University in Talladega, Alabama. In 1966 Clifton Johnson, a white professor at Fisk, was named director. While the RRI did maintain its broad commitment throughout its tenure to utilize the social sciences, education, and legislation to secure civil rights, the embittered struggle for those rights had caused changes within the project. By the time the RRI ended, it had explored—and in some cases encompassed—more direct methods to be used in civil rights efforts.

In "A Southern Negro's View of the South," thought to be the last article Johnson wrote, a seemingly disenchanted Johnson chastises America as he reflects on government's failure to provide definitive measures that would right the wrong of racial oppression. He wrote:

> It is the tragic truth today that in the face of the world's turning away from the crass inhumanities of racial snobbery and imperial domination, we have a substantial part of an entire region asserting defiance of freedom and the laws that support it. It is a tragic pity that while the rest of the world is giving new attention and respect to basic human rights, every device from subversion of law to violence is being employed to defeat the Constitution, and with such frantic desperation that no voice of stern national statesmanship dares defy, without apology and compromise, this organized retreat from freedom to tyranny and feudalism.
>
> There has been no bold and forthright national statesmanship that would dare look at the nation as a whole and its intractable parts, and face a common destiny in the new kind of world we have today.[3]

That Johnson would have abandoned his belief in the role the social sciences, education, and legislation could play in securing civil rights had he continued to live is doubtful. However, it is clear that years of white resistance to legislative efforts designed to address unequal practices had caused black hope in legislation to wane. While the RRI continued to enlist the aid of scholars and educated leaders after Johnson's death, the program could not ignore black America's overall changing mood during the late 1950s and '60s. Black communities throughout the South were calling for direct action, and the RRI knew grassroots efforts and developing organizations like the Student Nonviolent Coordinating Committee (SNCC) and the Southern Christian Leadership Conference (SCLC) were increasingly answering those calls.

The Nashville community was an example of those changing thoughts. While Nashville was home to numerous black institutions of higher learning including the American Baptist Theological Seminary, Fisk University, Meharry Medical College, and Tennessee State University, it was a segregated city. During the fall of 1959 black students from those institutions and several adult community members met to discuss Nashville's racial issues and desegregating the city's downtown. The group started attending weekly workshops on nonviolence led by James Lawson, a black student at Vanderbilt's Divinity School. Lawson had studied nonviolence and Mahatma Ghandi's techniques while going to school in India. Diane Nash, a Chicago native who had transferred to Fisk from Howard University in Washington, DC, was among those students.[4]

On February 13, 1960, in efforts to secure the desegregation of downtown Nashville, 124 mostly black and mostly college students began a formal sit-in at segregated white-only lunch counters in downtown Nashville. Three months later—after continued demonstrations, student arrests, and the bombing of the home of their attorney, Z. Alexander Looby, on April 19—the mayor of Nashville ended segregated lunch counters.[5] The RRI had operated in Nashville since the summer of 1944, but had not taken a stance on the city's discriminatory practices or become an active supporter of the student sit-in efforts. However, in 1961, by adding a clinic on sit-in strategies to its roster, the RRI found a way to blend its tradition of being the objective observer and a clearinghouse of civil rights information with its desire to promote more direct methods of social action. The sit-in clinic, which Lawson co-directed, allowed the RRI to enter into the realm of direct social protest methods without raising the concern of financial backers or board members.

Sessions on sit-in strategies and tactics ran daily for six days between June 20 and June 28. The first session focused on the philosophy and theology of nonviolence. They discussed the "psychological make-up" and "motivation" of a people in nonviolent movements and were given a list of reading materials including Mahatma Ghandi's *Non-Violence in Peace and War* and the UNESCO Study *All Men Are Brothers*; Martin Luther King's *Stride Toward Freedom*; Louis Fisher's *The Life of Mahatma Ghandi*; Joanne Bonderat's *The Conquest of Violence*; and Leo Tolstoy's *The Kingdom of God Is Within You*. The clinic promoted non-violence as perhaps the "most significant approach to segregation and many other problems" because they felt "past efforts [had] not been fast enough."[6] The previous concentration and "dependence on legalities" left other critical issues that also impacted race relations untouched. Participants at the clinic learned they had to deal with a "clock of fear" that supported segregation.[7] The clock of fear depicted the law being surrounded by attitude, custom, habit, and attitudes. On subsequent days participants discussed the definition of nonviolence, methods and overall strategies of nonviolence methods, the contradiction of nonviolence leading to violence, leadership, and the use of nonviolent methods outside of the South.[8]

The RRI continued efforts to make their ideologies applicable to black America's growing desire for action. During the 1963 RRI approximately 200 delegates "sent a telegram" to Tennessee Governor Frank G. Clement and 15 other southern governors requesting that they follow the lead of Kentucky Governor Bert Combs and halt racial discrimination by executive order. Governor Combs' executive order "banned discrimination in the state licensed businesses and professions in Kentucky."[9] The telegram, however, did not sway Governor Clements who "acknowledged receipt of the appeal" at a press conference but noted that he did not plan to issue an "executive order of that type."[10] The delegates also sent a telegram to Kentucky Governor Combs and commended his "forthright courageous and humanitarian action in issuing such an order."[11] They noted that Combs' stand was "a milestone in the march of progress toward justice and human rights for all citizens of your state and the United States."[12] The RRI delegates also sent copies of the telegram to President Kennedy and Attorney General Robert Kennedy.[13]

The delegates were well aware, however, that executive orders like the one issued by Governor Combs were only valuable if implemented.[14] That, perhaps, was the reason some RRI presenters were cautious when they heard the 1963 Civil Rights Bill passed. While the RRI as a whole acknowledged the bill was of "'high significance' and a renewal by Congress of the principles of the Declaration of Independence," one RRI speaker at the 21st annual meeting noted that the bill "'[would] not soften the hearts of segregationists nor cleanse the stain of hate from the souls of racists.'"[15] The speaker felt the bill was, however, "'an indication that the majority of the people of the nation tend[ed] to conform to standards of conduct fixed and supported by the established authority of the community and nation.'"[16] He noted the bill had already impacted some "restaurant, hotel and theater operators who have previously wavered in discriminatory practices as a result of the 'combined weight of protest from without and guilty consciences.'"[17]

Invited speakers continued to point to a need for direct action and vocalized concerns during their presentations. In July 1964, Robert Johnson, son of the late Fisk University President Charles S. Johnson, told members of the RRI "in some areas where there is no voluntary compliance with the civil rights law groups may need to use demonstrations." Johnson noted that the purpose of the demonstrations was not to "flout the law, but to invoke a higher law of morality."[18] He noted that "persons involved in demonstrations usually feel that the means to the end must be appropriate to the ends resolved."[19] The fact that the RRI invited such speakers as James Farmer, former head of the Congress on Racial Equality (CORE); Baynard Rustin, executive director of the A. Philip Randolph Institute and key organizer of the 1963 March on Washington; and Whitney Young, executive director of the National Urban League to present at the RRI also highlights the projects desire to support methods of direct action.[20]

In 1968, the RRI for the first time in its twenty-five-year history turned its lense on its own backyard. Although the RRI had held sessions on sit-in strategies and had sent telegrams to governors and the President of the United States, it had never directly taken a stance against the city's practice of segregation or the impact of social inequality. However, after Martin Luther King Jr.'s assassination that April, Nashville feared the erupting riots. The RRI added a special afternoon session on "human relations in Nashville" to its traditional schedule of addresses and panel discussions.[21] Topics for the seminar included "discussions of Nashville's employment, housing, health, mass media, public welfare, police-community relations education and urban renewal and highway planning—all with emphasis on opportunities and obstacles which affect the ability of white and black Nashvillians to relate to the society they share." According to Dr. Clifton Johnson, the third RRI director, the session was not designed to "have either race lecture the other on its shortcomings—but rather to 'supply an open atmosphere which can bring together different points of view.'"[22] Johnson hoped "for the first time representatives of significant elements of the city's white population" would be on hand "to listen and talk about the problems and progress which characterize the relationship between the races" in Nashville.[23]

The session did not go as smoothly as organizers had hoped. At the seminar a man who identified himself as a student from Tennessee A&I State University and who the newspaper described as an "angry...Black Power advocate, who later walked out of the meeting," openly challenged the assistant police chief, John Sorace, to join the panel.[24] Sorace had been sitting in the audience. The young man charged police brutality during disturbances in North Nashville and since Sorace was "the general" and the other "cops [didn't] give orders" wanted Sorace to answer for the behavior.[25] The student insisted that during disturbances in the black area surrounding Fisk, police used excessive force, including shooting into a girls' dormitory and wounding a Fisk coed. Another student, a former vice president of the A&I student association, also charged the police department with spying on A&I students and employing "various harassments such as 'stop and frisks.'"[26] He noted that "North Nashville was under siege after King's death." Sorace noted that police were "not perfect human beings" and detailed a proposal to improve relations.[27] The proposal included organizing "neighborhood complain bureaus, increased sensitivity training and a community relations section for police-community relations."[28]

Besides adding methods of direct action to its roster, the RRI once again experienced changes in its directorship during the 1960s. As mentioned earlier, Herman H. Long had taken over the helm of the RRI after Johnson was named president of Fisk University. Long remained director until 1964, when he left Nashville to become president at Talladega University in Talladega, Alabama. Long, however, continued to help direct the RRI until the AMA selected Clifton Johnson, a white professor, in 1966 as the new director. Although the AMA had selected blacks to head their black colleges, they had never selected a white man to direct the RRI. Clifton Johnson reflects that the AMA was having difficulty finding a qualified director for the amount of money that they were willing to pay. A friend living in New York prompted AMA officials to consider Clifton Johnson for the position. Reminding the AMA officials that the organization had traditionally frowned on selecting people because of color, the friend noted that Clifton Johnson was already at Fisk University. The AMA was familiar with Clifton Johnson because a couple of years earlier he had presented a proposal for them to fund an African American archival project. In 1966 Johnson accepted the RRI directorship with the understanding that the AMA would fund his archival project. Clifton Johnson thus became the first white director of the RRI.[29]

Clifton Johnson's presence at the RRI as the director did not go unnoticed. Johnson recalls that he was often challenged by blacks questioning his ability, as a white man, to direct a conversation on race and civil rights. Supporters of the Black Power movement also questioned the RRI's ability to facilitate change through what they considered "tea sipping" strategies.[30] Johnson recalls that during the late 1960s people who came to the RRI thought the project should devote more attention to "building black pride and building black power." Some even wanted "to rid the RRI of white participation." Once while giving a presentation on stage, Johnson was even told by one participant to "sit down" because he "had no business up there anyway."[31]

Although remaining records of the RRI clearly show the project expanding and encompassing different ideas of what constituted effective strategies in achieving racial tolerance and social justice, they also show that the RRI, like the National Association for the Advancement of Colored People (NAACP) did not support the growing calls of black power and black nationalism. On a whole, speakers at the RRI did not believe in a separate black culture. They believed in integration. Speakers consistently urged participants to find ways to keep the civil rights revolution from being engulfed by the "extremes" of the "rising tide of pure black nationalism."[32] In his 1966 address to the RRI, Herman Long warned that "Black nationalism defeats the goals and purposes of the revolution."[33] Invited back to speak at the 1967 RRI, Long again cautioned participants that black power had "essentially the same logical consequences" as white supremacy.[34] He said it led to "segregation—to separation" and criticized black leaders for failing to confront what he termed the "'new left'" movement among black students. Long declared that "any concept" of black power as "absolute" was an illusion and that blacks needed to "exercise political strength in balance of power bargaining with the community as a whole."[35] "Black Power," he contended, remained a "generalized, highly emotional slogan" without any clearly defined means or ends.[36] He felt black power tended to "be divisive since it has taken on some of the language which has attempted to divide the Negro community on a class basis."[37] Long felt cries for black power tended to "cast suspicion" on blacks who "may just happen to be educated, or just happen to be doctors or dentists, or just happen to own small businesses."[38] Dr. Vivian W. Henderson, president of Clark College, Atlanta, echoed Long's views. She also warned the 1967 RRI of "mis-guided conceptions as Black Power" and other methods.[39]

The warnings against black power continued at the RRI throughout the last meeting in 1969. Roy Wilkins, executive director of the NAACP, warned participants that the "cult" of black separatism could harm the freedom struggle.[40] Wilkins noted:

> Although the Negro citizens of the United States have a long list of legitimate grievances, there is grave danger that the present enthusiasm for things black, with its thinly-veiled drive toward racial separatism, will produce a havoc, worse by far, than the evils sought to be eliminated.[41]

Wilkins made it a point to clarify that he had "no patience with those who advocate retreating into blackness or dictatorship—that is to conform or be banned into outer darkness."[42] He noted that was "Hitler's war" and not black America's.[43]

Wilkins comments echoed the beliefs of black intellectual leaders who thought the only way blacks could survive in America was to become fully integrated into American society. Wilkins told participants:

> The only way for a minority to survive in this rich and powerful nation is to drive for inclusion into the majority. We are a small minority in a powerful majority. Elements of the majority are just looking for a reason to destroy us. In a war the minority would be anihilated.[sic][44]

Wilkins went on to explain that the "vast majority of Negroes believe in integration. They want 'in' not 'out.'"[45] That desire to integrate was also " true of the young people, too, despite what you hear from the minority of militants on college campuses."[46] Wilkins reminded the audience that blacks had been in America for 350 years, and argued that America was home and that blacks had put too much into it "to want to burn it down or destroy it."[47]

But speakers at the RRIs during the 1960s were clearly not monolithic in thought. Some speakers went on record and argued militant demonstrations had helped the civil rights movement. NAACP's chief counsel Jack Greenberg, director of the NAACP Legal Defense and Education fund, told the 1965 RRI, "It is unquestionably the demonstrations which made possible the Civil Rights Act of 1964."[48] He believed the demonstrations in Selma, Alabama, would facilitate the Civil Right Act of 1964. Greenberg argued civil rights laws had "to a large extent been unobserved" until someone checked and reported a violation.[49] He noted "inspection and follow-up" were necessary; otherwise the paper plans were "nonsense."[50]

Other speakers cautioned participants that media often misrepresented the meaning of "Black Power." For example, the Rev. Charles E. Cobb, executive director of the Committee for Racial Justice Now of the United Church of Christ, charged the news media with "distortion" and "lifting out of context" civil rights news.[51] He also blamed the news media for facilitating the "rhubarb" between conservative older black leaders and the younger ones.[52] Cobb told participants that he had even found areas on which he and SNCC president Stokely Carmichael, who popularized the term "Black Power," agreed. Explaining this he said:

> At this point I guess I sound like Mr. (Stokely) Carmichael, and at this point I agree with him...The country which we love so well and to which we have contributed so much must be classified as racist and will be, so long as it denies human dignity to the Negro sector or any other sector of the society...The Negro American is saying almost frighteningly to society that either we all have the good life or no one can have it.[53]

Even though Cobb found commonalities between his views and Carmichael's, he quickly reaffirmed that he did not accept the strategy of separatism or the tactics of violence. Cobb maintained that he wouldn't "give up on America," and advocated a continuance of "boycotts, demonstrations and block voting—and especially the use of economic pressure by such institutions as churches" to secure social justice.[54]

By 1969 Clifton Johnson's African American archival project, the Amistad Research Center, had grown to 3 million manuscript papers. That surprised many who thought the project would not be successful because they believed blacks as a race had not been very literate and had not kept documentation and papers. But after finding out about the project, people had approached Johnson to make donations. With their resources stressed, the AMA could not afford to maintain funding for the RRI and Johnson's archival project. Considering numerous other organizations with larger budgets were holding similar types of meetings and attracting many of the same speakers who presented at the RRI; invited RRI speakers asking for larger honorariums; and charges that the RRI was out of touch with black America's changing needs, Johnson suggested that if the AMA had to cut funds, they do everything possible to maintain support for the archive. He felt that the archive would make the longest contribution to the field. With that, the RRI, which had operated since 1944, closed its doors.[55]

Although remaining records fail to offer any indication, one has to ask if calls for more direct action, black power, and student demonstrations might have also influenced the AMA's decision to abandon the RRI. Fisk made other attempts during the 1970s, 1980s, and most recently, late 1990s to revive the prominent project, but has yet to reinstate and maintain the program at its former level of national prominence.

A hurried first glance of the RRI might lead one to believe that the project was little more than an elite, feel-good, "tea-sipping"[56] academic conference organized and made available to the public by black intellectuals and do-good white liberals. Although the lectures, panels, and workshops presented at the RRI reflect years of scholarly discourse focused on race relations and promoting civil rights efforts, they do not reflect any evidence of the project mobilizing to challenge the establishment outside of the 1963 letters to southern governors. There are no records of the RRI filing a lawsuit. There are no records of the RRI organizing a boycott, a sit-in, or a protest march. The records only show research, scholarship, and discourse. But subsequent and more reflective examination of that research, scholarship, and discourse reveals a project that was undergoing its own metamorphosis while steadily working to improve American society by arming participants with material that would allow them to make informed decisions about methods they could utilize in the struggle for freedom.

EPILOGUE

Reflecting on Charles S. Johnson as a sociologist and a black leader, S.P. Fullinwider notes in *The Mind and Mood of Black America: 20th Century Thought* that "Johnson, however much he may have wanted to do so, never led a crusade for the removal of the oppression; instead, he called for treatment of the patient."[1] An analysis of the RRI, however, proves otherwise. The RRI, a unique, twenty-six-year experiment that sought to utilize the social sciences as its primary tool for securing social justice in the United States, was Johnson's crusade.[2] Although the concept may appear conservative in light of later grassroots movements, the RRI stood on the tradition of black scholars and intellectuals who believed legislation was the way America would correct its social wrongs. They believed that legislation would be driven and supported by the data they collected on the treatment of blacks in America and how that treatment impacted their lives.

This belief is clearly seen in the monumental *Brown v. Board of Education* case. Reflections on the Brown case remind us that there were scholars, like Kenneth Clark, who worked, without end, utilizing their research abilities to gather data that would help secure such monumental decisions. Charles H. Houston, the man who started America on "The Road to Brown," and a contemporary of Charles S. Johnson, once said that a lawyer is either "a parasite on society or a social engineer."[3] While I hope scholars are not perceived as societal parasites, I trust that they are viewed as social engineers as were the anthropologists, sociologists, psychologists, and educators who attended the RRI and utilized their research to vigorously argue against pseudo-scientific notions that propelled and maintained a system of oppression in the United States. Their scholarship and involvement with the RRI was a true testament and legacy to Johnson's beliefs that

... man is made both good and bad by his institutions; that these institutions are responsible for the shaping of personalities, our morals, and the patterns of our social relations; and that the re-shaping of our institutions are our responsibility.[4]

ILLUSTRATIONS

Fig. 1—Charles S. Johnson, RRI founder. United Church Board for Homeland Ministries Archives, Race Relations Department, 1944, Amistad Research Center at Tulane University.

Fig. 2—Charles H. Houston; Willard Townsend, and Frayser T. Lane at the 1944 RRI. United Church Board for Homeland Ministries Archives, Race Relations Department, 1944, Amistad Research Center at Tulane University.

Fig. 3.—1952 RRI participants. Charles S. Johnson, eighth from left, holding hat. United Church Board for Homeland Ministries Archives, Race Relations Department, 1952, Amistad Research Center at Tulane University.

Fig. 4—1952 RRI participants attending a lecture. United Church Board for Homeland Ministries Archives, Race Relations Department, 1952, Amistad Research Center at Tulane University.

ILLUSTRATIONS

Fig. 5—Galen Weaver (far right) with Native American Participants, 1955 RRI. United Church Board for Homeland Ministries Archives, Race Relations Department, 1955, Amistad Research Center at Tulane University.

Fig. 6—Martin Luther King, Jr. at the 1956 RRI. United Church Board for Homeland Ministries Archives, Race Relations Department, 1956, Amistad Research Center at Tulane University.

Fig. 7—*Thurgood Marshall presenting at the 1956 RRI. United Church Board for Homeland Ministries Archives, Race Relations Department, 1956, Amistad Research Center at Tulane University.*

Fig. 8—*RRI Participants at a social (women dancing together). United Church Board for Homeland Ministries Archives, Race Relations Department, 1956, Amistad Research Center at Tulane University.*

ILLUSTRATIONS 121

Fig. 9—*Thurgood Marshall on a coffee break with 1957 RRI Participants.* United Church Board for Homeland Ministries Archives, Race Relations Department, 1957, Amistad Research Center at Tulane University.

Fig. 10—*Young RRI participant "cutting a rug" at the 1960 RRI.* United Church Board for Homeland Ministries Archives, Race Relations Department, 1960, Amistad Research Center at Tulane University.

Fig. 11—*RRI participants at lunch. United Church Board for Homeland Ministries Archives, Race Relations Department, 1956, Amistad Research Center at Tulane University.*

APPENDICES

APPENDIX A
Program Schedule Eighth Annual Institute of Race Relations July 2–14, 1951*

FIRST WEEK—BASIC ORIENTATION TO WORLD PROBLEMS OF RACE AND THE DOCTRINE OF HUMAN RIGHTS

Monday, July 2

Morning
8:30 – 11:30   Registration—Social Science Building Foyer
11:30 – 12:15 Discussion of material in packet; briefing on procedure
               Herman H. Long
Afternoon
2:30 – 3:10   Introductory Statement—Keynote of Institute
               Charles S. Johnson
3:10 – 4:00   The Institute and the AMA
               Philip Widenhouse
Evening
8:00   Acquaintance Meeting—International Student Center

Tuesday, July 3

Morning
9:00 – 9:45   Growth of World Civilization
               Gene Weltfish
9:45 – 10:30   Discussion

---
* RRD Papers, Amistad, box 47, file 5, 1951

11:00 – 11:50   Planning and Management of Intergroup Relations in Community Agencies, Margaret McCulloch
11:50 – 12:30   Discussion

Afternoon
2:00 – 2:45   The Role of the United States in the International Economy
                Walter S. Salant
3:00 – 4:00   Discussion
2:00 – 4:00   Workshop on Economic Education

Evening
8:00   World Civilization and World Crisis
                Gene Weltfish

Wednesday, July 4

Morning
CHANGING CUSTOMS AND POLICIES IN THE CIVIL RIGHTS CONTEXT
9:00 – 9:45   The Anatomy of Prejudice
                Carey McWilliams
9:45 – 10:30   Discussion
11:00 – 11:50   "Growing Pains": It Is Happening in the South
                Mrs. M.E. Tilly
11:50 – 12:30   Discussion

Afternoon
2:00 – 4:00   Clinics
                Workshop on Economic Education
4:00   Tea

Evening
8:00   Untenable Hypotheses in Race Relations
                Ira De A. Reid

Thursday, July 5

Morning
9:00 – 9:45   Minority Personality and Character: An Examination of the Kardiner Thesis, Ira De A. Reid
9:45 – 10:30   Discussion
11:00 – 11:45   Labor and Race in the New National Economy
                Mark Starr
11:50 – 12:30   Panel and Discussion
                McWilliams, Reid, Starr, Tilly

Afternoon
2:00 – 4:00   Clinics
               Workshop on Economic Education

Evening
8:00   Beyond Civil Rights
               Carey McWilliams

Friday, July 6

Morning
9:00 – 9:45   Minorities and the Present Crisis
               Rabbi Arthur Hertzberg
9:45 – 10:30   Discussion
11:00 – 11:45 Participation in Community Affairs, an Effective Means of
               Education for Democracy, Max Wolff
11:50 – 12:30 Panel and Discussion
               McWilliams, Reid, Starr, Tilly

Afternoon
2:00 – 4:00   Clinics
               Workshop on Economic Education
4:00   Tea

Saturday, July 7

Morning
9:00 – 9:45   Economic Motivations Underlying Race Relations
               Ralph Ireland
9:45 – 10:30   Discussion
11:00 – 11:45 Parallels and Contrasts in British American Racial Patterns,
               Kenneth Little
11:50 – 12:30 Discussion

Sunday, July 8

Morning
11:00   Morning Worship
               Address, Rev. Samuel Kincheloe
               Memorial Chapel

APPENDICES

SECOND WEEK—PROBLEM AREAS

Monday, July 9

Morning
9:00 – 9:45	Double-Timing for Urban Survival Frayser T. Lane
9:45 – 10:30	Occupancy Patterns of Public Housing Daniel M. Wilner
11:00 – 11:45	Legal Aspects of Industrial Democracy: Eight Questions for Friends of FEPC Frank Loescher
11:50 – 12:30	Discussion

Afternoon
2:00 – 4:00	Clinics Workshop on Economic Education
4:00	Tea

Evening
8:00	American Education: Its Status and Future Prospects Dr. Francis J. Brown

Tuesday, July 10

Morning
9:00 – 9:45	The Right to Life: Some Racial Implications of Social Security, Anna Hedgeman
9:45 – 10:30	Organized Labor and the Negro Attorney Robert Hall
11:00 – 11:45	The Task of Liberal Today Milton R. Konvitz
11:50 – 12:30	Panel and Discussion Hall, Hedgeman, Konvitz, Loescher

Afternoon
2:00 – 4:00	Clinics Workshop on Economic Education

Evening
8:00	Race Relations in the U.S. Navy Captain H. Pace Smith

APPENDICES 127

Wednesday, July 11

Morning
9:00 – 9:45   A Cultural Map of the South
               George S. Mitchell
9:45 – 10:30   The Present Status of Racial Integration in the South
11:00 – 11:45 Legislative and Community Strategy in Eliminating
               Segregated Schools in Indianapolis
               Attorney Willard B. Ransom
11:45 – 12:30 Discussion

Afternoon
2:00 – 4:00   Clinics
               Workshop on Economic Education
4:00   Tea

Evening
8:00   The Future of Legislation in Race Relations
               Thurgood Marshall

Thursday, July 12

Morning
POLITICS AND THE PRESS
9:00 – 9:45   Political Power and the Democratic Process
               Henry Lee Moon
9:45 – 10:30   The Role of the Press in Race Relations
               William Howland
11:00 – 11:45 Strategy and Community Planning in Current Race
               Relations Programs, Beulah T. Whitby
11:50 – 12:30 Panel and Discussion
               Howland, Looby, Scher, Moon, Whitby

Afternoon
THE ROLE OF THE ARTS IN THE FIELD OF RACE RELATIONS
2:00 – 2:45   The Negro in Post-War Novels
               Dr. Margaret Butcher
2:50 – 3:40   The Negro in Post-War Drama
               James Butcher
3:40 – 4:00   Discussion
2:00 – 4:00 (sic) Workshop on Economic Education

128   APPENDICES

Evening
8:00   Defense Mobilization and the "Integrated" Process
                Lester Granger

Friday, July 13

Morning
9:00 – 9:45   Current Trends in the Housing of Minority Groups
                Frank S. Horne
9:45 – 10:30   Discussion
11:00 – 11:45   The Navy's Program of Integration
                Lieutenant Dennis D. Nelson
11:50 – 12:30   Discussion

Afternoon
2:00 – 4:00   Workshop on Economic Education
4:00   Tea

Evening
8:00   Regional Education: Its Status and Future Prospects
                John Ivey

APPENDIX B
Lecturers, Consultants, and Clinic Leaders at the 6th Annual Institute of Race Relations, June 27–July 9, 1949*

FIRST WEEK: June 27–July 2

DR. SMILEY BLANTON, Psychiatrist; Director of Consultation Clinic, Marble Collegiate Church, New York; Associate Professor of Clinical Psychology, Vanderbilt University

CHARLES H. HOUSTON, Attorney; Vice-President, American Council on Race Relations; Legal Counsel, NAACP

M. F. ASHLEY MONTAGU, Anthropologist; Associate Professor of Anatomy, Hahnemann Medical College and Hospital and Lecturer at Harvard University

---

* RRD Papers, Amistad, box 41, file 1, 1949

APPENDICES 129

O.D. DUNCAN, Sociologist; Professor of Sociology, Oklahoma Agricultural and Mechanical College, Stilwater, Oklahoma

KENNETH L. LITTLE, Anthropologist; London School of Economics; Visiting Lecturer, Department of Sociology, Fisk University

BROOKS HAYS, Congressman, Arkansas

ARTHUR HERTZBERG, Rabbi, West End Synagogue, Nashville

KENESAW M. LANDIS, Lawyer and Columnist

RUTH A. MORTON, Director of Community Services, American Missionary Association, Board of Home Missions of the Congregational and Christian Churches

THOMAS H. WRIGHT, Executive Director, Commission on Human Relations, Chicago

SAMUEL L. STEVENS, President, Grinnell College, Grinnell, Iowa

REGINALD BARRETT, Cambridge University; Visiting Professor, Department of Sociology, Fisk University

ROGER BALDWIN, Director, Civil Liberties Union

MIKE MASAOKA, National Legislative Director, Anti-Discrimination Committee, Japanese American Citizens League

WILLIAM J. FAULKNER, Dean of the Chapel, Fisk University

HUBERT H. HUMPHREY, U.S. Senator from Minnesota

MRS. RUTH MUSKRAT BRONSON, National Congress of American Indians, Washington, D.C.

GEORGE L-P WEAVER, Director, National CIO Committee to Abolish Discrimination

SECOND WEEK: July 3–9

WILLIAM S. HOWLAND, Bureau Chief, Atlanta, *Time, Inc.*

REV. JOHN LAFARGE, S.J., Editor, *America*, National Catholic Weekly.

LESTER B. GRANGER, Executive Director, National Urban League

ROBERT E. CUSHMAN, Department of Government, Cornell University

JOSEPH D. LOHMAN, Sociologist; Department of Sociology, University of Chicago

FRANK S. HORNE, Assistant to the Administrator, Housing and Home Finance Agency, Washington, D.C.

HOWARD BONHAM, Vice-President, The American National Red Cross

JESSE O. THOMAS, Public Relations Consultant, The American National Red Cross

ARCHIBALD J. CAREY, JR. Minister, Woodlawn AME Church, Chicago

H.H. GILES, Director of Center for Human Relations Studies, School of Education, New York University

GEORGE S. MITCHELL, Executive Director, Southern Regional Council

FRAYSER T. LANE, Civic Director, Chicago Urban League

W.W. ALEXANDER, Formerly Vice-President, Julius Rosenwald Fund

VICTOR R. DALY, Chief, Personnel and Fiscal Division, Bureau of Employment Security, United States Employment Service, Washington, D.C.

BEN WEST, Vice-Mayor, City of Nashville

HENRY G. STETLER, Research Associate, State of Connecticut Inter-Racial Commission

JOHN J. MORROW, Personnel Manager, Pitney-Bowes Stamp Machine Co., Connecticut

APPENDIX C
OTHER NOTABLE SPEAKERS AT THE RRI 1944–1969*

WHITNEY YOUNG, Executive Director of the National Urban League

SAMUEL C. JACKSON, Member of the U.S. Equal Employment Opportunity Commission

BAYNARD RUSTIN, Executive Director of the A. Philip Randolph Institute

A. PHILIP RANDOLPH, Founder and Head of the Brotherhood of Sleeping Car Porters, and *Messenger*

MARTIN LUTHER KING, JR., Civil Rights Activist

CONSTANCE BAKER MOTLEY, NAACP Lawyer

BENJAMIN F. PAYTON, Executive Director of the National Council of Churches Department of Social Justice

JACK GREENBERG, Chief legal counsel of NAACP Legal Defense and Educational Fund

JAMES FARMER, Founder of CORE, Committee on Racial Equality

FANNIE LOU HAMER, Vice chairman of the Mississippi Freedom Democratic Party

ROY WILKINS, Journalist; Assistant executive Secretary of NAACP; editor of magazine *Crisis*

JAMES M. LAWSON, JR, SNNC, Student Nonviolent Coordinating Committee, Organizer

THURGOOD MARSHALL, NAACP Legal Defense and Educational Fund, Inc.

---

* Names taken from a compilation of programs from the RRI from 1944 to 1969 found in the RRD Papers, boxes 40–45, Amistad

APPENDIX D
AN ACTIVITY/TEST UTILIZED AT THE RRI

WHAT DO YOU KNOW ABOUT RACE?
A True-or-False Test
by
Edmonia W. Grant
Director of Education
Race Relations Division
American Missionary Association
287 Fourth Avenue
New York 10, N.Y.*

T F

I. The Germans are an Aryan race.
II. The Jews are a Semitic race.
III. The Germans are not a pure white race.
IV. Skin color is the most important physical characteristic.
V. The white, black and yellow people are as different from one another as dogs are from cats.
VI. Man's physical appearance is affected by his environment.
VII. The Jews are not a race.
VIII. All Jews have curved noses, which distinguish them from other people.
IX. All the Danish people are typical or average Caucasians.
X. American Negroes look to Europe, Africa for their ancestry.
XI. If we add all the characteristically black, white and yellow together, we have only some of the people of the world.
XII. The blood of Negro and white people is the same.
XIII. All children of parents who are from different racial groups are inferior to both parents.
XIV. All the foods we eat are a gift from ancient Europeans.
XV. American inventions provide us with only some of our basic comforts.
Total score_____

Directions: Put a check in the box in the T column if the statement is True, or in the F column if the statement is False.

After you finish taking the test your leader will give you the correct answer to each statement. Count the number of answers you had correct and place that number in the space after "Total Score." How does your score compare with that of your group. (sic) Is your score average, above average, or below average?

---

* RRD Papers, Amistad, box 243, file other records: CA 1944

APPENDIX E
Manuscript and Archival Material Utilized

American Missionary Association Papers	Amistad Research Center at Tulane University, New Orleans
Charles S. Johnson Papers, Microfilm Copy	Amistad Research Center at Tulane University, New Orleans
Charles S. Johnson Papers	Fisk University, John Hope and Aurelia Elizabeth Franklin Library Special Collection, Nashville
General Education Board Papers	Rockefeller Archive Center Sleepy Hollow, New York
Julius Rosenwald Papers, Microfilm Copy	Amistad Research Center at Tulane University, New Orleans
Julius Rosenwald Papers	Fisk University, Franklin Library Special Collections
Race Relations Archives Papers	Amistad Research Center at Tulane University, New Orleans
Race Relations Department, United Church Board for Homeland Ministries Archives	Amistad Research Center at Tulane University, New Orleans

APPENDICES

APPENDIX F
AN EXAMPLE OF SUGGESTED READINGS FOR RRI PARITICIPANTS

SELECTED BIBLIOGRAPHY
Prepared for the
FOURTH ANNUAL INSTITUTE OF RACE RELATIONS
AMERICAN MISSIONARY ASSOCIATION
Fisk University, Nashville, Tennessee
July 1 – 19, 1947

BIOGRAPHY

Bontemps, Arna W., *We Have Tomorrow*. New York: Houghton Mifflin Co., 1945. Inspiring career stories of twelve Negro men and women including Mildred Blount, Horace Cayton, Dean Dixon, Hazel Scott and Benjamin Davis.

DuBois, W.E.B. and G.B. Johnson (eds.) *Encyclopedia of the Negro; Preparatory Volume with Reference Lists and Reports*. New York: H.W. Wilson, Co.194 [sic] A four-volume encyclopedia of the Negro to parallel such volumes as the Catholic and Jewish encyclopedias. This preparatory volume contains an alphabetical list of the topics to be treated in the encyclopedia with bibliographical references under each head. A splendid student's guide to source materials and to secondary authorities concerning all aspects of Negro life.

Embree, E.R. *13 Against the Odds*. New York: The Viking Press, 1944. A collection of biographies of the following outstanding members of the Negro race: Mary McLeod Bethune, Richard Wright, Charles S. Johnson, Walter White, George Washington Carver, Langston Hughes, Marion Anderson, W.E.B. DuBois, Mordecai W. Johnson, William Grant Still, A. Phillip Randolph, Joe Louis, Paul Robeson.

Fisk University. Social Science Institute. *Unwritten History of Slavery*. Nashville: The Institute, 1945. A record of interviews with ex-slaves conducted during 1929 and 1930. "Glimpses into the mentality of a group so rigidly regimented by an unique economic structure and its supporting ideology. Valuable illustrations of 'the manner in which personality enters into social change.'"

Lotz, Phillip H. (ed.) *Rising Above Color*. New York: Association Press, 1944. Biographical sketches of the lives of thirteen Negroes including: George Washington Carver, Marian Anderson, W.E.B. DuBois, R.R. Moton, Samuel Coleridge-Taylor, Richard Allen, Frederick Douglas[sic], D.H. Williams, B.T. Washington, Roland Hayes, P.L. Dunbar, James Weldon Johnson, Walter White.

Maloney, Arnold Hamilton, M.D. *Amber Gold*. Boston: Meador Press, 1946. The life story of a Negro scientist whose work includes the discovery of an antidote for barbitol poisoning.

Meyer, E.H. *Our Negro Brother*. New York: Shady Hill Press, 1945. A picture book biography in short sentences and easy words designed for purpose of fostering better racial understanding on the part of elementary school children. It summarizes the lives of the following: Pedro Alonzo Nino, Crispus Attucks, Harriet Tubman, Frederick Douglass, Mathew Henson, George Washington Carver, Mary McLeod Bethune, A. Phillip Randolph.

Podbrey, P. *Famous American Negroes*. New York: The Thomas Y. Crowell Co. 1945.

Stevens, W.J. *Chip on My Shoulder*. New York: Meador Publishing Co., 1946. The autobiography of a Negro who has been a realtor, a restaurateur and a photographer and, in the field of public affairs, an ardent work for equal rights for Negroes.

ETHNOLOGY [SIC]

Benians, E.A. *Race and Nation in the United States*. Toronto: The Macmillan Co. 1946. *Race and Nation in the U.S.* is a historical sketch of the successive waves of immigration into the New World and the gradual development of the ideals of American democracy and American Unity.

Wheeler, Harold F.B. (ed.) *Peoples of the World Illustrated*. New York: William H. Wise & Co., Inc. 1944.

INTERCULTURAL EDUCATION

Clinchy, Everett R. *The Growth of Good Will*. New York: The National Conference of Christians and Jews. A brief history of persecution in the United States.

DuBois, Rachel D. *Build Together Americans*. New York: Hinds, Hayden & Eldredge, Inc., 1945. A report of intercultural-education initiated by the author and conducted in some hundred schools throughout the country over a period of twenty years. Aimed toward engendering individual pride in one's background and inheritance.

Duncan, E.M. *Democracy's Children*. New York: Hinds, Hayden, and Eldredge, Inc., 1945. Accounts of a variety of projects carried on with elementary school classes – projects intended to bring out American diversity of cultural backgrounds.

Dunham, Barrows. *Man Against Myth*. Boston: Little, Brown and Company. "The ideas behind such popular clichés as 'you can't change human nature, [sic] and 'words will never hurt me,' as well as the psychology behind racism are examined and found to be illogical and erroneous.

MacIver, Robert Morrison (ed.) *Unity and Difference in American Life*. New York: Harper & Bros., 1947. "Lectures and post-lecture discussions on racial, ethnic, economic and religious issues in American life and ways of resolving them by Allen Nevins, Vilkjalmur Stefansson, Ralph W. Sockman, Edward L. Bernays and others."

Taba, Hilda and William Van Til. *Democratic Human Relations: Promising Practices in Intergroup and Inter-cultural Education in the Social Studies*. [sic] Washington (D.C.): National Council for Social Studies, 1945. A manual of sources of data, ideas and methods for education designed to reduce racial and cultural conflict.

Vickery, W.E. and S.G. Cole. *Intercultural Education in American Schools*. New York: Harper & Brothers, 1944. The first of a series of manuals to help curriculum committees, public school teachers and their pupils to deal realistically with the problem of intercultural and interracial tensions. Its main theses are that intergroup conflicts threaten the well-being of the nation and that these conflicts can be lessened by a carefully planned educational program.

Watson, Goodwin B. *Action for Unity*. New York: Harper & Brothers, 1947. The case against racial discrimination and hatred presented by a psychologist of Columbia University and sponsored by the Commission on Community Interrelations.

Wise, J. W. *Springfield Plan*. New York: Viking Press, 1945. A record in pictures and text of the Springfield, Massachusetts plan for democratic living. How Springfield has put into practice a program that has reached beyond the schools and stimulated adult activity in the demonstration of good citizenship in a democracy.

Yeiser, I. *Curriculum as an Integrating Force for Ethnic Variations*. Cambridge. Harvard University Graduate School of Education, 1946.

Jews

Adler, Cyrus and Aaron M. Margolith. *With Firmness in the Right*. New York: American Jewish Committee, 1946. "A history of official American intervention in the rights of the other countries to protect the rights of oppressed Jews, 1840-1945."

Cohen, Harry. *Panorama of Prejudice*. New York: Bolck Publishing Co., 1945. A disclosure of the mistreatment and persecution of Jews even in unsuspected quarters.

Schneiderman, Harry et al. *The American Jewish Year Book*, 5707 (1946-1947) Philadelphia: Jewish Publishing Society of America, 1946.

Simmel, Ernst, M.D. ed. *Anti-semitism: A Social Disease*. New York: International University Press. 1946. "A psychoanalytic study of the motives behind anti-Semitism."

Wurhaftig, Zorach. Uprooted.[sic] New York: Institute of Jewish Affairs, 1946. The position of Jewish refugees in different parts of Europe today, and the operation of various international relief agencies which are trying to solve their problems."

Minorities

American Academy of Political and Social Sciences. *Controlling Group Prejudice* Philadelphia: American Academy, 1946. It is the editor's thesis that our failure to achieve human solidarity; to make the cooperative control of technology possible is largely due to a primary weakness in human nature which is usually referred to as group prejudice – the tendency to personify evil, to ascribe evil to groups or categories of persons rather than to impersonal forces or to single erring individuals. This volume constitutes a comprehensive collection of articles directed toward the purpose of controlling group prejudice in all its ramifications.

Brameld, T.B.H. *Minority Problems in the Public Schools*. New York: Harper & Bros., 1946. A study of administrative policies and practices in seven school systems. Demographic and occupational patterns are analyzed as well as such factors as community relations, administrative machinery, educational organization, activity programs and parent-teacher cooperation. Only a few of the school systems made deliberate efforts to meet the minority problem.

Herrick, A. and H. Askwith (eds.) *This Way to Unity*. New York: Oxford Book Co., 1946. "An anthology composed of stories, articles, speeches, and poetry by modern writers, civic leaders, and church men – Pearl Buck, Wendell Wilkie, Louis Adamic, Eric Johnson, Archbishop Spellman – for the purpose of promoting goodwill and teamwork among racial, religious and national groups."

MacIver, R.M. ed. *Group Relations and Group Antagonisms*. New York: Harper & Brothers, 1944. A symposium in which representatives of various minorities consider their problems from the viewpoints of (1) National welfare, and (2) the effects, intellectual and spiritual, within the minorities themselves. Some of the groups included are: Lost Europeans, Italian – Americans, Negro, Chinese in the United States, Roman Catholic, Jewish, Society of Friends, Europe's Conflict of cultures, Minorities in Latin American [sic], Soviet Minorities and India.

MacIver, R.M. (ed.) *Civilization and Group Relationships*. New York: Harper & Bros., 1946. A symposium of the addresses delivered at the second course of the Institute for Religious Studies held at the Jewish Theological Seminary of America in New York City for the purpose of providing a rich source of suggestions as to practical ways by which individuals and groups can aid in the solution of the problem created by discrimination.

Stegner, W. *One Nation*. Boston: Houghton Mifflin Co., 1945. Brief text, with pictures, describing the lives of several minority groups in the United States, including the Pacific races; Mexicans; Indians; Negroes; Catholics; and Jews

NEGRO

Aptheker, H. *Essays in the History of the American Negro*. New York; International Publishers Co., 1945. This study belies the old impressions of Southern life, during ante-bellum days, as pleasant and easy for plantation Negroes. It is a statistical, documentary record of the grim living conditions of the Negroes, their revolts against these conditions, their patriotism in the Revolutionary War, from the 17th century through the civil war. A valuable research source.

Aptheker, Hubert. *The Negro People in America*. New York: International Publishers, 1946. A severe criticism of Gunnar Myrdal's *American Dilemma*.

Becker, John L. *Negro in American Life*. New York: Julian Messner, Inc. Publishers, 1944. (Sponsored by the Council Against Intolerance in America) A primer on better racial understanding. Presents the Negro as a people, capable and willing to share in the American life.

Bontemps, Arna W. and J. Conroy. *They Seek a City*. New York: Doubleday Doran and Co., 1945. A study of Negro migration from the south [sic] to the North and West beginning with the flight of slaves from the antebellum South via the Underground Railroad, and ending with the recent movements to industrial centers beyond the Mason-Dixon Line.

Cable, G.W. *A Southerner Looks at Negro Discrimination*. New York: International Publishers Co., 1946.

Drake, St. C. and H.R. Cayton. *Black Metropolis*. New York: Harcourt, Brace & Co., 1945. A sociological study of Negro life in Chicago. A description and analysis of the structure and organization of the Negro community, both internally, and in relations to the metropolis of which it is a part. A mature and penetrating view of race relations in America.

Funderburg, J. H. *March of the Negro*. Boston: Christopher Publishing House, 1945.

Furr, Arthur. *Democracy's Negroes*. Boston: House of Edenboro, 1947. "A factual account of the work of American Negroes in the different branches of the armed forces during World War II."

Gysin, Brion. *To Master – A Long Goodnight*. Toronto: McClelland & Stewart, Ltd., 1946. The true story of the man, Josiah Henson, who was the prototype of Harriet Beacher Stowe's fictional Uncle Tom.

Halsey, Margaret. *Color Blind*. New York: Simon and Schuster, Inc., 1947. An experiment in human courtesy; the record of a personal experience turned into a revealing social document which shows what Americans can do to expedite the inclusion of the Negro into full citizenship.

Hercules, E.E.L. *Democracy Limited*. Central Publishing House, 1945.

Klineberg, Otto. *Characteristics of the American Negro*. New York: Harper & Brothers, 1944. A collection of studies made under the direction of Gunnar Myrdal. Contents: The Stereotype of the American Negro; Tests of Negro Intelligence; Experimental Studies of Negro Personality, 'Race' Attitudes; The Hybrid and the Problem of Miscegenation; Mental Disease Among Negroes: A statistical analysis.

Logan, R.W. *The Negro and the Post War World*. Washington: Minorities Publications Bureau, 1946. A brief review of the status of the Negro in all parts of the world today.

Logan, S. *A Negro's Faith in America*. Toronto: The Macmillan Co., 1946. Not an autobiography but rather an attempt to speak for all Negroes in America.

Maloney, A.H. and others. *Pathways to Democracy*. Boston: Meador Publishing Co., 1945.

Moon, B. (ed.) *Primer for White Folks*. New York: Doubleday, Doran & Co. 1945. An anthology of prose writings by and about the American Negro from slavery to the present. Contirbutors include: W.E.B. DuBois, Henrietta Buckmaster, Sara Haardt, Tess Slesinger, L.W. Robinson, Dorothy Parker, Langton Hughes, Righard Wright, Erskine Caldwell, Wendell Wilkie, S.A. Brown, Roi Ottley, Earl Brown, R.C. Weaver, Lillian Smith. A significant work.

Murray, Florence. *Negro Handbook*, 1946-1947 edition. (Published biennially) New York: Current Books, Inc., 1947. A manual of current facts, statistics and general information concerning Negroes in the United States.

Myrdal, Gunnar. *An American Dilemma: the Negro Problem and Modern Democracy.* New York: Harper & Brothers, 1944. A comprehensive study of the Negro question in America. An analysis of anthropological, cultural, social, economic, legal, political, educational, and spiritual aspects of the Negro minority, set against the background of the "American Creed." The dilemma between American ideals and social concepts and the actual behavior of white towards Negro and Negro towards white represents a "moral lag in the development of the nation."

Nelson, B.H. *Fourteenth Amendment and the Negro Since 1920.* Washington: Catholic University of America, 1946. Study of sixty-nine federal cases showing the nationalization of civil liberties most of which have extended the protection granted the Negro against state government as stated in the Fourteenth Amendment.

Ottley, Roi. *New World A-Coming.* New York: World Publishers, 1945. A journalist's account of what American Negroes are doing and thinking and of how they are living presented against the background of Harlem in the great Metropolis. He tells what Negroes want in the New World that's coming and what is being done about it.

Powell, Adam Clayton. *Marching Blacks.* Toronto: Longmans, Green and Co., 1946. An interpretative history of the rise of the black common man in which is outlined the technique of nonviolent but direct social action – the boycott; the protest march, and so forth by which it is believed the Negro can gain his full rights in a free country.

Powell, Adam Clayton. *Riots and Ruins.* New York: Richard S. smith, 1945. The personal document of a Negro leader whose life has spanned the years of the rise of the Negro out of slavery to his present position. It reflects it a more than ordinary insight into both Negro and white feelings.

Sachs, W. *Black Anger.* Boston: Little, Brown and Company, 1947. Begun as a psychoanalytic study of an African witch doctor, *Black Anger* is the story of a whole people in conflict between black and white cultures on interest to anthropologists, sociologists, and students of race and race relations?

Schomburgh, Meg. Gehrts. *Negro Types.* London: George Routledge and Sons, Ltd., 1944.

Tannenbaum, F. *Slave and Citizen.* New York: Alfred Knopf, Inc., 1947. A history of the Negro in the whole western hemisphere which shows why and in what respects Negro status varies in different parts of the Americas. The writer demonstrates that the national history and religious background of the European home communities strongly affected attitudes toward slavery.

Thompson, R. W. *Black Caribbean.* London: MacDonald & Co., Publishing, 1946.

Weaver, Robert C. *Negro Labor: A National Problem.* New York: Harcourt, Brace and Co., 1946. A consideration of the Negro during reconversion with an appraisal of his change of status during the war.

ORIENTALS

Constantino, Sam A., Jr. *Tale of the Twain.* New York: Harper and Brothers 1946. "A sincere and earnest appeal for goodwill between nations and races."

Konwitz, Milton R. *The Alien and the Asiatic in American Law.* Ithica: Cornell University Press, 1946. A study of Supreme Court decisions on matters relating to the alien and the American citizen of Asiatic extraction.

Lind, Andrew W. *Hawaii's Japanese*. Princeton: American Council, Institute of Pacific Relations, Princeton, New York, 1946. History of the Japanese in Hawaii stressing their status during the war years considered by the author "a significant experiment in democracy."

Martin, Ralph G. *Boy From Nebraska, The Story of Ben Kuroki*. New York: Harper & Brothers, 1946. "The courage of an American boy of Japanese descent who fought not only the enemy during the war but a powerful racial prejudice."

Okubo, Mini. *Citizen 13660*. New York: Columbia University Press, 1946. The diary of a Nisei girl in pictures and text, at the Tanforan assembly center and at Topas Relocation Center in Utah.

Thomas, Dorothy Swaine and Richard S. Nishimato. The Spoilage. Berkeley: University of California Press, 1946. A factual record documenting the causes that produced the group of Japanese Americans classified as "disloyal" and the consequences that accompanied such classification.

RACE

Adamic, Louis. *Nation of Nations*. New York: Harper and Brothers, 1945. American history rewritten to include the part played by races and nations other than Anglo-Saxon. The author's thesis is that consciously and unconsciously, historians and other writers have looked upon the American way of life as White – Protestant – Anglo-Saxon in origin whereas it is actually founded on a wide diversity of cultures and beliefs.

Ashley-Montagu, [sic] M.F. *Man's Most Dangerous Myth: The Fallacy of Race*. New York: Oxford University Press, 1944. An expose of the false ideas of race being propagated in the modern world presenting the biological, psychological and cultural aspects of the race question.

Benedict, Ruth F. *Race: Science and Politics*. New York: The Viking Press, 1945. This book seeks to distinguish between races as biological realities and the body of doctrine and dogma that operates to define and control interracial contacts and relations and to expose the scientific fallacies and sinister motives of the racialists.

Boas, Fraz [sic]. *Race and Democratic Society*. New York: J.J. Augustin, Inc., 1945. Thirty-three articles and addresses made by Boas over a period of almost 40 years, selected by him to aid in the struggle against Facism.

Delos, Joseph T. and others. *Race: Nation: Social Aspects of the Race Problems* (a symposium) New York: Barnes and Noble, Inc. 1944. A symposium of 10 monograms by Catholic scholars of Europe and America. An attempt to counteract the race theories of the Nazi party from the viewpoint of the Christian concepts of the dignity of the individual and the brotherhood of man.

Dingwall, E.J. *Racial Pride and Prejudice*. London: C.A. Watts and Co., Ltd., 1946.

DuBois, W.E.B. *Color and Democracy: Colonies and Peace*. New York: Harcourt, Brace & Co., 1945. A survey of the situation of colonial and colored peoples through out the world, with arguments against imperialism and for the freedom of dependent nations.

Herskovits, Melville J. and Frances S. *Trinidad Village*. New York: Alfred Knopf, 1947. An anthropological study of Negroes with a small community in the West Indian island of Trinidad as a base. The authors carefully examine the family structure, economic standards, marriage and death customs, religion, songs, and other means of self-expression. A scientific study.

Jones, F.N. and M.G. Arrington. *Explanations of Physical Phenomena Given by White and Negro Children*. Baltimore: The Williams and Wilkins Co., 1945.

McCleary, George F. *Race Suicide?* London: George Allen and Unwin, Ltd., 1945.

Odum, Howard W. *Race and Rumors and Race*. New York: Oxford University Press, 1944. A study of racial tensions in the United States during the year of global war from mid-1942 to 1943. "An...appeal to all the people of the nation and challenge to its leadership...in facing truth...in asking of essential questions, in the search for correct answers."

Rife, David C. *Dice of Destiny*. Columbus: College Book Co., 1945.

Van Deusen, John G. Black Man in White America. Washington: Associated Publishing, Inc., 1944.

Walker, A.K. *Tuskegee and the Black Belt*. Richmond: Dietz Press, 1944. "Portrait of a race." A study of the issues troubling the Negro today prefaced with a sympathetic account of Booker T. Washington's early struggles and the founding of Tuskegee Institute.

RACE PROBLEM

Baruch, Dorothy. *Glass House of Prejudice*. New York: William Morrow & Co., Inc., 1946. An analysis of prejudice and bigotry towards Negroes, Jews, Mexicans and Chinese Americans as it exists in the United States today, including a section or cure.

Bilbo, Theodore G. *Take Your Choice – Separation of Mongrelization*. Poplarville (Miss.): Dream House Publishing Co., 1947.

DuBois, W.E.B. *The World and Africa*. New York: The Viking Press. An inquiry into the part which Africa has played in world history. A condemnation of exploitation of Negro Africa particularly in the 19th century.

Hartley, E.L. *Problems in Prejudice*. New York: King's Crown Press, 1946. Using several eastern colleges, including one Negro institution, the writer presents a study in social psychology based on the assumption that "life histories and community studies may serve to show where race friction reaches its maximum and where it is inconsequential or altogether lacking."

Huszar, George B. *Anatomy of Racial Intolerance*. New York: The H.W. Wilson Co., 1946. Reprints of scientific and semi-popular articles on race, race relations and race prejudice.

Landry, Stuart O. *Cult of Equality: A Study of the Race Problem*. New Orleans: Pelican Publishing Co., 1945. A presentation of the point of view of one who maintains that there are racial inequalities and whites are superior.

Lerner, A.R. and Hervert Pester. *Challenge of Hate*. New York: F.F.F. Publishing Co., 1947. A photo-record of democracy's struggle against disruption, examines twenty-eight topics briefly showing positive and negative aspects.

Leiper, H.S. *Blind Spots: Experments [sic] in the Self-cure of Race Prejudice*. New York: Friendship Press, 1944. Race prejudice and the need of recognizing our own irrational views as studied by a religious worker. The cure of prejudice, like charity, begins at home.

Linton, R. *Science of Man in the World Crisis*. New York: Columbia University Press, 1945. A symposium by 21 contributors emphasizing the place of anthropology, sociology, and economic geography in the application of the techniques of science to the solution of human problems.

Roback, A.A. *Dictionary of the International Slurs*. (ethnophaulisms) With a supplementary Essay on Aspects of Ethnic Prejudice. Cambridge: Sci-Art Publishers, 1944.

Russell, A.G. *Colour, Race and Empire*. London: Victor Gollanz, Ltd., 194[unclear]

Sperry, W.L. (ed.) *Religion In the Post-War World*. Cambridge: Harvard University Press, 1945. A series of four volumes: (1) Religion of our Divided Denominations, (2) Religion of Soldier and Sailor (3) Religion and our Racial tensions, (4)Religion and Education. Including essays by leaders in the various retegious denominations, these volumes attempt to state present facts and to indicate future problems.

Tenenbaum, Samuel. *Why Men Hate*. New York: Beechhurst Press, 1946. The typical bigot analyzed and racial prejudices and hate for minorities and 'foreigners' discussed with examples and curatine [sic] programs."

Tuck, R.D. *Not With the Fist*. New York: Harcourt, Brace & Co., 1946. An account of the Mexican-American problem in a typical California City. The writer traces the origin of Mexican immigration, the attitude of indifference assumed by the United States, the lack of any plan for Mexican education and assimilation, and suggest plans for amelioration.

RACE RELATIONS

Brown, F.J. and J.S. Roucek. *One America*. New York: Prentice Hall, 1945. A compendium of information about our foreign population. Formerly published under the title: *Our Racial and National Minorities*, 1937.

Hardy, Arthur W. and Owen E. Penn. *The Racial Factor in YMCA's*. New York: Association Press, 1946. A report on Negro-white relationships in twenty-four cities.

Johnson, Charles S. and associates. *Into the Main Stream*. Chapel Hill: University of North Carolina Press, 1947. A study which depicts active racial cooperation taking place between Negroes and whites in the South today...in the fields of education, religion, health, employment and housing.

Johnson, Charles S. and others. *To Stem This Tide: A Survey of Racial Tension Areas in the United States*. Chicago: Pilgrim Press, 1944. A survey of the country at large with respect to racial tension in industry in rural districts and on public carriers. Attention is given to the sources and kinds of friction peculiar to the various sections of the country.

Logan, R. W. (ed.) *What the Negro Wants*. Chapel Hill: University of North Carolina Press, 1944. A symposium comprising the contributions of fourteen prominent Negroes. Though of varying careers and reputations, they are of one accord on what the Negro wants.

Lumpkin, K.D. *The Making of a Southerner*. New York: Alfred Knopf Co., 1947. The autobiography of a Southern woman whose story points up the enormous difficulties in the way of changing human prejudice. The story of the childhood and youth of a distinguished sociologist; an illumination of character formation, environmental influences and Negro-white relations.

Powdermaker, Hortense. *Probing our Prejudices*. New York: Harper & Bros., 1944. An attempt to help high-school students become awarw of their prejudices, to understand the nature, origin and effect of prejudices, and to suggest activities that can be employed to help reduce them.

Smith, R. *White Man's Burden*, New York: Vanguard Press, 1946. The record of a young white woman's struggle to abide by her conscience, in the matter of race relations, in a country where the minds of men speak one language, their feeling another.

RELIGION

DeHueck, Catherine. *Friendship House*. New York: Sheed & Ward, 1946. "The founder of Friendship House, a Catholic settlement house in Harlem, tells the story of the origin and growth of her work among Negroes which has spread to several other cities in America and Canada.

Gallagher, Buell G. *Color and Conscience: The Irrepressible Conflict*. New York: Harper and Borthers, 1946. A refutation of racial superiority from the viewpoint of a Christian.

Link, Henry Charles. *The Rediscovery of Morals*. with Special Reference to Race and Class Conflict. New York: E.P. Dutton & Co., Inc., 1947. Antagonism and hatred between different races, religious and class groups are viewed as essentially moral problems that can be corrected only by a resurgence of Christian ethical belief.

McKinney, Richard I. *Religion in Higher Education Among Negroes*. New Haven: Yale University Press, 1945. A study of the place occupied by religion in more than thirty Negro colleges, with a summary of findings and recommendations.

Shackelford, J.D. *My Happy Days* [sic]. Toronto: Associated Publishers, 1944. A description of the daily life of a little Negro boy in a middle class Northern home. A book aimed at the demolition of the walls of prejudice between Negroes and whites.

Soper, Edmund D. *Racism, A World Issue*. New York: Abingdon-Cokesbury, 1947. The outgrowth of several religious seminars and conferences, the purpose of this study is to interpret and guide Christian thinking on racial matters. It is also a resume of the composition of people within various boundaries in all parts of the World. [sic].

GENERAL

Adams, Evelyn C. *American Indian Education*. New York: King's Crown Press, A record of government policy with regard to the education and economic development of the Indian from the colonial period to the present day.

Arnall, Ellis G. *The Shore Dimly Seen*. Philadelphia: J.B. Lippincott Company, 1946. Democratic program in Georgia – National issues.

Brownlee, Fred L. *New Day Ascending*. Boston: Pilgrim Press, 1946. A history of the first one hundred years of the American Missionary Association.

Carlson, John Roy. *The Plotters*. New York: E.P. Dutton & Co., Inc., 1946. "A startling account of the post-war activities of our native fascists" using veterans organizations to spread race and class hatred.

Gould, Kenneth M. *They Got the Blame*. New York: Association Press, 1944. A discussion of the history of scapegoating.

Kennedy, Stetson. *Southern Exposure*. New York: Doubleday, Doran & Co., 1946. A factual word picture of the problem of the South, exposing the Southern subversive elements and their Yankee collaborationists, but concluding that "the region is ripe for democracy and that total equality between the races can be achieved."

Mukerjee, Radhakamal. *Races, Lands and Food*. New York: Dryden Press, 1947. An Indian sociologist appraises problems of overpopulation.

Northrup, H.R. *Organized Labor and the Negro*. New York: Harper & Bros., 1944. A study of the racial policies of trade unions and the status of Negroes in industry since the last depression. Shows how exclusion exists through ritual, constitutional provisions, tacit consent and segregated auxiliary status, how external factors also have influenced policy: regional differences, labor supply, the presence of Negroes in industries being unionized by C.I.O., and future prospects of Negro labor.

Odum, Howard Washington, *The Way of the South*. New York: The Macmillan Company, 1947. "The cultural heritage of the South, its problems, social and economic and the past and future stages in their solution; an analysis of the southern people by a famous sociologist."

NOTES

INTRODUCTION

1. "Prospectus for an Institute of Race and Culture: The Need for Integrated Training and Experience in the Field of Race and Culture" n.d. Charles Johnson Papers, box 28, file, 14, Amistad Research Center, New Orleans.
2. Daryl Michael Scott, *Contempt and Pity: Social Policy and the Image of the Damaged Black Psyche, 1880–1996* (Chapel Hill: University of North Carolina Press, 1997), xii.
3. Ibid., 62.
4. Ibid., 63.
5. Kevin K. Gaines, *Uplifting the Race: Black Leadership, Politics, and Culture in the Twentieth Century* (Chapel Hill: University of North Carolina Press, 1996), 3.
6. Ibid., 3-4.
7. See Vernon J. Williams Jr., *From a Caste to a Minority: Changing Attitudes of American Sociologists Toward Afro-Americans 1896–1946* (New York: Greenwood Press), 1989.
8. For more information on Charles H. Houston, see Genna Rae McNeil, *Groundwork: Charles Hamilton Houston and the Struggle for Civil Rights* (Philadelphia: University of Pennsylvania Press), 1983.

CHAPTER ONE

1. S.P. Fullinwider, *The Mind and Mood of Black America: 20th Century Thought* (Homewood, IL: Dorsey Press, 1969), 12.
2. Ibid., 13.
3. Ibid., 14.
4. Ibid., 72.
5. Ibid., 14.
6. Aldon Morris, *The Origins of the Civil Rights Movement: Black Communities Organizing for Change*, (New York: Free Press, 1984), 3.
7. For more information on the riots of the 1940s see Charles R. Lawrence Jr., "Race Riots in the United States, 1942–1946," in Jessie Parkhurst Guzman, ed. *Negro Year Book: A Review of Events Affecting Negro Life, 1941–1946* (Tuskegee, Alabama: The Department of Records and Research, Tuskegee Institute, 1947), 232; James N. Upton, *A Social History of Twentieth Century Urban Riots* (Bristol, IN: Wyndham Hall Press, 1984); Michael Newton and Judy Ann Newton, *Racial and Religious Violence in*

America: A Chronology (New York: Garland Publishing, 1991); and Herbert Shapiro, *White Violence and Black Response: From Reconstruction to Montgomery* (Amherst, MA: University of Massachusetts Press, 1988).

8. John Egerton, *Speak Now Against the Day: The Generation Before the Civil Rights Movement in the South* (New York: Alfred A. Knopf, 1994), 414. Gunnar Myrdal, *An American Dilemma: The Negro Problem and Modern Democracy* (New York: Harper & Brothers, 1944), 414.
9. Egerton, *Speak Now Against the Day*, 203. Myrdal, *An American Dilemma*, 414.
10. Jessie Parkhurst Guzman, "Housing" in Jessie Parkhurst Guzman, ed. *Negro Year Book, 1952: A Review of Events Affecting Negro Life*, 11 ed. (New York: W. H. Wise & Co., Inc.), 184.
11. Charles R. Lawrence Jr., "Race Riots in the United States 1942–1946," *Negro Year Book* 1 (1947): 232.
12. Ibid., 232.
13. E. Franklin Frazier, *The Negro in the United States*, Revised Edition (New York: Macmillan Company, 1957), 699.
14. Lawrence, Jr., "Race Riots," 232
15. Ibid., 234.
16. Ibid., 328.
17. Ibid., 210–211.
18. Ibid., 242–243.
19. Ibid., 243.
20. Ibid., 243.
21. Egerton, *Speak Now Against the Day*, 410. Willis D. Weatherford and Charles S. Johnson, *Race Relations: Adjustment of Whites and Negroes in the United States* (New York: Negro Universities Press, 1934), 520–523.
22. The symbolic theories are also referred to as the psychological theories.
23. Charles S. Johnson, *A Preface to Racial Understanding* (New York: Friendship Press, 1936), 175.
24. Brewton Berry, *Race Relations: The Interaction of Ethnic and Racial Groups* (Boston: Houghton Mifflin Company, 1951), 108.
25. Gordon W. Allport, *The Nature of Prejudice* (Cambridge, MA: Addison-Wesley Publishing Company, Inc., 1954), 216.
26. Berry, *Race Relations*, 108.
27. Gordon W. Allport, "ABCs of Scapegoating," 42–43 in Berry, *Race Relations*, 109.
28. Berry, *Race Relations*, 110.
29. Ibid., 176–177.
30. Ibid., 578–579.
31. Robert Ezra Park, "The Basis of Race Prejudice" in *Race and Culture* (Glencoe, IL: Free Press, 1950), 233.
32. Ibid., 233.
33. Ibid., 243.
34. Fullinwinder, *Mind and Mood*, 101.
35. Johnson, *Preface to Racial Understanding*, 191–192.
36. "The Sociology of Racial Conflict" ca. 1952, box 176, file 29, CSJ Papers, Fisk.
37. Ibid.
38. Ibid.
39. "Backgrounds of Race and Race Conflict," n.d., box 188, file 11, CSJ Papers, Fisk.
40. Ibid.
41. "Causes of Cultural Conflicts," n.d., box 158, file 17, CSJ Papers, Fisk.
42. Berry, *Race Relations*, 106.
43. Myrdal, *An American Dilemma*, lviii.
44. Ibid.

45. Ibid., xlv.
46. Ibid., li.
47. Ibid., 997.
48. Ibid., 418.
49. Ibid., 418.
50. "Memorandum of Conferences of WWA, CSJ, and ERE on the Fund's Program in Race Relations held June 27, 1942," 27 June 1942, box 313, file 2, Julius Rosenwald Papers, Amistad Research Center, New Orleans (hereafter cited as Rosenwald Papers, Amistad).
51. "National Organizations in the Field of Race Relations," March 1946, box 166, file 13, Charles S. Johnson Papers, Special Collections Library, Fisk University, Nashville, TN (hereafter cited as CSJ Papers, Fisk).
52. "American Missionaries Association," ca. 1944, box 243, file "Other Records Jan-March 1944," American Missionaries Association Addendum Papers, Amistad Research Center, New Orleans (hereafter cited as AMA Add., Amistad).
53. "Memorandum on the Race Relations Program of the American Missionary Association," 23 June 1943, box 29, file 3, Charles Johnson Papers, Amistad Research Center, New Orleans. (hereafter cited as CSJ Papers, Amistad).
54. "Article by Dr. Charles S. Johnson for June Herald," ca. 1943, box 243, file "Other Records: ca. 1943," AMA Add., Amistad.
55. "General Statement by the Director of the Race Relations Division of the American Missionary Association," 30 November 1943, box 243, file "Nov. – Dec. 1943," AMA Add., Amistad.
56. Ibid.
57. Ibid.
58. Edwin R. Embree and Julia Waxman, *Investment in People: The Story of the Julius Rosenwald Fund* (New York: Harper & Brothers Publishers, 1949), 28.
59. Ibid., 42.
60. Ibid., 155.
61. Ibid., 28.
62. Ibid., 182.
63. Edwin Embree to W.W. Alexander, 1 June 1942, box 313, file 2, Rosenwald Papers, Amistad.
64. Memorandum, Conference WWA. CSJ. amd ERE" 27 June 1942.
65. Edwin R. Embree to Howard W. Odum, 15 October 1942, box 313, file 2, Rosenwald Papers, Amistad.
66. Pearl S. Buck to Edwin R. Embree, 10 August 1942, box 313, file 2, Rosenwald Papers, Amistad.
67. John B. Kirby, *Black Americans in the Roosevelt Era* (Knoxville: University of Tennessee Press, 1980), 54.
68. Ibid., 56.
69. Ibid., 57.
70. Ruth Benedict, *Race and Racism* (London: George Routledge & Sons, Ltd., 1942), 163.
71. Ibid., 162.
72. Ibid., 164.
73. Gunnar Myrdal, *The Negro Problem and Modern Democracy* (New York: Harper & Brother Publishers, 1944), 109.
74. Ibid., 110.
75. Ibid.
76. Berry, *Race Relations*, 122.
77. Ibid.
78. Johnson, *Preface to Racial Understanding*, 188–189.

79. Ibid.
80. Ibid.
81. Ibid.
82. Ibid.
83. Arnold M. Rose, ed., *Race Prejudice and Discrimination: Readings in Intergroup Relations in the United States* (New York: Alfred A. Knopf, 1956), 539.
84. Ibid.
85. Ibid., 543.
86. Ibid., 544.
87. Egerton, *Speak Now Against the Day*, 413–414.
88. "Article by Dr. Charles S. Johnson for June Herald," ca. 1943.

CHAPTER TWO

1. "Prospectus for an Institute of Race and Culture: The Need for Integrated Training and Experience in the Field of Race and Culture," n.d., box 28, file 4, Charles S. Johnson Papers, Amistad Research Center, New Orleans, Louisiana (hereafter cited as CSJ Papers, Amistad).
2. Charles S. Johnson, "A Spiritual Autobiography," n.d.,p. 3 manuscript, Charles S. Johnson Papers, Fisk University Special Collections, Nashville, TN (hereafter cited as CSJ Papers, Fisk).
3. Ibid., 6.
4. Sarah L. Delaney and A. Elizabeth Delaney with Amy Hill Hearth, *Having Our Say: The Delaney Sisters' First 100 Years* (New York: Dell Publishing), 1993, p. 95.
5. C. Vann Woodward, *The Strange Career of Jim Crow*, 3rd ed. (New York: Oxford University Press), 1974, pp. 6–7.
6. Ibid., 7.
7. Delaney, p. 92.
8. Johnson, "A Spiritual Autobiography," 1.
9. Ibid., 6.
10. Edwin R. Embree, *13 Against the Odds* (New York: Viking Press, 1944), 48.
11. Johnson, "A Spiritual Autobiography," 2.
12. Ibid., 2.
13. Ibid., 5.
14. Ibid., 2.
15. Embree, *13 Against the Odds*, 50.
16. Ibid.
17. Ibid.
18. Interview with Jeh V. Johnson, New York, Oct. 2002.
19. Johnson, "A Spiritual Autobiography," 6.
20. Ibid.
21. Ibid.
22. Ibid.
23. Other archival biographical information lists 1916 as the year Johnson he gained his AB.
24. Johnson, "A Spiritual Autobiography," 8.
25. Embree, *13 Against the Odds*, 54.
26. Johnson, "A Spiritual Autobiography," 8.
27. Richard Robbins, *Sidelines Activist: Charles S. Johnson and the Struggle for Civil Rights* (Jackson: University Press of Mississippi, 1996), 4. For more information on the Chicago School, see Martin Bulmer, *The Chicago School of Sociology: Institutionalization, Diversity, and the Rise of Sociological Research* (Chicago: University of Chicago Press, 1984); and James E. Blackwell and Morris Hanowitz, eds., *Black Sociologist: Historical and Contemporary Perspectives* (Chicago: University of Chicago Press, 1974).
28. Johnson, "A Spiritual Autobiography."

29. Charles S. Johnson, "The Mission of the Urban League," p.1. in Ralph L. Pearson, Charles S. Johnson: The Urban League Years. A Study of Race Leadership," diss. 1971.
30. Johnson, "A Spiritual Autobiography," 7.
31. A second black man, James Crawford, was later killed by police who had gathered at the beach to calm tensions. The Chicago Commission on Race, *The Negro in Chicago: A Study of Race Relations and a Race Riot* (Chicago: University of Chicago Press, 1922), 1.
32. Embree, *13 Against the Odds*, 56.
33. Johnson as quoted in Embree, *13 Against the Odds*, 56–57.
34. Ibid., 57.
35. For details on the Chicago 1919 riot, see the Chicago Commission on Race Relations, *The Negro in Chicago: A Study of Race Relations and a Race Riot* (Chicago: University of Chicago Press, 1922). Note: It is a widely held belief among scholars that Charles S. Johnson wrote *The Negro in Chicago*, but did not receive credit because of the social constraints of the day. Also see "Chicago: Riot and Response" in Arthur I. Waskow, *From Race Riot to Sit-In, 1919 and the 1960s* (Gloucester, MA: Peter Smith, 1975), Chicago Riots of 1919.
36. Chicago Commission on Race Relations, *Negro in Chicago*, p. 1, Introduction. Also see Allen D. Grimshaw, ed. *Racial Violence in the United States* (Chicago: Aldine Publishing Company, 1969), pp. 97–105. Note: The coroner's jury determined Williams drowned from "fear of stone-throwing" which kept him from the shore.
37. Ibid.
38. Ibid., xv
39. Embree, *13 Against the Odds*, 57.
40. Nancy J. Weiss, *The National Urban League 1910–1940* (New York: Oxford University Press, 1974) 141, and John Egerton, *Speak Now Against the Day* (New York: Alfred A. Knopf, 1994), 46.
41. Egerton, *Speak Now Against the Day*, 46–47. Seventy Southern African Americans, "some still wearing the uniform of their country, were shot, beaten, or burned to death by lynch mobs." Upton, *Social History of 20th Century Urban Riots*, 8. Twenty-three African Americans and fifteen Euro-Americans were killed during the Chicago riot.
42. For information on other 20th century riots see Waskow's *From Race Riot to Sit-In*; J. Paul Mitchell, ed. *Race Riots in Black and White* (Englewood Cliffs, NJ: Prentice-Hall, 1970); and Allen D. Grimshaw, ed. *Racial Violence in the United States* (Chicago: Aldine Publishing Company, 1969).
43. Embree, *13 Against the Odds*, 57–58.
44. Ibid., 58.
45. The Ph.B was a common degree during the early 1900s. Although referred to as Dr. Johnson, Johnson did not hold a Ph.D. In 1928 Virginia Union University awarded him an honorary Litt. D. degree.
46. Johnson, "A Spiritual Autobiography,"
47. Charles S. Johnson, "Mental Measurements of Negro Groups," *Opportunity*, February 1923, vol. 1, no. 2, p. 21.
48. Ibid., 21.
49. Ibid., 21.
50. Charles S. Johnson, "Public Opinion and the Negro," *Opportunity* 1, no. 7, July 1923, 204. Johnson did not give statistics to support this claim, however, the U.S. Bureau of the Census, Historical Statistics of the Colonial Times to 1970, "Illegitimate Live Births and Birth Rates by Age and Race of Mother 1940–1970, under Vital Statistics and Health and Medical Care, 1975, p. 52, lists 90,000 total illegitimate births for 1940. Of that, 49,000 were black and 40,000 were white. Documentation could not be found for illegitimate births prior to 1940.

51. Johnson, "Public Opinion and the Negro," 204.
52. Ibid.
53. Ibid.
54. Ibid.
55. http://www.lucidcafe.com/library/96jun/rousseau.html.
56. Johnson, "A Spiritual Autobiography," 11.
57. Ibid.
58. Vincent P. Franklin, "Black Social Scientist and the Mental Testing Movement, 1920–1940" in *Black Psychology*, 2nd Ed., Reginald Jones, ed., New York: Harper & Row, 1980, 201–202.
59. Charles U. Smith and Lewis Killian "Black Sociologists and Social Protest" in *Black Sociologists: Historical and Contemporary Perspectives*, edited by James E. Blackwell and Morris Janowitz (Chicago: University of Chicago Press), 1974, 196.
60. Ibid., 195, 201.
61. Franklin, "Black Social Scientist," 201–202.
62. Ibid., 205.
63. In *Sidelines Activist*, Robbins points out that Johnson also conducted similar workshops at Cheney State and New York University. Robbins, *Sidelines Activist*, 122.
64. "Institute of Race Relations, Swarthmore College" 1–29 July 1934, box 319, file 8, Julius Rosenwald Papers, Special Collections Library, Fisk University, Nashville, TN (hereafter cited as Rosenwald, Fisk).
65. "Institute of Race Relations," n.d., box 137, file 5, Charles S. Johnson Papers, Fisk University Special Collections Library, Fisk University, Nashville, TN (hereafter cited as CSJ Papers, Fisk) "The Institute of Race Relations," n.d., box 136, file 10, CSJ Papers, Fisk.
66. Ibid.
67. Ibid.
68. "The Institute of Race Relations," 1–30 July 1933, program in Johnson Papers. See also "Institute of Race Relations Open," Swarthmorean, 6 July 1934, and Charles Spurgeon Johnson, "An Approach to Race Relations," in "The Speeches of Charles Spurgeon Johnson: Addresses Delivered to Institutes of Race Relations, 1939–1949," 10:1 (26 July 1938); unpublished typescript, Special Collections Library, Fisk; cited in Patrick Joseph Gilpin, *Charles S. Johnson: An Intellectual Biography*, unpublished dissertation, Vanderbilt University, Ph.D. 1973, 525.
69. "Institute of Race Relations, Swarthmore," 1934, box 319, file 8, Rosenwald, Fisk. "Institute of Race Relations," n.d., box 137, file 5, CSJ Papers, Fisk.
70. "Institute of Race Relations" program, n.d., box 319, file 8, Rosenwald, Fisk.
71. "Institute of Race Relations," n.d., box 137, file 5, CSJ Papers, Fisk.
72. "Institute of Race Relations," n.d. box 136, file 8, CSJ Papers, Fisk.
73. Fred L. Brownlee, "The American Missionary Association Division: Race Relations," 6 March 1944, box 243, file "Other Records: Jan. – March 1944," AMA Add., Amistad.
74. In *Sidelines Activist*, Robbins points out that Johnson also conducted similar workshops at Cheney State and New York University. Robbins, *Sidelines Activist*, 122.
75. "Prospectus for an Institute of Race and Culture: The Need for Integrated Training and Experience in the Field of Race and Culture," box 28, file 4, CSJ Papers, Amistad, 1–3.
76. Ibid.
77. Ibid.
78. Ibid., 3.
79. Ibid.
80. Ibid., 8–13.
81. Ibid. For a history of Fisk University see Joe M. Richardson, *A History of Fisk University, 1865–1946* (Tuscaloosa, Alabama: The University of Alabama Press, 2002).

82. Fred L. Brownlee, "The American Missionary Association Division: Race Relations," 6 March 1944, box 243, file "Other Records Jan.–March 1944," American Missionary Association Archives Addendum, Amistad Research Center, New Orleans (hereafter cited as AMA Addendum, Amistad); This quote shows that the AMA agreed with Johnson's life choices.
83. "Prospectus for an Institute on Race and Culture," 3.
84. Robert E. Park used the term "Great Society."
85. "Announcing...The Third Annual Institute of Race Relations," box 36, file 1, RRD Papers, Amistad.
86. "Statesmanship in National Crisis: 13th Annual Institute of Race Relations, July 2–July 14, 1956," 1956, box 52, file 1, RRD Papers, Amistad.
87. "Human Rights in the Great Society: 22nd Annual Institute of Race Relations June 28–July 10, 1965," 1965, box 68, file 1, RRD Papers, Amistad.
88. Ibid.
89. "Race Institute Opens Today," 29 June 1964, *The Nashville Tennessean* in Johnson Scrapbook, box 67, file 7, RRD Papers, Amistad.
90. Ibid.
91. Patrick J. Gilpin, "Charles S. Johnson: An Intellectual Biography" (Ph.D. diss., Vanderbilt University, 1973), chapter 13.
92. "Prospectus on Institute of Race and Culture," ca. 1942, box 34, file 32, CSJ Papers, Amistad.
93. Ibid., 4.
94. "Prospectus on Institute of Race and Culture," Amistad; and "The Institute of Race Relations: An Instrument of Societal Change," 1944, box 36, file 9, CSJ Papers, Fisk.
95. "Announcing...The Third Annual Institute of Race Relations," and "The 6th Annual Institute of Race Relations, June 27th to July 9th," 1948, box 41, file 1, RRD Papers, Amistad.
96. "Comments on the Institute of Race Relations and Suggestions of Additions Regarding Future Programs," 1944, box 34, file 35, RRD Papers, Amistad.
97. Analysis based on the following news releases on Institute: "News Release, 1949 Institute," 1949, box 50, file 22, RRD Papers, Amistad; "News Release, 1958 Institute," 1958, box 54, file 24, RRD Papers, Amistad; "News Release, 1962 Institute," 1962, box 62, file 22, RRD Papers, Amistad.
98. "Announcing...The Third Annual Institute of Race Relations," and "Lecturers, Consultants, and Discussion Leaders," 1947, box 38, file 10, RRD Papers, Amistad.
99. Ibid.
100. Richard Robbins, *Sidelines Activist: Charles S. Johnson and the Struggle for Civil Rights* (Jackson: University Press of Mississippi, 1996), 123.
101. Robbins, *Sidelines Activist*, 123.
102. W.E.B. Du Bois, *The Autobiography of W. E. B. Du Bois: A Soliloquy of Viewing My Life from the Last Decade of Its First Century* (New York: International Publishers Co., Inc, 1968), 311–325.
103. Robbins, *Sidelines Activist*, 123.
104. Ibid., 122. Robbins notes that the ratio of black to white participants evened over the years.
105. "Eighth Annual Institute Announcement," 1951, box 47, file 1, RRD Papers, Amistad.
106. Analysis based on Institute news releases from 1949, 1958, and 1962, Amistad.
107. "Announcing...The Third Annual Institute of Race Relations."
108. Robbins, *Sidelines Activist*, 181.
109. Ella Baker quoted in Charles M. Payne, *I've Got the Light of Freedom: The Organizing Tradition and the Mississippi Freedom Struggle* (Berkeley, California: University of California Press, 1995), 77.

110. Analysis taken from John M. Glen, *Highlander: No Ordinary School 1932–1962* (Lexington, KY: University Press of Kentucky, 1988) 129–130; and Payne, *I've Got the Light*, 70.
111. Egerton, *Speak Now Against the Day*, 161.
112. Payne, *I've Got the Light*, 71.
113. Aldon Morris, *Origins of the Civil Rights Movement* (New York: Free Press, 1984), 139–140, quoted in Payne, *I've Got the Light*, 70; and Egerton, *Speak Now*, 161.
114. Payne, *I've Got the Light*, 74.
115. Correspondence from Septima P. Clark to Dr. Herman Long, 6 January 1958, box 21, file 1, RRD Papers, Amistad.
116. Correspondence from Septima P. Clark to Dr. Clifton H. Johnson, 23 May 1967, box 73, file 8, RRD Papers, Amistad.
117. Clark to Johnson, 23 May 1967; and Clifton H. Johnson to Mrs. Septima P. Clark, 26 May 1967, file 8, box 73, RRD Papers, Amistad. For more information on the financial contributions to the RRI, see the General Education Board Papers, Rockefeller Archive Center, Sleepy Hollow, New York
118. Johnson, *Preface to Racial Understanding*, 192.

CHAPTER THREE

1. Richard Robbins, *Sidelines Activist: Charles S. Johnson and the Struggle for Civil Rights* (Jackson: University Press of Mississippi), 1996, pp. 180–181.
2. Race relations specialist Ina C. Brown was a professor of social anthropology at Scarrit College for Christian Workers in Nashville.
3. Gordon W. Allport was also chairman of the Department of Psychology at Harvard University.
4. Psychologist Smiley Blanton was an associate professor of clinical psychology at Vanderbilt University.
5. "What Is Race and Are Race Differences Significant? By Ina C. Brown," 1944, box 34, file 12, Race Relations Department Papers, Amistad Research Center, Tulane University, New Orleans (hereafter cited as RRD Papers, Amistad).
6. Brown, "What Is Race and Are Race Differences Significant?."
7. "What Can You Say When They Ask You?" n.d., Ethel Alpenfels, RRD 1943–1970, box 36, file 12, RRD Paters, Amistad.
8. Alpenfels, "What Can You Say When They Ask You?"
9. "Press Release—American Missionary Association Race Relations Division, Fisk University Social Science Department, Nashville 8, Tennessee. July 6, 1945 'Psychoanalysis of Race Relations,'" pp. 2–3. box 35, file 26, RRD Papers, Armistad.
10. "Frightened People" Dr. Helen V. McLean, n.d. box 35, file 18, RRD Papers, Amistad.
11. McLean, "Frightened People."
12. "Press Release—American Missionary Association Race Relations Division, Fisk University Social Science Department, Nashville 8, Tennessee. July 6, 1945 'Psychoanalysis of Race Relations,'" p. 3.
13. "Summary of Unconscious Factors in Racial Prejudice" 1945, Helen B McLean, box 35, file 19 RRD Papers, Amistad.
14. Ibid.
15. "A Philosophy of Race Relations" Margaret Halsey, n.d., box 44, file 18, RRD Papers, Amistad, 3–4.
16. Ibid., 3–5.
17. Ibid., 5.
18. Ibid., 9.
19. Ibid., 15.
20. Ibid.

21. Ibid.
22. "Press Release, American Missionary Association Institute of Race Relations, Fisk University Social Science Department, Nashville 8, Tennessee, July 5, 1944, RRD Papers, Amistad, box 34, file 32, pp 2–3.
23. Ibid.
24. Ibid.
25. "Comments on the Institute of Race Relations and Suggestions of Additions Regarding Future Programs," 1944, box 34, file 35, RRD Papers, Amistad.
26. "An Analysis of the Race Relations Institute Sponsored by the American Missionary Association at Fisk University, July 3/21, 1944," box 36, file 9, CSJ Papers, Fisk.
27. "'Next Voter' Criticizes Race Institute," *The Nashville Banner*, 1949, box 43, file 11, in RRD Papers, Amistad.
28. Ibid.
29. Ibid.
30. "The Eighth Annual Institute of Race Relations, July 2–14, 1951," box 46, file RRD Papers Amistad. A separate race and racial theories component at the Institute was not listed in this or subsequent programs.
31. "Problem in Education: Tests Show Race Prejudice," by Edwin A. Lahey in *Chicago, Ill. News*, July 10, 1947, RRD box 39, file 62.
32. Ibid.
33. Ibid.
34. Press Release: Race Relations Department American Missionary Association Board of Home Missions Congregational Christian Churches, Fisk University Nashville, Tennessee, July 4, 1953, "Immediate Abolition of Segregation Urgent National Need, Noted Psychiatrist Tell Race Relations Institute: Tenth Session of Intergroup Leaders Gives Emphasis to Problems of Prejudice," RRD box 49, file 14.
35. Margaret Connell Szasz, *Education and the American Indian: The Road to Self-Determination Since 1928*, 3rd ed. (University of New Mexico Press, 1999), 20.
36. Ibid., 120.
37. Ibid., 121.
38. American Missionary Association Addendum Papers, box 243, file 1950–51 Minutes: Meeting of the National Advisory Committee of the Race Relations Department of the Congregational and Christian Churches—Held at Nashville, Tennessee, July 2, 1951. (Note: Minutes are stamped with a Mar 18, 1952 date.)
39. Ibid.
40. Guadalupe San Miquel Jr. *"Let All of Them Take Heed": Mexican Americans and the Campaign for Educational Equality in Texas, 1910–1981* (College Station: Texas A&M University Press, 1987), 68.
41. Ibid.
42. Ibid.
43. As quoted in San Miquel, 69.
44. Press Release, 7/2/53 Race Relations Department American Missionary Association Congregational Christian Churches Fisk University, Nashville 8, Tennessee— "'Airborne Migration' Brings New Intergroup Problems Fisk Institute Told" in RRD box 49, File 14.
45. Sonia Nieto, *Puerto Rican Students in United States Schools*, (Mahwah, N.J.: Lawrence Erlbaum Associates, 2000), 5–33.
46. Press Release, 7/2/53 Race Relations Department American Missionary Association Congregational Christian Churches Fisk University, Nashville 8, Tennessee— "'Airborne Migration' Brings New Intergroup Problems Fisk Institute Told."
47. Ibid.

48. Press Release, "Special for Atlanta Daily World from: John H. McCray, Information Officer, Race Relations Institute, Fisk University, Nashville, Tennessee" in RRD box 72, file 20, 1966.
49. Ibid.
50. Ibid.
51. "Press Release—American Missionary Association Institute of Race Relations, Fisk University Department of Social Sciences, Nashville, Tennessee, July 18, 1944: For Immediate Release, Alma G. Forrest, Herman H. Long," RRD box 34, file 32, 1944.
52. Ibid.
53. V.P. Franklin, Nancy L. Grant, Harold M. Kletnick, and Genna Rae McNeil, eds. *African Americans and Jews in the Twentieth Century: Studies in Convergence and Conflict* (Columbia: University of Missouri Press, 1998), 3.
54. Ibid., 2.
55. Ibid., 2–3.
56. "Minority Groups Urged to Unite for Common Goal at Race Relations Meet," Kansas City, MO *CALL*, July 25, 1947, in RRD box 39, file 26.
57. "Community Action Clinic Report: Race Relations Institute, Fisk University, Nashville, Tennessee, June 28–July 10, 1965" RRD Papers.
58. Ibid.
59. "Memorandum to Dr. Charles S. Johnson from W. H. Grayson, Jr., Coordinator of Institutes of Race Relations, November 4, 1946. RRD Box 82, Folder 1.
60. "Community Race Relations Institute, St. Louis, Missouri. February 1946," RRD Box 82, File 16.
61. "Division of Race Relations, American Missionary Association, Fisk University, Tentative Suggested Outline of Area Institute of Race Relations, W. H. Grayson, Jr. Coordinator," p. 3 in RRD Box 89, File 1.
62. Ibid., 2.
63. Memorandum to Dr. Charles S. Johnson, Director from W.H. Grayson, Jr., Secretary. April 11, 1947." RRD Box 82, Folder 1; and "Summary of Institute on Race Relations in Baltimore, p. 2. RRD Box 82, File 3, no date.
64. "City Ignores Race Problems, View" *Baltimore Evening Sun*, January 15, 1947 in RRD Papers, Box 82, File 8. Also in "Summary of Institute on Race Relations in Baltimore, p. 2. RRD Box 82, File 3, no date.
65. "Slum Conditions Held Cause of High TB Rate" *Baltimore Evening Sun*, January 16, 1947, in RRD Papers, Box 82, File 8.
66. Ibid.
67. Ibid.
68. "Speakers Present Method to Oppose Racial Prejudices," *Baltimore Morning Sun*, January 18, 1947, in RRD Papers, Box 82, File 8.
69. "What Now, Baltimoreans?" Editorial, *Baltimore Afro-American*, January 21, 1947, p. 4 in RRD Papers, Box 82, File 8.
70. Ibid.
71. Ibid.
72. "Race Relations Institute Set to Encourage Discussions," *Baltimore Evening Sun*, January 14, 1947, in RRD Papers, Amistad Box 82, File 8.
73. Nicholas V. Montalto, *A History of Intercultural Educational Movement, 1924–1941* (New York: Garland Publishing, Inc. 1982), 20.
74. "Summary Report: July 2–21, 1945," 1945, box 35, file 25, RRD Papers, Amistad. pp. 85–93.
75. Ibid.
76. Lecturers at the Institute referred to intergroup education as intercultural education until 1951 when the Institute initialized a separate Intergroup Education clinic.

77. "Summary Report: RRI 1943–1976, Intercultural Education in School," 1946, box 37, file 21, RRD Papers, Amistad.
78. "Summary Report: Fisk University Race Relations Institute, 1946" 1943–1970, box 37, file 21, RRD Papers, Amistad, 82–86.
79. Ibid., 89.
80. Ibid., 89–90.
81. Ibid., 91–92.
82. Ibid., 82–86.
83. Numerous school districts across the country had some form of intercultural education program. Most notable were programs in Springfield, MA; Detroit; Cincinnati; Santa Barbara, CA; and New York. Analysis from C.I. Chatto (1944, November) "What the Schools Are Doing: The Springfield Program for Democratic Citizenship." *Intercultural Education News*, 1–3, in General Education Board Collection, Box 567, File 6052, Series 13; Rockefeller Center Archives, N. Tarrytown, New York (hereafter GEB Papers, Rockefeller). Also from E. Mickelson (June, 1945) "Toward Better Intercultural Understandings: IV. What the Schools Are Doing, *Intercultural Education News*, 1–2, GEB Papers, Rockefeller.
84. "Findings of the Clinic on Church and Race", Race Relations Department American Missionary Association, Fisk University, Nashville, Tennessee, Fifth Annual Institute of Race Relations, June 28–July 16, 1948.
85. Ibid.
86. Ibid.
87. "Clinic on Church and Race: Summary of Discussion, Race Relations Department, American Missionary Association, Fisk University, Nashville, Tennessee, Sixth Annual Institute of Race Relations, June 27–July 9, 1949." RRD box 46, file 2, RRI, 1950.
88. Ibid.
89. Ibid.
90. "Summary of Discussion in the Clinic on 'Religion and Race', Chairman: Galen R. Weaver, July 1–9, 1954" RRD box 50, file 25.
91. "Fisk Institute on Race Relations – 1960, Clinic on Church and Race, Summary," RRD box 58, file 15.
92. Ibid.

CHAPTER FOUR

1. Charles S. Johnson "The New Frontier of Negro Labor," *Opportunity* 10, no. 6 (June 1932): 169–170.
2. Ibid.
3. Nancy L. Grant, *TVA and Black Americans: Planning for the Status Quo* (Philadelphia: Temple University Press, 1990), xix.
4. John B. Kirby, *Black Americans in the Roosevelt Era* (Knoxville: University of Tennessee Press, 1980).
5. Paul Burnstein, *Discrimination, Jobs, and Politics: The Struggle for Equal Employment Opportunity in the United States Since the New Deal* (Chicago: University of Chicago Press, 1982) pp. 3–5. Quoted in Grant, *TVA and Black Americans*, xx.
6. Charles S. Johnson and Associates, *To Stem This Tide: A Survey of Racial Tension Areas in the United States* (AMS Press: New York, 1943), 4–6.
7. Aldon Morris, *Origins of the Civil Rights Movement* (New York: Free Press, 1984), 1.
8. J. Weston Walch, *Complete Handbook on Fair Employment Practices Law* (Portland, ME: J. Weston Walch Publisher, 1952), 9; "H" jobs from Fair Employment Practice Committee, *Final Report, June 28, 1946* (Washington, DC: United States Government Printing Office, 1947), 33–37.

9. James A. Mitcham, *Fair Employment Practices Legislation: A Summary of Its History and Development with Statements on Both Sides* (Washington, DC: Library of Congress Legislative Reference Service, 1952), 4.
10. Committee on Fair Employment Practice, *FEPC How It Operates* (Washington, DC: Committee on Fair Employment Practice, Division of Review and Analysis, 1944), 2.
11. Analysis taken from Louis Coleridge Kesselman, *The Social Politics of FEPC: A Study in Reform Pressure Movements* (Chapel Hill: University of North Carolina Press, 1948), 15–16; Library of Congress Legislative Reference Service, *Fair Employment Practices Legislation*, 4.
12. "FEPC Member Makes Talk at Race Meeting," *Nashville Banner*, 14 July 1945, box 35, file 27, Race Relations Department, United Church Board for Homeland Ministries Archives, Amistad Research Center, New Orleans (hereafter cited as RRD Papers, Amistad).
13. "FEPC Member Makes Talk at Race Meeting," July 1945.
14. "South and the FEPC," *Nashville Banner*, 13 July 1945, box 35, file 27, RRD Papers, Amistad.
15. Untitled newspaper clipping, ca. July 1945, RRD papers, box 35, file 27, Amistad.
16. Mitcham, *Fair Employment Practices*, 4–5; and Fair Employment Practice Committee, *Final Report June 28, 1946*, 12.
17. Ibid., viii.
18. "Memorandum: From Grace C. Jones, October 25, 1951," in Race Relations Department, American Missionary Association Papers, Special Collections Library, Fisk University; statistics taken from *Nairo Reporter* 1, no. 2, April 1951, 3; and *Nairo Reporter* 1, no. 5, July 1951: 1.
19. Mitcham, *Fair Employment Practices*, 5–6.
20. Ibid., 6.
21. "Memorandum: From Grace C. Jones," October 25, 1951.
22. Mitcham, *Fair Employment Practices*, 6.
23. Ibid.
24. "Prospectus for the Industry and Labor Management Clinics: 7th Annual AMA Race Relations Institute, Fisk University by John Hope II Consultant on Industrial Relations: Fair Employment Practices Through the Normal Labor-Management Relations Machinery," n.d., box 42, file 13, RRD Papers, Amistad.
25. Ibid., 1–2.
26. Ibid.
27. Jane Carter, "Racial System Held Test of Sincerity: Paper by Fisk's Dr. Johnson Read to Institute Notes Improvements," *Nashville Tennessean*, 1 July 1953, box 48, file 17, RRD Papers, Amistad; this paper was read by Carter to RRI participants as Johnson was in Europe during the 1953 RRI.
28. "A Suggested Prospectus for Guidance of the Industrial Relations Clinics, June–July, 1949," John Hope II., n.d., box 42, file 13, RRD Papers, Amistad.
29. "The Role of Management in the Integration of Minorities," Joseph J. Morrow July 8, 1949, box 42, file 13, RRD Papers, Amistad.
30. Ibid., 9.
31. Ibid., 8.
32. Participant requests and comments are discussed in detail in Chapter 5.
33. "Ninth Annual Institute of Race Relations, June 30–July 12, 1952: Report of Clinic of Employment and Industry, John Hope II, Leader," RRD Archives, box 48, file 14; and "Employment and Industry Clinic, 7 July 1952, Chairman – John Hope II," box 48, file 14, RRD Papers, Amistad, 2–3.
34. Ibid., 3.
35. Ibid.
36. Ibid., 3–4.

37. Ibid., 4.
38. Ibid., 5.
39. Ibid., 4.
40. Ibid.
41. Ibid.
42. "Report of Clinic Discussion on Employment Eleventh Annual Institute of Race Relations June 25–July 10, 1954," box 50, file 24, RRD Papers, Amistad.
43. Ibid., 1.
44. Ibid., 2–3.
45. Ibid.
46. "Report of the Industrial Relations Clinic: John Hope—Discussion Leader," ca. 1953, box 49, file 11, RRD Papers, Amistad, 2–3.
47. Ibid., 7.
48. Ibid.
49. "Clinic on Equal Job Opportunity: Causes and Cures of Minorities Discrimination in Employment: A Summary of the Group Discussions and Findings," box 53, file 11, RRD Papers, Amistad, 3.
50. Ibid.
51. Theodore W. Keel, *Guide to Fair Employment Practices*, (Englewood Cliffs, New Jersey: Prentice-Hall, Inc, 1964), 18.
52. Ibid., 18–19.
53. *The Guide to American Law: Everyone's Legal Encyclopedia*, vol. 2 (New York: West Publishing Company, 1983).
54. Ibid.
55. "Employment Clinic Report, July 9, 1965," box 70, file 11, RRD Papers, Amistad.
56. Ibid.
57. "Summary Report: June 29th to July 11, 1953," 1954, box 50, file 15, 1954, RRD Papers, Amistad, 35–37.
58. "Some Principles Related to the Problems of Desegregation," by Kenneth B. Clark, box 51, file 11, 1955; for detailed information on Clark's study see Kenneth B. Clark "Desegregation: An Appraisal of the Evidence." *The Journal of Social Issues*, 9: no. 4, 176, 1953.
59. Ibid.
60. Ibid.
61. Ibid.
62. Ibid.
63. Ibid.
64. Ibid.
65. Ibid.
66. Ibid.
67. Ibid.
68. Ibid.
69. Ibid.
70. Ibid.
71. Ibid.
72. Ibid. Most of the violent reactions to desegregation centered around housing, and Clark felt research needed to be done on the violence associated with housing desegregation.
73. Ibid.
74. Ibid.
75. Ibid.
76. Ibid.
77. Ibid.; Clark also pointed out that there was some evidence that contradicted this idea.

78. "NAACP to Press Fight for Integration, Marshall Says" by Robert Churchwell, *Nashville Banner*, 7 July 1955, RRD Papers, box 51, file 21, 1955, Amistad.
79. Ibid.
80. Ibid.
81. Ibid.
82. Ibid.
83. Ibid.
84. Ibid.
85. Ibid.
86. "Thurgood Marshall Denies Desegregation 'Long Pull,'" *Nashville Banner*, 5 July 1955, box 51, file 21, RRD Papers, Amistad.
87. Ibid.
88. Ibid.
89. "Negro on Spot in Integration, Says Speaker" *Nashville Banner*, 1 July 1955, box 51, file 21, RRD Papers, Amistad.
90. "The Present Status of Desegregation in Education and Some Suggestions as to Future Action—What are some of the important problems involved in the implementation by the Court's decision and what to do?" 1956, box 52, file 10, RRD Papers, Amistad.
91. Ibid.
92. Ibid.
93. Ibid.
94. Ibid.
95. Ibid.
96. Ibid.
97. Ibid.
98. Ibid.
99. Ibid.
100. Ibid.
101. Ibid.
102. Ibid.
103. Ibid.
104. Ibid.
105. Ibid.
106. Ibid.
107. Ibid.
108. "Summary Report: The 20th Annual Institute of Race Relations, June 24–July 6, 1963," 1963, box 64, file 14, RRD Papers, Amistad, 42; "The Status of Public School Desegregation," 1958, box 54, file 18, RRD Papers, Amistad, 1–2.
109. "The Status of Public School Desegregation," 1–2.
110. Ibid.
111. Ibid., 2.
112. Ibid.
113. Ibid.
114. Ibid.
115. Ibid., 3
116. Ibid., 7.
117. Ibid., 7–8.
118. Richard Shapiro, "Secretary of Christian Social Action Report on the 19th Annual Institute on Race Relations Fisk University June 24–July 7, 1962, Theme: Human Rights and the Public Interest, Summary IV, The American School System and the Races: Community preparation for School Desegregation," 1962, box 62, file 26, RRD Papers, Amistad.
119. Ibid.

120. Ibid.
121. Ibid.
122. Ibid.
123. Ibid.
124. Ibid.
125. Ibid.
126. Ibid.
127. "Summary Report: The 20th Annual Institute of Race Relations, June 24–July 6, 1963, Developments in Educational Segregation—Desegregation, 1954–1963," 1963, box 64, file 14, RRD Papers, Amistad, 42.
128. Ibid.
129. Ibid.
130. Ibid.
131. Ibid.
132. Ibid.
133. Ibid.
134. Ibid.
135. Ibid.
136. Ibid.
137. Ibid.
138. Ibid.
139. Ibid.
140. Ibid.
141. Ibid.

CHAPTER FIVE

1. Telephone interview with John Hope Franklin, Dec. 11, 2001.
2. Ibid.
3. Ibid.
4. Constance Baker Motley, *Equal Justice Under Law* (New York: Farrar, Straus and Giroux), 1998, p. 48.
5. See John Lewis with Michael D'Orso, *Walking With the Wind: A Memoir of the Movement* (New York: Simon & Schuster), 1998, for a discussion on the lives of Fisk students in Nashville.
6. Videotaped interview with John Hope Franklin, conducted by Chike Kani Omo, Blackwing Productions.
7. Ibid.
8. The young man to which John Hope Franklin refers is believed to be Cordie Cheek, a seventeen-year-old boy. Cheek was lynched after a grand jury returned a "no bill" on a charge that Cheek molested a white girl. See Jessie Parkhurst Guzman, ed., "Race Riots in the United States 1942–1946: The Columbia, Tennessee Riot" in *Negro Year Book: A Review of Events Affecting Negro Life, 1941–1946*. (Tuskegee, AL: Tuskegee Institute, 1947), 248.
9. Ibid., 250.
10. Ibid.
11. Ibid.
12. Ibid.
13. Quoted in Patrick Joseph Gilpin, "Charles S. Johnson," PhD diss., Vanderbilt University, 1973, chapter 13, 515.
14. Ibid.
15. "Picture of Human Rights 'War' Emerges at Fisk." *The Nashville Tennessean*, July 4, 1965 in RRD Papers, Amistad, box 70, file 15, 1965.
16. Ibid., 540.

17. Ibid.
18. Ibid., 541.
19. For more information on educators and the Red Scare see Stuart J. Foster, *Red Alert! Educators Confront the Red Scare in American Public Schools, 1947–1954* (New York: Peter Lang), 2000.
20. "Communist Daily Worker Comes to Southern Conference for Human Welfare Here—And Workers Seem to Follow 'Line'" *Nashville Banner*, 30 July 1945, box 35, file 31, RRD Papers, Amistad.
21. "Fisk Race Institute Unfair, Communist Party Man Says" The *Nashville Tennessean*, 12 July 1947, box 39, file 25, RRD Papers, Amistad.
22. Ibid.
23. John M. Glen, *Highlander: No Ordinary School, 1932–1962*. (Lexington, KY: University Press of Kentucky), 1988. p. 41.
24. Ibid., 41.
25. "'Next Voter' Criticizes Race Institute," *Nashville Banner*, 1949, box 43, file 11, in RRD Papers, Amistad.
26. Ibid.
27. "Comments on the Institute of Race Relations and Suggestions of Additions Regarding Future Programs," 1944, box 34, file 35, Race Relations Department Papers, Amistad Research Center, New Orleans (hereafter referred to as RRD Papers, Amistad).
28. Ibid.; Alonzo Moron later became the president of Hampton University, Hampton, Virginia.
29. Ibid.
30. Ibid.
31. Ibid.
32. Ibid.
33. Ibid.; Benjamin Quarles later became a distinguished historian at Morgan State University, Baltimore, Maryland.
34. Ibid.
35. Ibid.
36. Ibid.
37. Ibid.
38. Ibid.
39. Ibid.
40. Ibid.
41. Ibid.
42. Ibid.
43. "Comments...1944," RRD Papers, Amistad.
44. "Comments on the Institute of Race Relations....," RRD Papers, Amistad.
45. Ibid.
46. Ibid.
47. Ibid.
48. "Fisk Institute Speaker Blasts Greed of Appalachia Leadership," *The Nashville Tennessean*, June 30, 1967, Box 75, file 6 RRD Papers, Amistad; "Indian Raps U.S. Philosophy As One of 'Self-Interest,'" *The Nashville Tennessean*, July 4, 1950. box 46, file 7 RRD Papers, Amistad; "Race Relations Institute Sessions Continue," *The Nashville Banner*, July 7, 1951, Box 47, file 27, RRD Papers, Amistad.
49. Ibid.
50. Ibid.
51. Ibid.
52. Ibid.
53. Ibid.

NOTES FOR PAGES 98 TO 106 159

54. John Lewis with Michael D'Orso, *Walking With the Wind: A Memoir of the Movement*. (New York: Simon & Schuster), 1998. p. 89.
55. Comments—Institute of Race Relations—1944, box 34, file 35, RRD Papers, Amistad.
56. Ibid.
57. Ibid.
58. Ibid.
59. Ibid.
60. Ibid.
61. Ibid.
62. Ibid.
63. Ibid.
64. Ibid.
65. Comments about Second Annual Institute of Race Relations, box 35, file 34, RRD Papers, Amistad
66. Ibid.
67. Ibid.
68. Ibid.
69. Ibid.
70. Ibid.
71. Ibid.
72. Ibid.
73. Ibid.
74. Ibid.
75. Memo in re: Race Relations Institute, June 16, 1945 to Dr. Johnson from Margaret C. McCulloch, box 35, file 34.
76. Ibid.
77. Ibid.
78. Ibid.
79. Ibid.
80. Weaver to Brownlee, "Evaluation of the 1948 Institute," 2 July 1948, box 36, file 5, RRD Papers, Amistad.
81. Ibid.
82. Correspondence to Mr. Ed. Grief from Herman H. Long, July 16, 1946, in box 36, file 3, RRD Papers, Amistad.
83. Ibid.
84. Ibid.
85. Grief to Long, 16 July 1946, box 36, file 3, RRD Papers, Amistad.
86. Ibid.
87. "Evaluations—1969," box 81, file 13, RRD Papers, Amistad.

CHAPTER SIX

1. The exact year Herman Long became director of the RRI is not clear. Remaining data at times list Johnson as director of the RRI as late as 1949 as well as Long. It is likely that Johnson continued to keep a paternal eye on the project until his death in 1956.
2. For more on the life and death of Charles S. Johnson, see *Richard Robbins Sidelines Activist: Charles S. Johnson and the Struggle for Civil Rights* (Jackson: University Press of Mississippi, 1996).
3. Charles S. Johnson, "A Southern Negro's View of the South" manuscript submitted to *New York Times Magazine*. Provided by JEH V. Johnson, October 18, 2001.
4. Taylor Branch, *Parting the Waters: America in the King Years 1954–1963* (New York: Simon and Schuster, 1988).

5. For more information on the Nashville student sit-in movement, see David Halberstam, *The Children* (New York: Fawcett Books), 1998.
6. "Sit-In Strategy and Tactics Clinic of the 18th Annual Institute of Race Relations, Race Relations Department, American Missionary Association, Fisk University, Nashville, Tennessee. Reverend James Lawson and Reverend J. Metz Rollins, Clinic Leaders," p. 1. RRD Papers, box 60, file 25: RRI 1961 Report of the Clinic on Sit-In Strategy and Tactics.
7. Ibid.
8. Ibid.
9. "Clement Balks on Race Edict," *The Nashville Tennessean*, Saturday, June 29, 1963, in RRD box 64, file 17.
10. Ibid.
11. Ibid.
12. Ibid.
13. Ibid.
14. Ibid.
15. "Rights Bill Called Very Significant," *The Nashville Tennessean*, Thursday, July 9, 1964, RRD Papers box 67, file 7.
16. Ibid.
17. Ibid.
18. "Stop Self-Hate Minority Urged," *The Nashville Tennessean*, July 10, 1964, in RRD Papers box 67, file 7.
19. Ibid.
20. "Fisk Race Relations Institute: Rustin, Young to Speak Here," *The Nashville Tennessean*, June 18, 1967. RRD Papers box 75, file 6.
21. "Fisk Race Institute Focuses on Nashville," *The Nashville Tennessean*, June, 23, 1968 RRD box 78, file 7, 1968
22. Ibid.
23. Ibid.
24. "Sorace Cites Plans After Race Institute Challenge" *The Nashville Tennessean*, July 3, 1968 in RRD Papers, box 78, file 7, 1968.
25. Ibid.
26. Ibid.
27. Ibid.
28. Ibid.
29. Interview with Clifton Johnson, September 19, 2000, Amistad Research Center, Tulane University, New Orleans, Louisiana.
30. Video Interview with Clifton Johnson by Chike Kani Omo; also see "White Power Corrupts Culture: Fisk Speaker," *The Nashville Tennessean*, July 5, 1969, RRD Papers box 81, file 9.
31. Interview with Clifton Johnson, Amistad Research Center.
32. "Dr. Long Urges Rights Work to Avoid Extremes," *The Nashville Banner*, June 27, 1966. RRD Papers, box 72, file 21.
33. Ibid.
34. Ibid.
35. Ibid.
36. Ibid.
37. Ibid.
38. "Race Institute Told: Superficial News Tied to Rights Riots," *The Nashville Tennessean*, July 5, 1967. RRD Papers, box 75, file 6.
39. "Speaker Decries Lack of Employment for Negroes," *The Nashville Banner*, July 3, 1967, RRD Papers, box 75, file 6, 1967.

40. "'Could Ruin Black' Cause': Wilkins Warns On Separatism," *The Nashville Tennessean*, July 10, 1969, RRD Papers, box 81, file 10.
41. Ibid.
42. Ibid.
43. Ibid.
44. Ibid.
45. Ibid.
46. Ibid.
47. Ibid.
48. "Militant Demonstrations Called Rights Drive Aid," *The Nashville Tennessean*, July 2, 1965, RRD Papers, box 70, file 15.
49. Ibid.
50. Ibid.
51. "Distortion Charged: Press "Criminals of Hour' Says Race Relations Speaker," *The Nashville Tennessean*, July 2, 1967, RRD Papers, box 75, file 6.
52. Ibid.
53. Ibid.
54. Ibid.
55. Interview with Clifton Johnson, Amistad Research Center.
56. "White Power Corrupts Culture: Fisk Speaker," *The Nashville Tennessean*, July 5, 1969, RRD Papers, box 81, file 9.

EPILOGUE

1. S.P. Fullinwider, *The Mind and Mood of Black America: 20th Century Thought*. (Homewood, IL: Dorsey Press), 1969, p. 108.
2. Note that the RRI initially ran from 1944–1969 at Fisk University. The project was briefly resurrected during the early 1980s under the directorship of Dr. Manning Marable and again during the late 1990s under the directorship of Dr. Raymond A. Winbush.
3. "The Road to Brown" [videorecording] (San Francisco: California Newsreel), 1990. For more on Charles H. Houston see Genna Rae McNeil, *Groundwork: Charles Hamilton Houston and the Struggle for Civil Rights*. (Philadelphia: University of Pennsylvania Press), 1983.
4. Charles S. Johnson, "A Spiritual Autobiography," p.11 n.d., manuscript, Charles S. Johnson Papers, Fisk .

INDEX

13 Against the Odds (Embree), 26, 27, 42
1963 Civil Rights Bill, 107
1963 March on Washington, 108

African Americans and Jews in the Twentieth Century (Franklin), 54
Alexander, W. W., 18, 42
All Men Are Brothers (UNESCO), 107
Allport, G. W., 42, 48
Alpenfels, E., 48
American Baptist Theological Seminary, 106
American Council on Race Relations, 15, 42, 66, 73
American Jewish Committee, 73
American Jewish Congress, 52
American Missionary Association, 2, 15, 16, 22, 36, 38, 59, 102, 109, 112
American Sociological Society, 36
Amistad Research Center, 112
Ammerman, H., 59
An American Dilemma (Myrdal), 13, 14, 15, 19
A. Philip Randolph Institute, 108
Atlanta University, 36, 42, 43
Atlanta University Studies of Negro Life, 34

Baltimore Evening News, 56
Baltimore Institute of Race Relations, 56
Bean, R. B., 32
Benedict, R., 18, 19, 20
Bennington College, 42

Berea College, 100
Berry, B., 13, 19
Black Americans in the Roosevelt Era (Kirby), 18
Black Boy (Wright), 14
Black Power, 109, 110, 111, 112
Blanton, S., 42, 48
Boas, F., 32, 36
Bond, H. M., 42
Brameld, T., 57
Brigham, C., 34
Brooklyn College, 59
Brotherhood of Sleeping Car Porters, 6, 63
Brown Americans (Embree), 42
Brown, I. C., 42, 48, 50
Brownlee, F., 42
Brown v. Board of Education, 88, 113
Buck, P. S., 18
Bunche, R., 36
Burgette, M. A., 31, 32

Caliver, A., 36, 42
Carmichael, S., 111
Carnegie Corporation, 15
Cheek, C., 90
Chicago Commission on Race, 17
Chicago Race Riot of 1919, 1, 30
Chicago Urban League, 28, 29
citizenship schools, 44
Clark College (Atlanta), 110
Clark, K., 42, 76, 77, 78, 79, 80, 82, 113
Clark, S., 44, 45, 98
Clement, F. G., 107

clock of fear, 107
Cobb, C. E., 111
College of the City of New York, 76
Color and Conscience (Gallagher), 14
Columbia University, 36
Combs, B., 107
Commager, H. S., 42
Committee on Fair Labor Standards, 37
Congress on Racial Equality, 14, 15, 69, 108
Contempt and Pity (Scott), 3
Cox, O. C., 34

Davis, A., 102
Davis, B. J., 92
Delany, A. E., 2, 25
Delany, S. L., 2, 25
Detroit City Planning Commission, 7
Detroit Riot of June 1943, 8
Dillard University, 36
Dollinger, I., 66
Du Bois, W. E. B., 34, 36, 43

Ebony, 14
Economic Status of Negros, 35
Education and the American Indian (Szasz), 52
Education of the Negro in the American Social Order (Bond), 42
Egerton, J., 44
Eisenhower, D. D., 74
Embree, E. R., 17, 18, 26, 27, 31, 42, 91
Equal Justice Under Law (Motley), 89
Evers, M., 105

Fair Employment Practices Committee, 7, 65, 66, 67
Farm Security Administration, 42
Farmer, J., 108
Federal Council of Churches, 59
Fisher, L., 107
Fisk University Race Relations Institute (RRI), 2, 3, 4, 11, 15, 16, 22, 23, 24, 25, 36, 37–45, 106, 109, 113
   closing of, 105
   communities and, 55–57
   curriculum of, 41–42
   education legislative efforts of, 75–88
   employment legislative efforts of, 63–75

   Mexican Americans and 53
   Native Americans and, 52–53
   participant evaluations of, 93–104
   people og, 51–55
   Puerto Ricans and, 53–54
   scholarship at, 48–51
   school, church and, 57–61
Fleming, W., 90
Ford Foundation, 83
Franklin, J. H., 14, 89, 90
Franklin, V.P. (Vincent P.), 54
Frazier, E. F., 8, 28, 34, 36
From Slavery to Freedom (Franklin), 14
frustration-aggression theory, 10
Fry, C. L., 38
Fullinwider, S. P., 5, 6, 113

Gaines, K. K., 3
Gardner, R. A., 45
Garvey, M., 15
General Education Board, 15
Ghandi, M., 106, 107
Gilpin, P., 40, 91, 92
Globe-Independent (Nashville, TN), 91
Goldberg, Arthur J., 87
Gone With the Wind, 14
Governor's Commission on Race Relations (IL), 30, 31
Graham, F., 42
Granger, L. B., 42
Grant, N. L., 64
Grayson Jr., W. H., 57
Greenberg, J., 111
Growing Up in the Black Belt (Houston), 4

Halsey, M., 49, 50
Harlem Riot of 1943, 8
Harvard University, 42
Having Our Say (Delany and Delany), 2, 25
Hays, B., 42
Henderson, V. W., 110
Henry, C., 25
Herskovits, M., 36
Highlander (Glen), 92
Highlander Folk School, 44, 45, 92, 98
Hope III, J., 42, 68, 74
Horton, M., 44
Houston, C. H., 3, 4, 36, 42, 65, 99, 113
Howard University, 4, 36, 106
Hughes, E., 28
Hughes, H., 28

INDEX

In a Minor Key (Reid), 42
Intergroup Education in Cooperating Schools, 42, 56
Into the Main Stream (Johnson), 14

Jahoda, M., 52
Jewish Vocational Services, 73
Jim Crow laws, 2, 3, 4, 25, 27, 102
Johns, H. B., 91
Johns Hopkins University, 32
Johnson, C., 105, 108, 109, 112
Johnson, C. S., 1, 2, 3, 4, 11, 14, 16, 18, 22, 33, 90, 92, 99, 102, 105, 108, 113
   college years of, 28
   early life, 24–25, 26
   education and, 23, 24, 41
   employment Legislative Efforts of, 63–75
   later career of, 106
   marriage of, 31–32
   military career of, 29
   race relations and, 24
   racial conflict theories and, 12, 13
   racist scientific notions and, 47
   research on blacks and, 34
   social organizations and, 19
Johnson, L. B., 74
Johnson, R., 108
Johnson, W. B., 25
Jones, G. C., 59
Jones, L. W., 47
Journal of Abnormal and Social Psychology of Radio, 42
Julius Rosenwald Foundation, 14, 15, 16, 17, 18, 22, 36, 37, 42, 96, 99

Killian, L., 34
King Jr., M. L., 42, 44, 105, 107, 108
Kingdom of God Is Within You (Tolstoy), 107
Kirby, J. B., 18
Kleinberg, O., 36
Ku Klux Klan, 58

Labor and Industry Clinic, 72
La Farge, J., 42
Lawson, J., 106, 107
League of United American Citizens (LUCAC), 53
"Let All of Them Take Heed," (San Miquel Jr.), 53

Life, 14
Life of Mahatma Ghandi (Fisher), 107
Lincoln University, 42
Long, H. H., 39, 44, 45, 109, 110
Looby, Z. A.. 106
Lowden, F. O., 30

MacKenzie, B., 59
Mall, F. P., 32
Man's Most Dangerous Myth (Montagu), 42
March on Washington Movement, 9, 65
Marshall, T., 42, 71, 75, 76, 79, 80, 81, 82
Mather Junior College, 45
McDaniel, H., 14
McLean, H. V., 48, 49
Meharry Medical School, 106
Miller, L., 71
Mind and Mood of Black America (Fullinwider), 5, 113
Minneapolis Joint Committee for Employment Opportunity, 72
Mitchell, G., 80
Montagu, M. F. A., 42, 48, 102
Monthly Summary of Trends and Events in Race Relations, 40
Morris, A., 6
Morrow, J. J., 69, 70
Motley, C. B., 89
Myrdal, G., 13, 15, 19, 20

Nashville Banner, 66, 69, 92, 93
Nashville Tennessean, 91, 92
National Association for the Advancement of Colored People, 15, 30, 34, 36, 42, 75, 79, 102, 110, 111
National Defense Advisory Commission, 64, 65
National Labor Relations Board, 68, 72
National Survey of the Higher Education of Negroes, 42
National Urban League, 15, 32, 34, 36, 42, 108
Negro in American Civilization, 34
Negro Housing: Report of the Committee on Negro Housing, 35
Negro In Chicago, 31
Negro in the United States (Frazier), 8
Non-Violence in Peace and War (Ghandi), 107
Northside Center for Child Development, 76
Northwestern University, 36

OASIS, 84
Odum, H., 36
Opportunity, 3, 32, 63
Origins of the Civil Rights Movement (Morris), 6

Park, R. E., 3, 10, 11, 12, 13, 28, 30, 32, 33, 36, 37, 38, 44
Patterns of Negro Segregation (Johnson), 37
Payne, Charles M., 44
Pembroke State College, 99
Peterson, J., 34
Phelps Stokes Fund, 15
Plessy, H., 25
Plessy v. Ferguson, 2, 25
Preface to Racial Understanding (Johnson), 11
President's Committee on Civil Rights, 7, 21
President's Committee on Equal Employment Opportunity, 74

Queens College, 42

Race and Racism (Benedict), 18
Race Relations (Berry), 19, 35
Race Relations Institute (RRI). *See* Fisk University Race Relations Institute
racial conflict theories, 9–15
Randolph, A. P., 6, 7, 15, 63, 65
Redfield, R., 28
Red Summer, 30
Reid, I. DeA., 36, 42
Reuter, E. B., 36, 38
Robbins, R., 28, 42, 43, 47
Robinson, J., 14
Rockefeller Foundation, 17
Roosevelt, F. D., 6, 7, 9, 64, 65
Rose, A. M., 20, 21, 42
Rosenwald, J., 16, 17, 31
Rousseau, J.-J., 33
Rustin, B., 108

Salzman, J., 54
Sarratt, 85, 86, 87, 88
scapegoat theory, 10
Scarritt College, 42
Scott, A. L., 45
Scott, D. M., 3

Sears, Roebuck and Company, 16, 36
SERS. *See* Southern Education Reporting Service
Shadow of the Plantation (Houston), 4
Shoemaker, D., 83
Sidelines Activist (Robbins), 47
Simpson, J., 27
Smith, C. U., 34
Society of Friends, 35
Sojourner Truth Housing Project, 7, 8
Sorace, J., 109
Southern Christian Leadership Conference, 69, 75, 106
Southern Education Reporting Service, 83, 85
Southern Interracial Commission, 36
Southern Regional Council, 80, 102
Stephenson, G., 90, 91
Stephenson, J., 90, 91
Strange Career of Jim Crow (Woodward), 25
Stride Toward Freedom (King), 107
Struggles in the Promised Land (Salzman), 54
Student Nonviolent Coordicating Committee, 106
Swarthmore College Institute of Race Relations, 35, 37, 43
Szasz, M. C., 52

Taba, H., 42, 56, 58, 59
Talladega University, 105, 109
Teachers College, 56
Tennessee State University, 106, 108
Till, E., 105
To Stem This Tide (Johnson), 37
Townsend, W., 42
Truman, H. S. 21, 67
Tuskegee Institute, 8
TVA and Black Americans (Grant), 64

United States Employment Services, 72, 73
University of Chicago, 3, 10, 20, 29, 31, 36, 37, 42, 58, 59
University of Iowa, 36
University of Kansas, 76
University of Minnesota, 57
University of North Carolina, 36
University of Texas Law School, 76
Uplifting the Race (Gaines), 3
Urban League, 31, 36, 73, 102
U. S. Housing Authority, 7

Vanderbilt University, 42

Wagner, H. M., 56
Watson, G., 56
Weaver, R., 66
West, D., 44
White, W., 15
Wilkins, R., 110, 111

Williams, E., 29, 42
Wirth, L., 28, 42
Woodward, C. V., 25, 42
Wright, R., 14

Yerkes, R., 34
Young, W., 108

THIS SERIES EXPLORES THE HISTORY OF SCHOOLS AND SCHOOLING in the United States and other countries. Books in this series examine the historical development of schools and educational processes, with special emphasis on issues of educational policy, curriculum and pedagogy, as well as issues relating to race, class, gender, and ethnicity. Special emphasis will be placed on the lessons to be learned from the past for contemporary educational reform and policy. Although the series will publish books related to education in the broadest societal and cultural context, it especially seeks books on the history of specific schools and on the lives of educational leaders and school founders.

For additional information about this series or for the submission of manuscripts, please contact the general editors:

>   Alan R. Sadovnik Susan F. Semel
>   Rutgers University-Newark The City College of New York, CUNY
>   Education Dept. 138th Street and Convent Avenue
>   155 Conklin Hall NAC 5/208
>   175 University Avenue New York, NY 10031
>   Newark, NJ 07102

To order other books in this series, please contact our Customer Service Department:

> 800-770-LANG (within the U.S.)
> 212-647-7706 (outside the U.S.)
> 212-647-7707 FAX

Or browse online by series at:

> www.peterlangusa.com